The Great Basin

The publication of this volume was made possible in part
by a generous gift from Don Frazier.

The Great Basin

People and Place in Ancient Times

Edited by Catherine S. Fowler and Don D. Fowler

A School for Advanced Research Popular Southwestern Archaeology Book

School for Advanced Research Press
Santa Fe, New Mexico

School for Advanced Research Press
Post Office Box 2188
Santa Fe, New Mexico 87504-2188
www.sarpress.sarweb.org

Co-Director: Catherine Cocks
Copy Editor: Jane Kepp
Designer and Production Manager: Cynthia Dyer
Maps: Molly O'Halloran
Proofreader: Margaret J. Goldstein
Indexer: Ina Gravitz
Printed in China by C&C Offset Printing Co., Ltd

Library of Congress Cataloging-in-Publication Data
The Great Basin : people and place in ancient times / edited by Catherine S. Fowler and Don D. Fowler.
    p. cm. — (Popular Southwestern archaeology book)
Includes index.
ISBN 978-1-930618-95-4 (cl : alk. paper) — ISBN 978-1-930618-96-1 (pa : alk. paper)
    1. Indians of North America—Great Basin—Antiquities—Popular works.
    2. Paleo-Indians—Great Basin—Popular works.
    3. Great Basin—Antiquities—Popular works.
    I. Fowler, Catherine S. II. Fowler, Don D., 1936-
E78.G67G75 2008
979—dc22
2008016298

Cover photographs: front, Deep Grooves site, photograph courtesy of
Alanah Woody, Nevada Rock Art Foundation; back, Lagomarsino, photograph
courtesy of Angus Quinlan, Nevada Rock Art Foundation.
Frontispiece: Coso-Style patterned body anthropomorphs, Coso Range, California;
adapted by Cynthia Dyer from Heizer and Baumhoff, *Prehistoric Rock Art of Nevada and Eastern California*
(Berkeley: University of California Press, 1962): ii.

Contents

Color plates follow page 50.

Acknowledgments

This book had its genesis in conversations with James F. Brooks, president of the School for Advanced Research (SAR), in May 2006, when we were in Santa Fe for Don to deliver a lecture on the founder of SAR, the inimitable Edgar Lee Hewett. SAR Press had previously published excellent works on Chaco Canyon, Bandelier National Monument, and Mesa Verde in its popular archaeology series, and a volume was under way on the Hohokam. James felt that a book focused on a broader region, the Great Basin, would be a logical next step in the series.

We had each devoted four decades and counting to working with many Indian people, archaeologists, ethnohistorians, and ethnographers to better understand the lives and times of the peoples who have lived in the Great Basin for more than 12,000 years. James thought we would be logical candidates to assemble such a regional volume. We had both been involved in writing and editing the Great Basin volume of the Smithsonian's *Handbook of North American Indians*, published in 1986. But much work had been done in the intervening two decades, particularly in contract, or cultural resource management (CRM), archaeology and in studies of Great Basin ancient environments. An up-to-date popular synthesis seemed both potentially useful and needed. We agreed to take on the task.

Archaeology and paleoenvironmental studies are team sports, as one of our authors, David Hurst Thomas, puts it, so we assembled an "A Team" at the October 2006 Great Basin Anthropological Conference in Las Vegas, Nevada. We gave our team members their agreed-upon topic assignments, and after numerous drafts and rounds of editing, the manuscript was assembled by the end of October 2007—to the mutual amazement of authors and editors.

We heartily thank our authors for their rapid and excellent work in distilling and presenting what is currently known about the peoples of ancient times and places in the Great Basin and the changing environments in which they lived. We particularly thank Don Frazier, longtime patron and active participant in Great Basin archaeology, for his generous financial support of the volume. We thank Jerry Lyon, of HRA Conservation Archaeology in Las Vegas, Nevada, for developing the excellent drafts of the shaded relief maps and Molly O'Halloran for putting them in final form. A special thanks to Linda Dufurrena, of Denio, Nevada, whose photographs of the diverse moods and beauty of Great Basin landscapes, in this and her own books, enhance our sense of the basin as a starkly beautiful place.

Louis Stancari, of the National Museum of the American Indian, Smithsonian Institution; Victoria Bradshaw, of the Hearst Museum, University of California, Berkeley; Eugene Hattori, of the Nevada State Museum; Kara Hurst, of the Utah Museum of Natural History; Shannon Arnold, of the Archaeological Center, University of Utah; and Steven LeBlanc, of the Peabody Museum of Archaeology and Ethnology, Harvard University, were of inestimable help in providing key images for the book, and we thank them all.

Catherine Cocks, executive editor of SAR Press, performed wonders in keeping us on time and on track and reminding all of us that brevity, clarity, and the active voice are virtues to be continually cultivated. Jane Kepp, copy editor extraordinaire, has worked her usual magic and made us and our authors read even better than we deserve. Finally, our thanks to James Brooks for urging us to take on this task. It's been a pleasure.

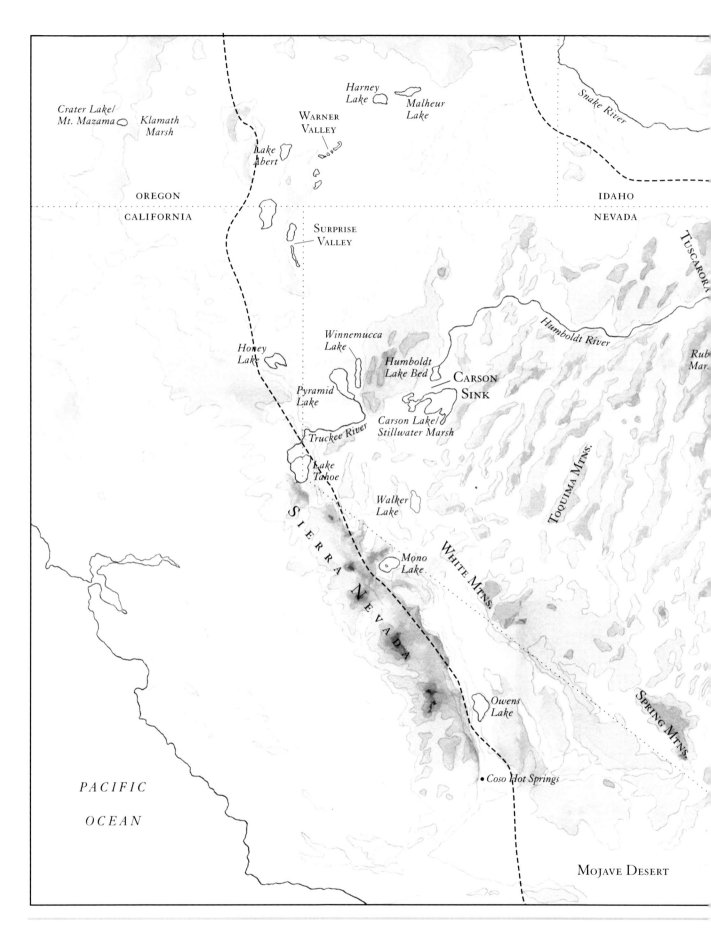

Map 1.The Great Basin region. The dotted line marks the approximate boundary of the hydrographic Great Basin.

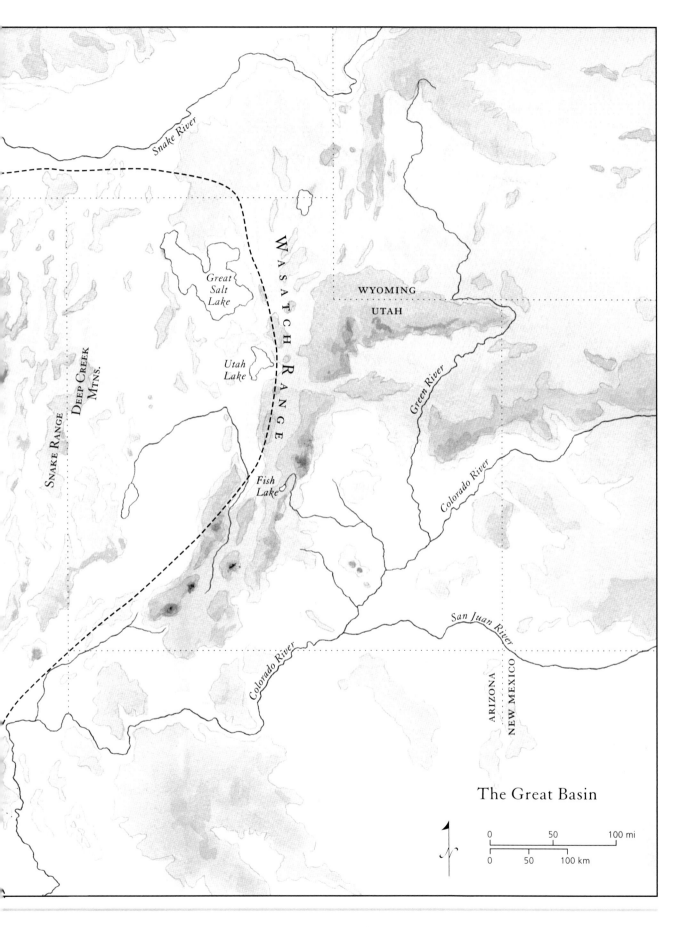

Snake River

Great
Salt
Lake

WYOMING
UTAH

Utah
Lake

W
A
S
A
T
C
H

R
A
N
G
E

SNAKE RANGE

DEEP CREEK
MTNS.

Green River

Fish
Lake

Colorado River

Colorado River

San Juan River

ARIZONA
NEW MEXICO

The Great Basin

N

| 0 | | 50 | | 100 mi |
| 0 | 50 | | 100 km | |

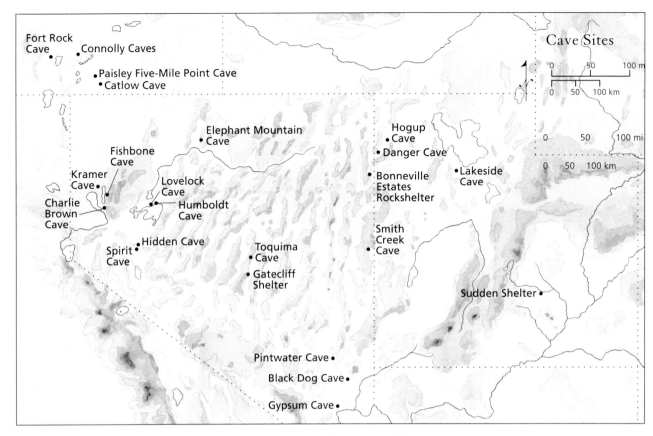

Map 2. Some major cave sites in the Great Basin. Horizontal scale exaggerated.

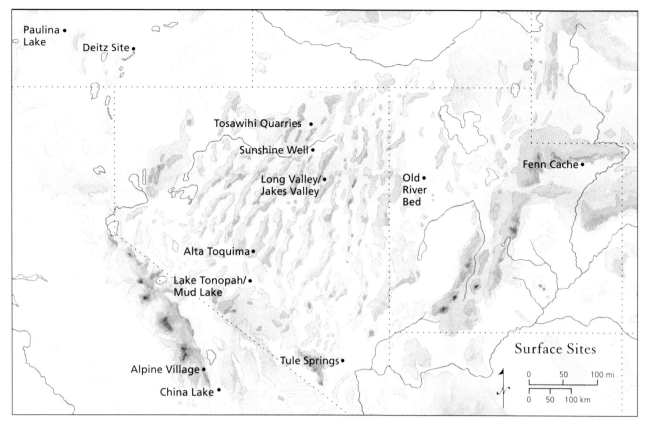

Map 3. Surface sites in the Great Basin mentioned in the book. Horizontal scale exaggerated.

Chronology of the Great Basin

Dates are given as BCE (before the common era) and CE (of the common era).

Climatic Periods and Geological Events

9700 BCE	End of the Pleistocene epoch, or last Ice Age; start of the Holocene epoch, marking the inception of modern climates
9700–6500 BCE	Early Holocene: warming climate and the waning of late Ice Age, or Pluvial, lakes
6500–2000 BCE	Middle Holocene: global warming and droughts of different intensities
5670 BCE	Eruption of Mount Mazama and formation of Crater Lake caldera; Mazama ash plume spreads widely across Great Basin and northern Rocky Mountains
2000 BCE–present	Late Holocene: cooler and wetter, with the gradual advent of modern climate
1450–1850 CE	Little Ice Age: cooler climate, resurgence of mountain glaciers
1850 CE–present	Period of warming; drier climate

Cultural Periods

Approx. 12,000 BCE	Earliest evidence of people in northern Great Basin
11,000–10,700 BCE	Clovis era
10,700–6500 BCE	Paleoarchaic period: peopling of western and eastern sections of Great Basin; development of large stemmed projectile points
6500–4000 BCE	Early Archaic period: reduction in population in some parts of the Great Basin; advent of large, side-notched projectile points
4000 BCE–400 or 500 CE	Middle Archaic period: advent of smaller, notched and unnotched projectile points
400 or 500–1400 CE	Late Archaic period in central, western, and northern Great Basin; spread of bow and arrow technology and related small projectile points across Great Basin
400 CE	Beginning development of Fremont (Formative-stage) culture: farming and settled villages in present-day central and eastern Utah
1000–1400 CE (POSSIBLY EARLIER)	Present-day Indian peoples in place across the Great Basin
1300–1350 CE	Fremont farming villages abandoned
500 CE	Beginning of ancestral Pueblo ("Virgin Branch" Formative-stage) culture: farming and settled villages in southern Great Basin
1200–1300 CE	Southern Great Basin ancestral Pueblo villages abandoned
1600–1750s CE	Advent of first Euro-Americans in Great Basin

The Great Basin

Figure 1.1. Earth and Sky, Northern Humboldt County, Nevada.

Stories of a Place and Its Peoples

Don D. Fowler and Catherine S. Fowler

This book is about a place, the Great Basin of western North America, and about the lifeways of Native American people who lived there during the past 13,000 years. We do not attempt to tell a single story or to convey a complete view of the region over this long time span. Rather, we offer a set of smaller stories or vignettes about how people lived in this intriguing place, written by archaeologists who know it well.

By emphasizing the changing nature of the Great Basin, we highlight the ingenious solutions people devised over time to sustain themselves in a difficult environment. They did so largely by hunting and collecting the animals, fish, birds, and plants of the region rather than by depending on domesticated species, as some of their neighbors to the south did. Only for about the last 2,000 years, and only intermittently in what is now Utah and parts of southern Nevada, have some Great Basin Native groups lived as part-time farmers.

No matter how people made a living in the Great Basin, they and the place have always been deeply influenced by changing environments and climates. The Great Basin is, after all, a semiarid and often harsh land, but one with life-giving oases. As the weather fluctuated from year to year, and the climate from decade to decade or even from one millennium to the next, the availability of water, plants, and animals also fluctuated. Even in the best of times in such a place, only people who learned the land intimately and could read the many signs of its changing moods were successful. The evidence of their success is there, but it is often subtle

and difficult to interpret from the few and fragile remains left behind for archaeologists to discover. Every researcher soon feels the adventure of learning about this place and its people through time.

Anthropologists (including archaeologists), ecologists, hydrologists, and geologists define various Great Basins. One is the *hydrographic* Great Basin, an area of about 200,000 square miles that drains internally, with no outlets to the sea. On the map of his 1843–44 reconnaissance across the West, published by the US Congress in 1844, Captain John Charles Frémont placed a legend that read, "The Great Basin; diameter 11° of latitude, 10° of longitude: elevation above the sea 4 and 5,000 feet: surrounded by lofty mountains: contents almost unknown but believed to be filled with rivers and lakes which have no communication with the sea."

The *geological* Great Basin is part of the larger North American Basin and Range physiographic

province—the hundreds of generally north-south-trending mountain ranges separated by long, broad valleys extending from northern Mexico into central Oregon. Some 120 of these smaller basins and their intervening mountain ranges make up the Great Basin. The great nineteenth-century geologist Clarence Dutton said that a map of the many mountain ranges reminded him of a great army of caterpillars marching to Mexico.

The *biogeographic* Great Basin is for some ecologists larger and for others smaller than the hydrographic basin. In this book we consider the hydrographic and biogeographic basins to be identical. As Donald Grayson explains in chapter 2, plant life corresponds to elevation throughout the Great Basin, from the low-growing shrubs of the valley floors to the conifer forests of the high mountainsides.

There is also the *cultural* Great Basin, defined by anthropologists in the twentieth century. It is based on the distribution of present-day American Indian language families and material culture. This Great Basin encompasses the hydrographic Great Basin, parts of the Colorado Plateau, and the central Rocky Mountains.

Finally, for the purposes of this book, there is the *archaeological* Great Basin, which comprises the hydrographic Great Basin and a section of the western Colorado Plateau. As several of our authors tell the story, related peoples during what are called Archaic and Fremont times lived not only in the Great Basin proper but in a portion of the canyon country of the western Colorado Plateau. In its landforms, plant life, and patterns of water flow, this plateau area is somewhat different from the Great Basin. But the peoples who flourished there over thousands of years had relationships both with people to the west, in the Great Basin, and, after about 400 CE, with the farming-based, settled village cultures in the US Southwest. To properly tell our story of people's lives in ancient times, the western Colorado Plateau needs to be linked to the Great Basin proper.

In telling the archaeological stories of the Great Basin, our contributors generally look more at the deep past than at the immediate past or the present. Great Basin Indian people today do not distinguish between "history" and "prehistory," and we have adopted their view. It is a view of an ever-unfolding continuum from the time of the ancestors to the current-day people, all of whom shared parts of this one place. The story over that long span is a multifaceted one, many parts of which are incompletely known, especially when researchers have to rely on the subtle clues uncovered through archaeology. Many of the interpretations our authors make come from combining those clues with knowledge of lifeways in this place that Indian people have shared with others over time. It is this information that is so helpful in fleshing out the uses and meanings of artifacts and understanding environmental clues. To use only this knowledge to interpret the past would be to deny that present-day Indian people profited from the ancestors' experiences and changed over time, but their contemporary wisdom and counsel are nonetheless invaluable.

Because we emphasize the archaeological past, readers may wonder who the Native Americans of the Great Basin are today. They include roughly 10,000 residents in some 40 federally recognized tribes with land bases ranging from a few dozen acres to half a million. In addition, several thousand people live independently in urban settings rather than in reservation communities. Traditionally, anthropologists have grouped the tribes according to their indigenous languages. The Washoe people, centered on Lake Tahoe and several large valleys immediately east of it, speak a language affiliated with several languages in California, all part of the large, diverse Hokan language stock. Groups whose indigenous languages are affiliated with the so-called Numic branch of the widespread Uto-Aztecan language family cover most of the region. Linguists divide Numic into three pairs of languages: Mono and Northern Paiute in the western Great Basin, Panamint and Shoshone in the central Great Basin, and Kawaiisu and Ute in the southern and eastern Great Basin (see fig. 6.9). Different federally recognized tribes and cultural groups are included in each of these language divisions.

Today this way of dividing peoples is less useful, because everyone speaks mainly English. The groups maintain some differences in traditional culture, but they are more homogeneous than different. Some tribes and reservation communities are reasonably well-off economically, with viable tribal businesses, including casinos. Others, especially in rural settings, struggle to make ends meet and provide services for their members. Throughout the region, communities and individuals retain varying degrees of knowledge of older lifeways and skill in their indigenous languages.

Many Great Basin Natives are deeply concerned about their land, whether present-day reserved land or former larger territories. They feel a custodial relationship to the land that extends to its resources —animals, plants, and archaeological evidence of the ancestors. People still visit sacred sites, collect important food and medicinal plants, and pray to the many spirits who inhabit the land. Some take care of the land and its plants and animals in the old way, by selectively harvesting plant foods, cleaning and clearing springs, pruning, and burning overgrown areas.

Most tribes today have environmental and cultural preservation departments or committees and are seriously involved in consulting with land managing agencies both in their former territories and on reserved land. They routinely monitor archaeological and environmental activities, especially on federal and reserved land. Some are trained in the skills of archaeological survey, and more are seeking certification or professional degrees in scientific disciplines. As Brian Wallace, former chair of the Washoe Tribe of California and Nevada, said during a 2006 tribal environmental training session, "having the ability to read the land and interpret the world we live in is something that every Indian person should have as a skill. The traditional way,

that's what we Indian people come from. That's the way Indian people were. And one of the most important abilities and skills to have is to be out on the ground and be able to reconnect with that wisdom and from that place to our land. That comes from the history of our people, and the land's well-being rests and resides in that."

Native interpretations of the past do not always coincide with those of non-Native anthropologists, archaeologists, historians, and ecologists who carry out research in their regions—but Indian people are usually interested in others' results. More and more, Great Basin indigenous people are reviewing archaeological projects and requesting a say in decisions that affect their land and the region in general. They are especially interested in the designation and protection of sacred sites, whether specific places or larger districts, and they speak eloquently for their protection. The Washoe Tribe, for example, has partnered with the US Forest Service in a long battle to prevent climbing at Cave Rock, a site on the western shore of Lake Tahoe with important spiritual meaning for both Native persons of power and tribal members in general. Western Shoshone people, especially the Battle Mountain Shoshone Tribe, have similarly made their opinions known to federal agencies over the years about the sacredness of the Tosawihi quarries area in central Nevada.

Most tribes are concerned about the return of human remains and sacred objects under federal legislation known as the Native American Graves Protection and Repatriation Act (NAGPRA). They object to the disturbance or collection of such items in the region. Most are also concerned with protecting rock art sites throughout the Great Basin and

react with special revulsion to the vandalism of rock art. They are vocal about issues of access to and protection of naturally occurring hot springs and other important water sources. And they hold companies' and agencies' feet to the fire on issues of mine cleanup and acts of land contamination. Pauline Esteves, former chair of the Timbisha Shoshone Tribe of Death Valley, California, declared, "We never give up. The Timbisha people have lived in our homeland forever, and we will live here forever. We were taught that we don't end. We are part of our homeland and it is part of us. We are people of the land. We don't break away from what is a part of us."

From the stories that the land and peoples of the ancient Great Basin have to tell, we hope readers will gain a new appreciation for the human and environmental history of this place. The people and the land have much to reveal if only we stop to explore or pause long enough to truly listen.

Before turning to the stories themselves, we need to offer a few notes about maps, technical terms, dates, and further readings.

Cave and rockshelter sites figure prominently in this book, as do several of the thousands of recorded open and surface archaeological sites. Maps 2 and 3 show sites prominently mentioned in the following chapters.

Archaeologists, like other scholarly groups, have their own technical jargon, which is often impenetrable to the uninitiated. Our authors have kept technical terms to a minimum, but some are required. The contributors have tried to explain these terms the first time each appears.

Throughout the book, authors give dates of climatic and environmental phenomena, archaeological time periods, and artifacts as some number of "years ago." These statements are based on clusters of averaged radiocarbon dates. The radiocarbon (carbon 14) method of dating ancient organic materials yields ages in "radiocarbon years," usually given as statistical estimates such as "2000 ± 250 radiocarbon years." For complex reasons, there is no one-to-one correlation between radiocarbon years and calendar years, so researchers have developed correlation tables to produce "calibrated" radiocarbon years. For editorial simplicity we have substituted "years ago" for "calibrated radiocarbon years." The original radiocarbon dating method, first developed in 1949, and the later, refined radiocarbon dating method known as accelerator mass spectroscopy (AMS), are described in chapter 8.

Some of the chapter authors mention a "Mazama ash" layer as a time marker. The cataclysmic volcanic eruption of Mount Mazama in Oregon roughly 5,670 years ago, which left the caldera that became Crater Lake, spread a layer of ash over thousands of square miles of western North America. The distinctive ash fell into lakes, marshes, ponds, rockshelters, and caves. Any sediment or artifact found below the ash layer is older than 5,670 years, and anything above it is younger. How much older or younger has to be determined by other means.

When our contributors use conventional European calendar dates, they give them as BCE ("before the common era") and CE ("of the common era"), rather than as BC and AD. They also divide archaeological time into named periods such as Paleoarchaic and early, middle, and late Archaic. Consensus estimates of the lengths of these periods are given in the cultural chronology chart and in the various chapters.

Last, our use of the term *Archaic* and its divisions may appear inconsistent with usages in other archaeological regions of North America. In the Great Basin, as elsewhere in North America, "Archaic" refers to a mobile, hunting-gathering way of life. But in most parts of the Great Basin, unlike elsewhere, that lifeway continued, with some technological changes, from earliest times until the arrival of Euro-Americans in the 1770s. In other regions of North America, such as the Southwest, a farming-village lifestyle labeled "Formative" persisted into the Euro-American period, after 1540. A similar lifestyle, featuring settled villages, domesticated crops, and pottery making, had appeared by 400 CE in parts of the southern and eastern Great Basin, but it did not last much beyond 1350. After that time people returned to hunting and gathering, with minimal farming, until the advent of Euro-Americans disrupted their subsistence cycles and traditional modes of living.

The chapters in this book are distilled from the

information contained in an enormous number of scientific and historical studies. A suggested readings section at the end of the book provides introductory guidance to published studies that will help readers expand their knowledge of Great Basin archaeology and environmental history and their many facets.

Don D. Fowler is Mamie Kleberg Distinguished Professor of Anthropology and Historic Preservation Emeritus at the University of Nevada, Reno. Catherine S. Fowler is UNR Foundation Professor of Anthropology Emerita at the University of Nevada, Reno.

Figure 2.1. Death Valley's Badwater Basin, viewed from the top of Telescope Peak in the Panamint Range, 11,330 feet higher up.

Great Basin Natural History

Donald K. Grayson

"The Great Basin," the explorer John C. Frémont said, is that "intermediate region between the Rocky Mountains and the next range [the Sierra Nevada], containing many lakes with their own system of rivers and creeks…and which have no connexion with the ocean, or the great rivers which flow into it."

When Frémont named the Great Basin in 1844, he also noted that it was poorly explored. That is no longer the case. Not only has the modern Great Basin been explored in great detail, but we have also learned a remarkable amount about how the region came to be the way it is today. Most directly relevant to the basin's human history are its last 12,000 years.

The Great Basin Today

Perhaps the most striking features of the Great Basin are its many north-south-trending mountain ranges and intervening broad valleys. Many of these ranges are massive. Thirty-three have elevations exceeding 10,000 feet, and the highest of them all, the White Mountains (fig. 2.2), reaches 14,426 feet. In central Nevada, the Toiyabe Range is 126 miles long and nearly 20 miles wide, its tallest

peak reaching 11,788 feet. To its immediate east, the Toquima Range is 76 miles long and 13 miles wide and reaches 11,941 feet.

Even the valleys between these ranges stand at high altitudes. The highest valleys are found in central and eastern Nevada, with elevations decreasing

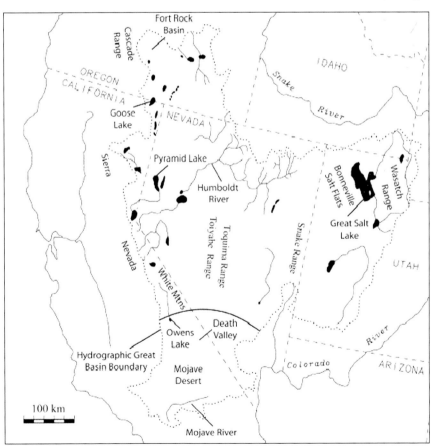

Figure 2.2. The hydrographic Great Basin. The curved line across southeastern California and southern Nevada indicates the approximate northern boundary of the Mohave Desert.

outward from there. For instance, the lowest elevation in Big Smoky Valley, between the Toiyabe and Toquima Ranges, is 5,430 feet. In Death Valley's Badwater Basin, some 200 miles to the south, the elevation falls to 282 feet below sea level, the lowest land surface in the United States. Valley bottom elevations fall in all other directions from the central area as well, but not nearly as much. For instance, Reno, Nevada, sits at about 4,400 feet; the Fort Rock Basin in south-central Oregon at 4,300 feet; and the Bonneville Salt Flats at 4,200 feet.

The combination of tall mountains and broad valleys creates tremendous elevational relief. The 11,000-foot peak of the Panamint Range, for instance, flanks the Badwater Basin to its immediate west, a vertical difference of more than two miles. The average elevational difference from valley bottom to adjacent mountaintop across the state of Nevada at 39 degrees north latitude (which cuts through the south end of Lake Tahoe) is a substantial 5,800 feet, or more than a mile.

X The great height of the Great Basin mountains helps determine the pattern of precipitation and the availability of water. The most important sources of precipitation are the winter storms that approach from the west. These Pacific storms quickly collide with the Cascade Range and the Sierra Nevada. Forced upward by the mountains and cooled, they let fall huge amounts of rain and snow on the western slopes. As they move eastward, they continue to drop rain and snow, especially where they meet high mountain ranges. The storms are most important in the western part of the Great Basin, which is closest to where the storms originate, and in the northern part, which receives the greatest number of frontal storms. This wintertime Pacific moisture, captured as snow, can feed streams and lakes well into the summer. In addition, the moisture contributed by these storms helps feed low-pressure systems, called Great Basin lows, that most commonly develop during the spring and bring a second source of precipitation to the central and eastern Great Basin.

X The eastern tropical Pacific and the Gulfs of California and Mexico are the third prime sources of precipitation. Storms from these areas, driven by the temperature difference between land and sea,

produce summertime rains that provide significant amounts of precipitation to the southern and eastern Great Basin.

Despite its multiple sources of rain and snow, the Great Basin as a whole is arid—in some places extremely so, as in the aptly named Death Valley, the hottest and driest place in the United States. Across the region, average annual precipitation in the valley bottoms measures between 4 and 12 inches a year, far less than the average annual evaporation rate. The result is a sere landscape of few lakes and streams. The lakes that do exist tend to be in the northern, far western, and far eastern portions. The western and eastern lakes exist because they are fed by streams from the Sierra Nevada and the Wasatch Range—streams born of the Pacific frontal storms. The lakes in the north exist because evaporation rates are lower there, and the area receives the greatest number of winter storms.

Given the Great Basin's extremes, from soaring peaks to sunken valleys, from arid plains to deep lakes, it should come as no surprise that its vegetation, too, differs from place to place. The Great Basin contains two areas defined on the basis of plants that typically grow there. One is the Mojave Desert, or "low desert," of southern Nevada and southeastern California, and the other is the "high desert" to the north, often called the Great Basin Desert. The dividing line between them is at roughly 36 degrees 30 minutes north latitude.

The creosote bush (*Larrea tridentata*), a gangly, sticky, dark green shrub that dislikes prolonged freezing temperatures and annual precipitation above about 7 inches, marks the divide between the two deserts. It thrives in the hot, dry Mojave Desert, which also hosts other plants not found in the high desert portions of the Great Basin. The most immediately recognizable is the Joshua tree (*Yucca brevifolia*) (fig. 2.3), said to have been named by immigrants who were reminded of Joshua of the Old Testament, beckoning them toward the promised land.

Most of the remaining Great Basin is covered by high desert vegetation. A standard set of plant zones, each with characteristic vegetation types and elevations, provides a convenient way to summarize what much of the basin's vegetation looks like (fig. 2.4).

Figure 2.3. Joshua trees in southeastern California's Mojave Desert.

Species of shrubs and herbaceous (soft-stemmed annual or perennial) plants that thrive in hot summers and on saline soils cover the floors of many Great Basin valleys. The most common is shadscale (*Atriplex confertifolia*), which gives its name to the entire zone. It has the ability to concentrate salts in its leaves, especially on their surfaces, which gives the plants a distinctive whitish-green color and enables them to reflect more sunlight than other plants. In many cases the salts are results of the evaporation of lakes that formed in some valleys more than 10,000 years ago. This set

Figure 2.4. The Monitor Valley and the Toquima Range as seen from Mosquito Creek in the Monitor Range, central Nevada. A, shadscale zone; B, sagebrush-grass zone; C, piñon-juniper zone; D, upper sagebrush-grass zone; E, limber pine–bristlecone pine zone; F, alpine-tundra zone.

Figure 2.5. View across the sagebrush-grass plant zone in south-central Oregon's Fort Rock Basin.

of adaptations gives shadscale access to water it could not otherwise use, keeps it cooler than it would otherwise be, and, because heavy doses of salts are not particularly palatable, gives it a chemical defense against herbivores.

Big sagebrush (*Artemisia tridentata*) (fig. 2.5) often dominates the zone just above the shadscale zone and the cooler, moister valley bottoms where shadscale does not grow. In his 1872 *Roughing It*, Mark Twain was impressed by this "imposing monarch of the forest in exquisite miniature," although he also felt that "as a vegetable, it is a distinguished failure," because nothing would eat it. As it happens, Twain was wrong. Many animals, from pygmy rabbits (*Brachylagus idahoensis*) to pronghorn antelope (*Antilocapra americana*), find it palatable, and pygmy rabbits rely on it almost entirely for their winter meals. It also was, and remains, an extremely important plant to Great Basin Native peoples for both medicinal and ritual purposes.

Although sagebrush dominates the sagebrush-grass zone, many other shrubs are found there, including Mormon tea (*Ephedra viridis*) and rubber rabbitbrush (*Chrysothamnus nauseosus*). Between the shrubs thrive many herbaceous plants, most obviously bunchgrasses, which used to be far more

abundant in the northerly parts of the high desert than to the south. Since the introduction of livestock and the invasion of exotic grasses, bunchgrasses are far less abundant than they once were. Unlike the grasses found on the Great Plains, which evolved in tandem with large herbivores, Great Basin bunchgrasses are poorly adapted to heavy grazing. The Great Basin also lacks native species of dung beetles, animals that are ubiquitous in areas that have significant numbers of herd animals. All this suggests a plant community that evolved in the absence of heavy grazing.

Even with all the shrubs and herbaceous plants, large parts of the sagebrush-grass zone are bare of plants, or so they look. Actually they teem with complex mixes of cyanobacteria (also known as blue-green algae), green algae, lichens, mosses, and other microorganisms, which form what scientists call "biological soil crusts" (or microbiotic or cryptogamic soil crusts). These crusts, which range from less than half an inch to more than 4 inches thick, are found throughout the relatively arid regions of the world. Although widely distributed in the Great Basin, the crusts tend not to develop on highly saline soils or in places with dense vegetation and heavy leaf litter. Once you know they are there, the crusts are easy to see. When walking in the sagebrush-grass zone, just look down, and chances are you will be standing on one. Unfortunately, the crusts are easily damaged by trampling, especially when dry. Although we do not yet understand how fast they recover from such injury, we know the recovery has to be measured in decades and centuries, not months and years.

The importance of these crusts is hard to overemphasize. They help prevent wind and water erosion; they fix nitrogen in the ground; they increase essential nutrients for vascular plants; and because they are dark and absorb the sun's heat, they increase soil warmth. All these benefits are lost when the crusts are destroyed. Like bunchgrasses, the crusts are ill equipped to deal with large-bodied organisms such as humans and cows, or with wheeled vehicles.

As the sagebrush-grass community laps against the flanks of the mountains adjoining the valley bottoms, small trees descend to meet it. The trees are almost always one of several species of juniper, often Utah juniper (*Juniperus osteosperma*), although in the northern Great Basin, roughly north of the Humboldt River, western juniper (*J. occidentalis*) replaces it. In much of the Great Basin—the Humboldt River is again the approximate northern boundary—piñons join the junipers at slightly higher elevations to form piñon-juniper woodlands.

The woodlands occupy the middle elevations of mountains throughout all but the northern area, covering some 17 million acres, or about 18 percent, of the hydrographic Great Basin. Juniper is more common below 6,600 feet, and piñon, above 7,200 feet. In most of these woodlands, the single-needled piñon (*Pinus monophylla*) abounds, but Colorado piñon (*P. edulis*) takes over on the far eastern edge of the Great Basin and extends onto the Colorado Plateau.

The preponderance of piñon and juniper in the Great Basin appears to be a recent phenomenon. The woodlands and the pure stands of western juniper in the northernmost Great Basin began to expand dramatically during the last half of the nineteenth century. Even though western and Utah junipers can live more than 1,000 years, and piñons more than 600, less than 10 percent of today's piñon-juniper woodland consists of trees established before 1860. During the period of intense mining in the Great Basin, from about 1850 to 1890, large sections of the woodlands were harvested to make charcoal for use in mine smelters. New trees grew back after the harvesting ended.

At the same time, the region experienced generally warmer, wetter weather, which discouraged fire and encouraged piñon-juniper or juniper woodlands to expand dramatically. This expansion continues today, a function of fire suppression and perhaps increased carbon dioxide in the atmosphere. But as these woodlands mature, they become increasingly prone to hot crown fires, which can destroy them. Unfortunately, this process is unlikely to return the landscape to anything resembling what it was before, because the burned areas become prime targets for invasion by introduced, fire-adapted Eurasian grasses, including cheat grass (*Bromus tectorum*).

The understory in a piñon-juniper woodland becomes impoverished as the trees close in, but the plants that do grow there are generally similar to those found in the sagebrush-grass zone. At the upper limit of the piñon-juniper woodland, the vegetation becomes very much like, though not identical to, that found just below the woodland. The similarities between the upper and lower versions of this sagebrush-grass zone are so striking that the piñon-juniper appears to be superimposed on an otherwise continuous sagebrush-grass community. And indeed it is, as we will see.

The upper sagebrush-grass zone extends all the way to the tops of some Great Basin mountains. On mountains that are high enough, however, it gives way to a second woodland—the limber pine–bristlecone pine zone (fig. 2.6). Although this zone is named after two of its most prominent members, it contains a fairly wide range of mountain conifers, including not only limber pine (*Pinus flexilis*) and bristlecone pine (*P. longaeva*) but also whitebark pine (*P. albicaulis*), Englemann spruce (*Picea engelmannii*), and subalpine fir (*Abies lasiocarpa*). Certainly the most famous of these trees is the bristlecone pine, because it is so long-lived. The oldest known bristlecone, from the Snake Range in eastern Nevada, reached the age of 4,844 years before it was cut down in the prime of life by an overzealous scientist. Now the oldest known tree, in the White Mountains of California, is about 4,800 years old.

The subalpine conifer zone generally falls between about 9,500 and 11,500 feet. Above it, dwarf shrubs and low-lying

herbaceous vegetation—
for instance, buckwheat
(*Eriogonum*), phlox
(*Phlox*), grasses, and the
wonderfully named sky
pilot (*Polemonium*)—
replace the trees. This
highest of all plant communities is called the alpine-
tundra zone. These cold
peaks, as we now know, are
home to some of the most
remarkable archaeological
sites in the Great Basin.

Figure 2.6. Limber pines and the alpine-tundra zone at the top of the Toquima Range, central Nevada.

Becoming Modern

Thanks to a large variety
of data about the ancient
environment, scientists
now well understand many
aspects of the natural history of the Great Basin,
especially during the past 12,000 years or so.

The period from the end of the Pleistocene
epoch, or last Ice Age, roughly 12,000 years ago,
until about 8,500 years ago is the early Holocene,
the beginning of modern climatic times. The period is important because it set the stage on which
the current environment began to play out its
drama. In most places, when rainfall increases or
evaporation decreases, excess water that enters a
lake basin flows away through streams leading to
the ocean. Nature doesn't work that way in the
Great Basin, because its rivers and streams have no
outlets. They generally flow into, but not out of,
low-elevation basins. As a result, when the amount
of water entering the basins increases, lakes grow
in places that shortly before had none. Lakes that
already existed get bigger. If they get big enough,
they can overflow, spilling into adjoining basins,
and then overflow again. This process continues
until an equilibrium is established between lake
level and water availability. It can even continue
until the lake rises so high that it finds a way to
spill out of the Great Basin altogether and ultimately
into the ocean. Northern California's Goose Lake
did just that in 1868.

This process has been going on in the Great

Basin for more than 2 million years, but the lakes
most relevant to us are those that grew toward the
end of the Pleistocene. During this time there were
about 80 such lakes in the Great Basin (fig. 2.7),
covering some 28 million acres, far more than is
now covered by piñon-juniper woodland. These
lakes formed in response to both lower temperatures and greater precipitation.

During the last glacial maximum, the time of
the greatest expanse of glaciers during the last Ice
Age, average annual temperatures in the Great
Basin fell by an estimated 14.5 to 23.5 degrees
Fahrenheit below present-day averages. As temperatures fell, glaciers formed in many Great Basin
mountains. Massive glaciers throughout North
America forced the jet stream and the storms associated with it southward. Later, as the glaciers
retreated northward, the jet stream migrated northward as well. Consequently, lakes in the southern
Great Basin reached their highest late Pleistocene
stands before those to the north. Lake Mojave I,
which formed in the Mojave River basin, reached
its highest late Pleistocene stand between 18,000
and 16,000 years ago, whereas Lake Bonneville,
once the size of Lake Superior, peaked between
about 15,000 and 13,500 years ago.

As far as we know, there were no people in the
Great Basin when the lakes were at their largest.

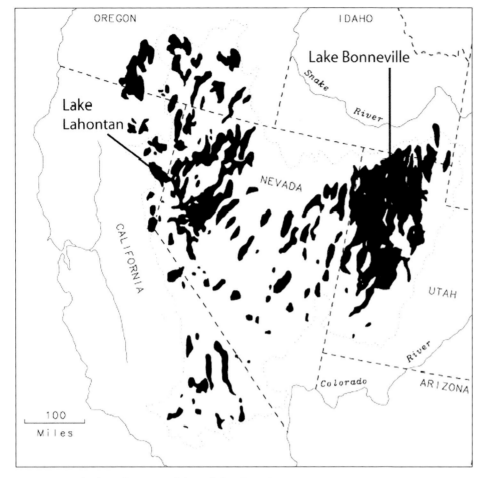

Figure 2.7. The late Pleistocene lakes of the Great Basin.

The late Pleistocene and early Holocene vegetation of the Great Basin differed as dramatically from that found today as the lakes and marshes did. In the Mojave Desert during the late Pleistocene, limber pine woodlands grew some 3,300 feet lower than they do now. The shrubby vegetation at lower elevations consisted not of the standard Mojave desert plants such as creosote bush but instead of plants now common in the high desert Great Basin to the north, such as sagebrush and shadscale.

After about 11,000 years ago, the low-elevation Mojave Desert woodlands gave way to woodlands of Utah juniper or both juniper and single-leaf piñon. The later woodlands, in turn, disappeared at different times in different places, often leaving behind desert vegetation such as sagebrush and shadscale, a situation that continued until about 8,500 years ago. Indeed, one of the defining plants of the Mojave Desert—creosote bush—did not appear in any abundance until after that time.

This sequence, in which shrubs characteristic of the high desert Great Basin replaced those now definitive of the Mojave Desert only after about 8,500 years ago, matches the evidence for lakes in the Mojave River basin. They disappeared about the same time the new vegetation spread throughout the region. The plant sequence also matches evidence for declining water tables and spring discharge in southern Nevada beginning about 8,500 years ago. The implication seems clear. The Mojave Desert was then wetter and cooler than it has been since.

However, many basins that are now dry or contain very shallow, saline lakes did hold lakes, or deeper ones, when people were certainly present. During the cold episode known as the Younger Dryas, about 11,000 to 10,000 years ago, small lakes existed in many Great Basin valleys, and water tables were generally high.

The end of the Pleistocene saw the end of most of these lakes. Their disappearance does not mean that valley bottoms were as dry as they are now. Evidence shows that many now-arid valleys harbored marshes between about 10,000 and 8,000 years ago, from the Mojave River drainage in the south to the lake basins of south-central Oregon in the north, and including the now bone-dry central Lake Bonneville basin. By the beginning of the middle Holocene, roughly 8,500 to 7,500 years ago, most of the low-elevation marshes had vanished as well.

To the north, in the high desert Great Basin, the vegetation sequence was much the same, although the plants involved may have differed substantially. Between about 12,500 and 10,000 years ago, many areas contained woodlands—sometimes dominated by Utah juniper and sometimes by limber pine, with other trees often present—at elevations far lower than today.

The understory of these woodlands was composed of plants characteristic of the cooler parts of the modern Great Basin, including sagebrush. In the northern Bonneville Basin, for instance, limber pine woodlands grew as low as 6,000 feet, with an understory that included sagebrush and the aptly named snowberry (*Symphoricarpos*). These woodlands began to retreat about 11,000 years ago and were replaced by shrubby vegetation dominated by sagebrush and shadscale.

Until about 8,000 years ago, many valleys where shadscale is now abundant were dominated by sagebrush. Other low-elevation settings supported shrubs that thrive in cool, moist settings no longer present at those elevations today. Just as in the Mojave Desert, the plant assemblages suggest that the Great Basin was cool and moist during the early Holocene. Our detailed knowledge of the small mammals that thrived during this period suggests exactly the same thing—a cool, moist Great Basin between about 10,000 and 8,000 years ago.

It is no accident that I have not mentioned piñon in discussing the plant life of the late Pleistocene and early Holocene in the high desert Great Basin. That is because it was not

present then, even though it grew just to the south in the Mojave Desert. Piñon seems to have begun its movement northward between 10,000 and 9,000 years ago. It reached central Nevada soon after 6,000 years ago and northwestern Utah about 7,000 years ago. The tree did not fill in the northwesternmost parts of its distribution until the last few hundred years, and it may still be moving northward.

Because people lived in the Great Basin by at least 11,500 years ago, we can be certain that they saw lakes and marshes where now there are none, and limber pine woodlands in places where the trees could not now survive. We can also be fairly certain they saw animals that have not existed for 10,000 years. Toward the end of the Pleistocene, North America lost some 35 genera of primarily large mammals, including the elephant-size mammoth (*Mammuthus*) and mastodon (*Mammut*), the 2,000-pound short-faced bear (*Arctodus*), and, at the other end of the size spectrum, the 30-pound diminutive pronghorn antelope (*Capromeryx*). Why, when, and how these extinctions took place remain unknown, but we do know that 19 of the genera lived in the Great Basin, and 7 of them—mammoths, the Shasta ground sloth (*Nothrotheriops*), some species of horses, the flat-headed peccary (*Platygonus*), the "yesterday's camel," the shrub ox (*Euceratherium*), and the giant short-faced bear—survived beyond 12,000 years ago and so into the time when people were present. Three species of mammals belonging to genera that still exist elsewhere in North America—the dire wolf (*Canis dirus*), the American lion (*Panthera leo*, and yes, a real lion), and Harrington's mountain goat (*Oreamnos harringtoni*)—also died out in the Great Basin during the late Pleistocene.

Researchers have no evidence that people hunted any of these animals in the Great Basin and thus no reason to think that humans played any role in their extinction. Although we don't know when the extinctions began—and it may have been long before 12,000 years ago—it certainly seems that none of these animals survived beyond 10,000 years ago, because archaeologists have found none of their bones in sites of that age. After 10,000 years ago, the only large herbivores known from the

Great Basin are those that
still live there or did so until
recently: mountain sheep
(*Ovis canadensis*), mule deer
(*Odocoileus hemionus*), pronghorn antelope (*Antilocapra
americana*), and, far less abundant, bison (*Bison bison*) and
elk (*Cervus elaphus*).

✗The middle Holocene,
from roughly 8,500 to 5,000
years ago, was a remarkable
time in the Great Basin. It
was, to put it briefly, very
hot and dry, the kind of
climate kangaroo rats might
like but people might not.
Many lakes and marshes
dried up completely or only
barely survived.

For example, the Ruby
Marshes of northeastern
Nevada (see fig. 11.1), the
site of a freshwater lake during the early Holocene and
now the heart of Ruby Lake
National Wildlife Refuge,
dried up entirely or close to
it between about 6,800 and
4,500 years ago. The central

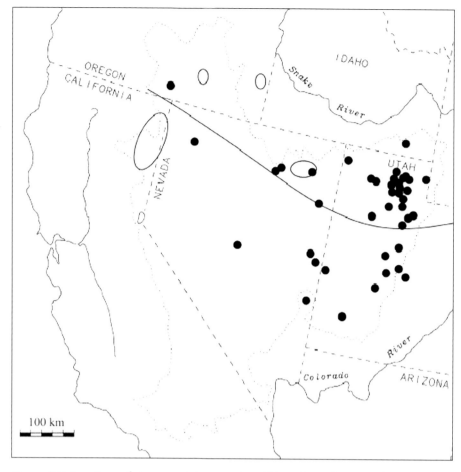

Figure 2.8. Locations of sites containing remains of bison dating between about 1,600
and 600 years ago. The ovals mark areas from which bison were reported in historic
times; distributions in present-day Utah not shown. After 600 years ago, Great Basin
bison were confined to areas north of the solid line.

part of the Humboldt River appears to have dried
up around the same time. Humboldt Lake, into
which the river normally flows, shrank substantially and perhaps disappeared. To the south and
west of the White Mountains, Owens Lake dried
up, and to the north, Lake Tahoe fell so much
between about 5,500 and 4,300 years ago that trees
grew 13 feet beneath the level at which the lake
now flows into the Truckee River. Because the
Truckee feeds Pyramid Lake, that lake, too, shrank.
Scientists have estimated that summer temperatures at the lake may have been about 9 degrees
Fahrenheit higher than they are now.

As a result of these changes in climate and the
availability of water, some animals went locally
extinct, and the creosote bush made its arrival in
the Mojave Desert. The bristlecone pine tree line in

the White Mountains moved upward some 500 feet
between 6,500 and 4,200 years ago. In short, the
middle Holocene, although not hot and dry everywhere all the time, was hot and dry enough to produce a Great Basin less welcoming to people than
what came before and after.

Only after about 5,000 years ago, during late
Holocene times, did the Great Basin become much
the way it is today, so that time travelers familiar
with the region's landscape would not be aston-
ished by what they saw. But the Great Basin of the
late Holocene was not yet an environmentally
modern Great Basin. Piñons did not fill in their
contemporary range until just a few hundred years
ago.✗In addition, detailed analyses of plant, animal,
and lake histories have all shown that the Great
Basin has undergone significant changes during the

last 5,000 years. For example, we have evidence of four severe droughts during the past 2,500 years, including one from 2,500 to 2,000 years ago. Two things that were especially relevant to the human history of the region need emphasis. First, the abundance of bison in the eastern Great Basin increased substantially between about 1,600 and 600 years ago. Second, two important episodes of drought struck during the past 1,000 years.

The Great Basin is not the kind of place one associates with bison, but they roamed there during the Pleistocene and lasted, to one degree or another, until Euro-Americans put an end to their existence in the region. They were most abundant between 1,600 and 600 years ago, particularly in the east and along the edges of the Bonneville Basin (fig. 2.8). This is the same area that saw the growth of the Fremont archaeological culture, and many Fremont sites contain bison bones.

The reason bison flourished in the Great Basin is that the summer rains I described earlier nourished the grasses on which bison fed. Because summer temperature differentials between land and sea drive these seasonal storms, rising land temperatures can fuel their strength. Stronger storms mean more summer moisture for grasses, which means more food for bison, as well as better conditions for the domesticated crops planted by Fremont people.

When the summer storm cycle ultimately weakened, the grasses that depended on summer moisture withered. As their food supply declined, bison dwindled as well. Indeed, the drop in the number of bison after 600 years ago correlates with evidence for a severe drought between about 1200 and 1350 CE, at least in northeastern Utah. After this change and the associated demise of the Fremont culture, bison shifted their range to the far northern Great Basin, where winter rainfall was increasing

The drought that affected northeastern Utah appears to have been widespread. It was one of two severe droughts that afflicted the Great Basin between about 1000 and 1500 CE. The first took place between about 1000 and 1150, and the second between about 1200 and 1350. Both happened during what scientists call the Medieval Climatic Anomaly, or the Medieval Warm Period.

Researchers have well-dated and convincing evidence for these droughts, including changes in tree line elevation and fire frequency and the trunks of dead trees that grew in places now under water. At Fallen Leaf Lake in the Tahoe Basin, for instance, 100-foot-tall trees dating back to 1215 CE are rooted 120 feet below the current lake surface. The drought that drew the water down far enough to allow trees to take root might have begun as much as 200 years earlier. The second drought (1200–1350) took hold at the time both the Fremont culture and bison declined in the Great Basin. These droughts also generally coincide with evidence that people began to use the uplands of the White Mountains and the Toquima and Toiyabe Ranges in ways distinctly different from earlier practices (see chapter 12). Humans, like plants, may have moved up the mountains in response to the pressures and opportunities that climate change offered.

Looking to the Future

The best archaeology and paleoecology satisfy our curiosity about the past while offering relevance for the future. Our knowledge suggests that the Fremont culture ebbed because climate change undermined people's ability to grow corn, beans, and squash, the staples of their diet. What might modern farmers living in the same area and subject to perhaps even greater climate change in the coming decades learn from their predecessors' fate? Between about 7,500 and 5,000 years ago, kangaroo rats flourished in the Great Basin, but people shunned it for milder, wetter places. Need we fear a return to similar conditions in the future? And if we do, what of Las Vegas and its apparently unlimited demand for water in a landscape that appears nearly devoid of it even now?

The histories of the plants and animals of the Great Basin over the last 12,000 years are tales of resilience. Where they lived and how many of them lived changed, but with rare exceptions none suffered extinction. This was true even of animals that people hunted during the entire time span—pronghorn, for instance, and mountain sheep. Does this resilience provide hope for the future of these animals, or might they join the bison in being no longer able to find a home in the Great Basin? Perhaps the most remarkable thing about the combination of archaeology and paleoecology is that it can provide, and in many case has provided, answers to questions of this sort. The principal answer may be that long-term drought cycles have occurred many times over the millennia and severely affected life as then lived in the Great Basin. It can easily happen again, despite the sophisticated technologies of the people currently living there.

Donald K. Grayson is a professor of anthropology at the University of Washington and author of *The Desert's Past: A Natural Prehistory of the Great Basin* (Smithsonian Institution Press).

Figure 3.1. Beach terraces of Pleistocene Lake Bonneville at the north end of the Oquirrh Mountains, Utah.

Building an Environmental History of the Great Basin

David Rhode

Soon after John C. Frémont first named the Great Basin in 1844, explorers and scientists began piecing together its rich environmental history, trying to understand what had created and shaped the present-day landscape. In 1849 Captain Howard Stansbury led a company of US Army Topographical Engineers through the Great Salt Lake basin. There he found a series of former beach terraces (fig. 3.1) that, like bathtub rings on a massive scale, proved this barren desert was once "a vast *inland* sea, extending for hundreds of miles; and the isolated mountains which now tower from the flats, forming its western and south-western shores, were doubtless huge islands, similar to those which now rise from the diminished waters of the lake."

In the 1880s the great geologist Grove Karl Gilbert named that ancient, island-studded sea Lake Bonneville, in honor of a French-born explorer of the region in the 1830s, Captain Benjamin L. E. Bonneville, and studied it in extraordinary detail. Israel C. Russell, Gilbert's colleague in the newly founded US Geological Survey, investigated another large former lake on the western edge of the Great Basin, Lake Lahontan, named for the seventeenth-century French explorer of North America Baron de Lahontan. Today their works are classics, revered by students of ancient lakes and landforms for the quality of their insights and reasoning.

Gilbert and Russell helped establish just how remarkably different a place the Great Basin was during the Pleistocene epoch, from about 1.8 million to 12,000 years ago. During that time the Great Basin was a land abounding in water. Besides Lakes

Bonneville and Lahontan, dozens of smaller lakes filled intervening valleys. Glaciers slowly advanced from the bordering Sierra Nevada and Wasatch Mountains and from some taller ranges inside the basin, leaving terminal moraines—telltale deposits of sediments and rocks—at valley margins where their advances ended. A menagerie of large Pleistocene animals left their remains embedded in cave and lake sediments. These were later discovered by nineteenth-century fossil hunters such as Othniel Marsh, Edward Drinker Cope, R. W. Shufeldt, and, in a later generation, John C. Merriam and others. The fossils verified that the lakes dated to the Pleistocene epoch. Israel Russell and his assistant W. J. McGee had seen bone beds of Pleistocene-age mammoths, rhinoceroses, horses, and camels in the Lahontan Basin. In one bed they found a well-fashioned obsidian knife or spear point, tantalizing but uncertain evidence of the possible coexistence of Ice Age animals with humans.

The Great Basin's post–Ice Age, or Holocene, environment was no less dynamic than that of the Pleistocene. Israel Russell was one of the first to appreciate this fact. Early explorers had noticed driftwood-strewn beaches several feet higher than the Great Salt Lake, showing recent fluctuations in lake levels. Russell recognized even more substantial changes. He calculated that Pyramid, Walker, and Winnemucca Lakes, which occupied sub-basins formerly inundated by Lake Lahontan, all contained less salt in their waters than would be expected if they were simply left over from a declining Lake Lahontan. Mollusks found in earlier lake deposits also differed from modern species. Russell reasoned that Lake Lahontan must have dried up completely, leaving chemicals from its water as dry concentrates in lake-bed playas. Pyramid, Walker, and Winnemucca Lakes were later refreshed, leaving the concentrates still buried. This interpretation led Russell to propose that the "post-pluvial" period, the time following the high lake levels, was significantly warmer and drier than today. Lacking adequate dating techniques, he suggested that the lakes had filled again only within the last 300 years.

Discovering the details and timing of this proposed sequence of post–Ice Age climate change —a warm, dry interval that desiccated the lakes, followed by a cooler, moister climate that reinvigorated some of them—later became a career-long quest for the brilliant Swedish geologist Ernst Antevs. Antevs was a student of Baron Gerard de Geer's, who had developed the counting of annually deposited layers of clay, called "varves," in lakes as a way to create glacial chronologies in Scandinavia. In 1920 de Geer and Antevs visited the United States to develop glacial chronologies for North America. Antevs stayed on when John C. Merriam, of the Carnegie Institution of Washington, asked him to tie the history of Great Basin lakes to North American glacial history. Antevs spent the next 40 years working across the continent, correlating the western record with the glacial sequences in eastern North America and northern Europe, an effort that culminated in his "Neothermal" climatic sequence.

The Neothermal sequence divided the Holocene into three parts: the early Holocene *Anathermal* (literally, "upward temperatures"), the middle Holocene *Altithermal* ("high temperatures"), and the late Holocene *Medithermal* ("temperatures of intermediate degree"). Antevs correlated his western record with the varve-dated record of lake and bog sediments in northern Europe and eastern North America, which reflected a similar three-part sequence: initial warming, then maximum temperature, followed by general temperature decline. Antevs relied on a variety of geochronological indicators to obtain age estimates, most of which, before radiocarbon dating, involved ingenious guesswork. His calculated guesses included the presumed age of volcanic ash layers in Oregon lake deposits, the rate of peat buildup in Klamath Marsh, Oregon, the time it took for salts to accumulate in Owens Lake in eastern California, and the glacial chronologies of the Sierra Nevada and the Wasatch Range. The uncertainty and scarcity of local evidence and the many assumptions Antevs had to make meant that his age estimates for the three climate periods were provisional and somewhat arbitrary.

Antevs intended the Neothermal sequence to provide a chronological framework for geological and archaeological deposits, but he happened to present it just as the radiocarbon dating method was being developed in the late 1940s. The radiocarbon revolution soon eclipsed the Neothermal sequence as a dating tool. More important than numerical age estimates, however, was Antevs's ordered sequence of recognizable climate periods, which allowed researchers to make rough correlations between disparate geological and archaeological deposits—a brilliant and practical achievement.

Later scientists developed sequences of Holocene environmental changes that offered greater temporal detail and focused on smaller areas. But Antevs's tripartite Neothermal climatic sequence for the Holocene continues to serve as an important framework for post-Pleistocene environmental changes. Those changes profoundly affect our concepts of western North America as a habitat for humans. What were the climatic periods really like? How much did they differ from the present day? How did the changing climates affect the plants, animals, people, and landscapes of the Great Basin? Many of the chapters in this book discuss these questions.

Measuring Past Environments by Proxy

Characterizing climatic periods in the Great Basin has meant figuring out how much warmer or cooler the climate was than at present, how much wetter or drier, and how variable it was from year to year. Researchers attempt to quantify these climatic traits using physical indicators of past conditions that can act as proxies, or substitutes, for direct measurements. Certain kinds of data can serve as indirect thermometers, rain gauges, and recorders of plants and animals.

Figure 3.2. View of the 1962 Tule Springs excavations in southern Nevada.

Many climatic proxies relate to the physical effects of water on the landscape, including the incising of arroyos and gullies by stream flow, the maintenance of wetlands by springs, and the formation of lakes and alluvial fans, places where streams drop sediments as they spread out onto a plain. Most important are studies of what scientists call "paleolakes," or ancient bodies of freshwater— studies that hark back to the days of Gilbert and Russell. The water level of a closed-basin lake is a function of how much water goes into the lake from precipitation, runoff, and discharge from springs, as well as how much is lost to evaporation, which is affected by air temperature, cloud cover, humidity, and wind. If we know a lake's present-day inputs of water and its evaporation rates and we can relate them to the lake's surface area and volume, then we can estimate the water inputs and rates of evaporation needed to support lakes of known sizes in the past.

Some proxy indicators of climate are chemical. Larry Benson and his colleagues, for example, measured the proportions of different types of oxygen and chemicals in lake sediments to determine variations in the amounts of water running into and evaporating out of Great Basin paleolakes. Such measurements highlight periods of diminishing and rising lakes and can be used to calculate the temperature and precipitation ranges needed to cause observed changes in lake water chemistry.

Among other water-related proxies, deposits of organic materials, often known as "black mats," reveal where ancient wetlands once flourished. And scientists have been able to work out the sequences in which layers of water-deposited sediments were laid down—so-called alluvial chronologies—for a few major Great Basin valley systems and rivers. Ages of artifact types found on and in dated alluvial layers can then be determined. Notable in this regard is the pioneering work carried out in the 1960s at Tule Springs in the Las Vegas Valley by C. Vance Haynes, Peter Mehringer, Richard Shutler, and their colleagues (fig. 3.2), which was subsequently refined by the geologist and geochemist Jay Quade.

Wood from long-lived trees provides another excellent proxy record of climate, one with a long research pedigree in the Great Basin. Tree-ring dating, or dendrochronology, relies on the fact that climate variability affects the widths of the rings that trees form every year as they grow. The Great Basin is blessed with the longest-lived tree on the planet, the bristlecone pine (plate 5). In the 1950s Edmund Schulman and his student C. W. Ferguson discovered living bristlecone pines more than 4,500 years old in the White Mountains of eastern California, along with much older dead snags and fallen wood. From these ancient trunks and scattered fragments they developed a continuous tree-ring sequence of more than 7,000 years (fig. 3.3). That is a record of annual weather covering more than two-thirds of the Holocene—an amazing feat. Later, Donald Graybill pushed that record back another thousand years, and researchers hope to extend it even further.

Tree-ring scientists have developed similar but shorter records for dozens of places in the Great Basin, the Sierra Nevada, and the Wasatch Range. The records are a tremendous resource for studying long-term trends in climate, documenting droughts and wet spells, reconstructing stream flow in major rivers, and examining historic patterns of fire frequency, to list just a few applications. The bristlecone pine chronology, for example, gave Valmore LaMarche the tools he needed to date timberlines in the White Mountains and to infer how they had moved up and down in response to temper-ature changes over the last 6,500 years. These were key data for determining the effects on Great Basin environments of the high temperatures experienced during the Holocene Altithermal.

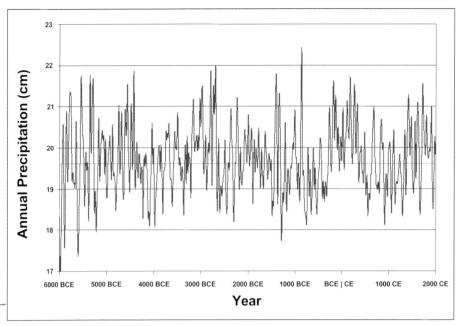

Figure 3.3. The 8,000-year bristlecone pine tree-ring record developed by Edward Schulman and C. W. Ferguson and later extended by Donald Graybill. The chart has been calibrated to reflect precipitation.

Researchers have used dendrochronology and the larger science of which it is a part, dendroclimatology, to identify the timing, extent, and severity of decades-long droughts over the past 1,000 years. Trees found submerged be-neath lakes or buried in river deposits in the Sierra Nevada and adjacent western Great Basin, most famously in Lake Tahoe, show that lakes were once lower than at present and that streambeds were dry enough to allow trees to grow in them. Scientists normally use radiocarbon dating to determine when these trees grew, and tree-ring dating gives their ages at death. Both pieces of information give an idea of the length of time the lakes were lower and the streambeds were dry.

Owl Pellets, Pollen, and Pack Rat Middens

Important clues to past environments also come from biogeography, the study of the distribution of organisms across the landscape. Modern distributions of species relative to their known past distributions; zones of hybridization, or genetic mixing, between populations of plant or animal species that are now geographically separated; and fossil remains of plants and animals in places where they no longer live all suggest that ranges of those plants and animals have shifted, expanded, and contracted in response to past climate changes. Fossil remains of plants and animals also serve as climate proxies. If we know, for example, that the subalpine limber pine grows only in places where the average July temperature does not exceed 72 degrees Fahrenheit,

and if we find fossil remains of limber pine in valleys where the average July temperature is now 86 degrees, then summers must have been at least 14 degrees cooler when limber pine grew in the valleys. By examining suites of plant and animal species, each with its own special climatic tolerances, we can build a climatic "envelope" that sets bounds on a region's possible climates.

Some of the most important biogeographic clues to past Great Basin environments have come from mammals that live in the basin's mountains but cannot now tolerate its hot, dry valleys. In 1971 the biologist James Brown proposed his now-classic concept of "island" biogeography, in which Great Basin mountain ranges were habitable "islands" for some species in otherwise uninhabitable "seas" of lower-elevation desert. The idea spurred a wealth of research on how and when animals and plants became extinct or moved into new areas, depending on the sizes of available habitats and the heterogeneity of the species. This kind of research tells much about the power of past climatic constraints in shaping where small mammals live today. It also helps in understanding how climate change stimulated the migration of species during the late

1 cm

Figure 3.4. Owl pellets.

a small shelter near Great Salt Lake, holds an 11,000-year record of faunal changes in the form of accumulated owl pellets (figs. 3.5, 3.6). This remarkable record, studied by Donald Grayson, Jack Broughton, and Stephanie Livingston, reveals dramatic changes in the kinds and abundances of animal species that once lived within the flying radius of a hunting owl. Among them were fish and waterfowl from Pleistocene Lake Bonneville and Holocene Great Salt Lake, sagebrush-loving pygmy rabbits and other small mammals from the cool and relatively moist early Holocene, desert-loving kangaroo rats from the warm, dry middle Holocene, and a few mountain-dwelling mammals during the cooler, wetter late Holocene—just as Ernst Antevs might have predicted.

These faunal changes accord well with the history of Great Basin vegetation. Paleoecologists have learned about that history by using two valuable tools in their arsenal. The first is palynology, the study of pollen and spores to deduce past vegetation patterns. Palynology was developed in the early twentieth century in Scandinavia, where layered peat bogs and lake sediments nicely trapped and preserved thousands of years of accumulated pollen grains. The science took a while to catch on in drier regions. Even so, the palynological pioneer Edward Deevey observed in the early 1960s that if "one digs under the mirage" of dry lake beds, much pollen could be found, both airborne pollen grains and pollen carried into lake beds and arroyos by intermittent streams.

In the early 1930s Frank Laudermilk and Philip Munz studied pollen in ground sloth dung from Gypsum Cave in southern Nevada, the first use of the technique in the Great Basin. Soon afterward, Henry Hansen, Paul Sears, Paul Martin, and others demonstrated the method's utility in archaeological sites, dry lake beds, and stream deposits. Peter Mehringer used pollen analysis to develop a number of records of ancient environmental change in the Great Basin. Many scholars working in a variety of settings have expanded on Mehringer's efforts, resulting in a maturing archive of Great Basin palynological records.

A complementary and equally useful product of biotic history augments the paleoecologist's tool

Holocene and, most pressingly, the fates of small mammal populations isolated on Great Basin mountaintops in the face of renewed warming and human settlement today.

Evidence from archaeology and paleoecology has played a crucial role in this research. The result, as Donald Grayson has pointed out, is that "our understanding of the history of Great Basin mammals during the past 10,000 years is arguably better than that for any other part of North America."

Rockshelters that have served as roosts for owls and other raptors are among the most useful places for studying changes in animal distributions over time. After a night of hunting and dining on small mammals, an owl finds a suitable resting roost, digests its meal, and regurgitates the indigestible bones and hair in compact balls called owl pellets (fig. 3.4). These pellets accumulate beneath the roost and over time and generations of owls build up into deposits that can contain millions of bones and other faunal remains. Homestead Cave,

Figure 3.5. Donald Grayson (right) and David Madsen at Homestead Cave, Utah, on the margins of Pleistocene Lake Bonneville. The site contains a record of small mammals, birds, and fish common to the area around the cave spanning the last 13,000 years. Most of the millions of bones there were deposited by roosting raptors, primarily owls.

Figure 3.6. Stratigraphic profile of Homestead Cave, Utah. Owl pellets and mammal, bird, and fish bones are heavily distributed throughout the deposit.

kit: the pack rat midden. The pack rat, or wood rat (genus *Neotoma*), a common Great Basin denizen (fig. 3.7), often builds a nest using sticks, cactus pads, and other plant parts in a protected rock overhang or crevice. The rat uses part of its nest as a latrine. The concentrated urine dries and crystallizes into a rock-hard mass, encasing whatever the rat has brought in from within a few hundred feet of its home: twigs, seeds, bones, feathers, and whatever else attracts its interest. These masses of crystallized urine, known to the cognoscenti as "indurated pack rat middens," can persist for tens of thousands of years if kept dry. Over time, new generations of rats may live in the same crevice and add new layers to the midden, which can accumulate to an impressive size (fig. 3.8). One has only to break open or dissolve layers of the midden to expose a trove of mummified biological remains in a remarkable state of preservation, ready for identification and radiocarbon dating.

Philip Wells and Clive Jorgensen first studied Ice Age pack rat middens in southern Nevada in the early 1960s. Thomas Van Devender, Geoffrey

Spaulding, Robert Thompson, Peter Wigand, and others quickly followed suit. Pack rat middens have allowed us to learn, for example, that subalpine conifers such as limber pine grew at elevations 3,300 feet lower than today in the late Ice Age Mojave Desert. We can trace the Holocene migration of single-leaf piñon from needles and cone fragments preserved in middens. Identifiable bones and fecal pellets tell us where pikas and other mountain-dwelling mammals formerly lived.

Pack rat middens have revolutionized the understanding of environmental history in the Great Basin. They can provide paleoenvironmental information for places where other records are lacking. Their remarkable preservation often allows researchers to identify plant and animal remains at the level of species. Many kinds of proxy records related to climate can be investigated from the same midden: faunal remains, plant parts, and pollen. An individual layer in a midden usually reflects the short time that a single rat lived there, and the layer's contents reflect environmental and climatic conditions within the rat's narrow collecting radius.

These local, temporally narrow midden records can complement the more continuous regional vegetation records provided by pollen from lakes and bogs. Putting the two together creates a powerful tool for establishing vegetation history.

My brief survey has covered only a few of the important sources of biological and physical informa-tion used to piece togeth-er Great Basin environmental his-tory. A great virtue of paleoenvironmental research is that so many different and com-plementary types of evidence are available to be used in combina-tion. Another virtue is the long tradition of close collaboration between scholars of past environ-ments and scholars of past human inhabitants, to the great benefit of both camps. Of course the paleoenvironmental information that archaeologists may wish for often goes beyond what paleo-ecologists are able to provide. As archaeologist Robert Kelly pointed out not long ago, paleoenviron-mental research provides general information about past climates and environments but relatively little about actual food, the pri-mary concern of ancient hunter-gatherers. We are now at the beginning stages of mapping the general distribution and rough abundances of principal Great Basin food resources across space and over time. Improvements in our understanding of these past distributions will tell us much more about the human experi-ence in the Great Basin.

Figure 3.7. A bushy-tailed wood rat on a typical pack rat midden.

Figure 3.8. Geoffrey Spaulding inspects a pack rat midden dating between 17,000 and 10,000 years ago in the Eleana Range in central Nevada.

David Rhode is an archaeologist and paleontologist with the Desert Research Institute in Reno, Nevada.

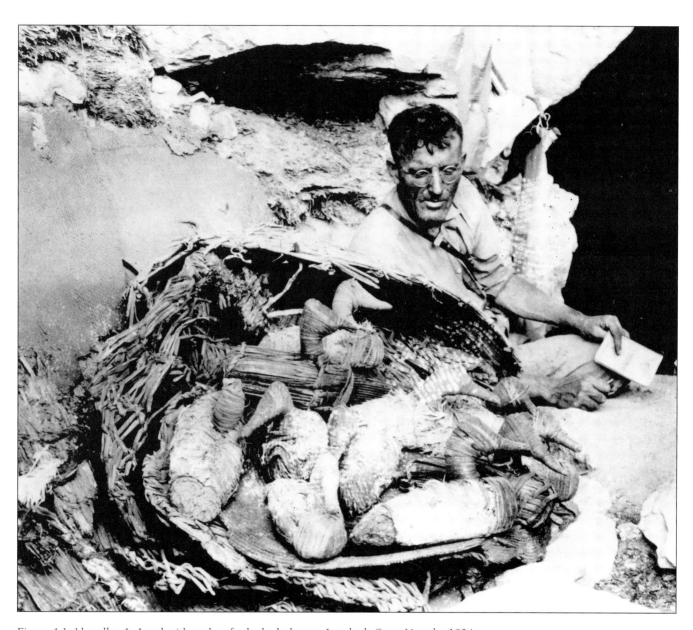

Figure 4.1. Llewellyn L. Loud with cache of tule duck decoys, Lovelock Cave, Nevada, 1924.

Great Basin Cave Archaeology and Archaeologists

C. Melvin Aikens

Ancient residents of the Great Basin were travelers in an endless cycle, always thinking about their next move to another spot, where they would find the things they needed to survive. During their travels they lived in caves and rockshelters, at least some of the time. Luckily for archaeologists, the combination of sheltered sites and the region's dry climate means that a rich record of more than 10,000 years of Great Basin life has been preserved. A wide array of normally perishable domestic items, including sandals, baskets, mats, bags, nets, snares, and rabbit-fur blankets, has survived. Excavators have unearthed feathered duck decoys, spear-throwers and darts, bows and arrows, and other items of plant fiber, wood, and bone. These artifacts embody and communicate the knowledge, skill, and artistry that sustained the Native peoples of the Great Basin over time.

Less obvious traces tell of past lives as well. Animal bones and plant fragments attest to a healthful diet rich in seeds, berries, roots, fish, and game. Nothing was too small or too large to have been hunted or trapped, from cottontail rabbits and muskrats to deer, mountain sheep, and occasionally bison. Dart points, arrow points, milling slabs, knives, drills, scrapers, and other stone tools found in the caves have counterparts at many sites in open terrain.

How archaeologists discover and piece together this human history is an interesting tale in its own right. The two story lines—those of ancient lives and archaeological science—commingle in the following accounts of excavations at three key sites

that did much to open up the field of Great Basin archaeology. Another theme is the research acumen of the colorful archaeologists who studied the caves. Lessons learned from their pioneering studies still guide archaeological research today.

Lovelock Cave

Llewellyn Lemont Loud was born in 1879 in Aroostook County, Maine. He graduated from the classical course at Caribou High School at the advanced age of 22, for work on the family farm let him study only in winter. After graduating in 1901, he traveled to the Klondike, Seattle, Oakland, and San Francisco, working as a miner, woodcutter, long-shoreman, book agent, laborer, and janitor, among other jobs. Loud gained his higher education over the years as work permitted. He took courses at the University of Washington, the Free Methodist Seattle Seminary, the University of California at Berkeley, and the Pacific School of Religion. Between 1905 and 1910 he regularly enrolled part-time as a special student at Berkeley. He did not seek a degree but took courses mainly in anthropology, geography, and natural history.

From 1911 until his death in 1946 Loud worked at the University of California Museum of Anthropology, at first in San Francisco and later on the Berkeley campus after the museum was moved there. His routine work was as guard, preparator, and janitor, depending on circumstances. He became an active socialist and for a time was a member of the International Workers of the World (the so-called Wobblies). He also distinguished himself as an ad hoc field archaeologist and ethnographer when called to those tasks by A. L. Kroeber, the legendary anthropologist of the University of California and Loud's boss at the University Museum.

In 1912 Kroeber sent Loud to make a collection at Lovelock Cave, Nevada (fig. 4.2), where he had heard about remarkable artifacts found by miners digging bat guano for use as fertilizer. Loud dug alone in the cave from April through July, collecting some 10,000 specimens. These included more than 3,000 pieces of basketry, matting, netting, and other items, including duck decoys fashioned from reeds and covered with feathered bird skins. He also collected some 1,500 stone tools from the edge of the old Humboldt Lake bed below the cave.

Figure 4.2. Lovelock Cave, Churchill County, Nevada, 1967. Archaeologist Robert F. Heizer stands in the cave mouth.

In 1924 Loud returned to the cave in the company of Mark Raymond Harrington for further excavations (fig. 4.3). Harrington, a professional archaeologist for the Heye Foundation Museum of the American Indian, was in charge. He excavated one unit stratigraphically—that is, following the natural layering of the sediments, with the youngest normally at the top and the oldest at the bottom—and recognized six main occupation levels, which he grouped into early, transitional, and late periods. The two researchers published a classic report on the site in 1929, with Loud describing the specimens and Harrington making interpretations.

The Lovelock Cave baskets and mats seemed very much like those already known from late-nineteenth- and early-twentieth-century excavations in dry Basketmaker and early Pueblo caves in the Four Corners area of the US Southwest. Tree-ring dates for such sites ranged from about 300 BCE to 900 CE. Unlike those sites, however, Lovelock Cave yielded no corn, beans, cotton, or pottery. Their absence gave rise to the theory that the Lovelock culture was a late derivative of the Southwestern Basketmaker-Pueblo cultures. Harrington postulated that the Lovelock people had lost the arts of agriculture and pottery in the high, cold deserts of the Great Basin. By extension, he suggested that all the Great Basin cultures known in historic times could be seen as later, devolved versions of Southwestern cultures. This theory would later be proved wrong.

Important later research at Lovelock Cave and other nearby sites by Robert F. Heizer (fig. 4.4) greatly extended archaeologists' knowledge of early Great Basin lifeways. Heizer was less colorful than Loud, but his work has been even more influential. Born in 1915, he grew up in Lovelock, Nevada, and was from boyhood aware of Loud's research and much interested in archaeology. He earned a BA in 1936 and a PhD in 1941 from the University of California, Berkeley, where he was a student of Kroeber's and a latter-day acquaintance of Loud's—both of whom he greatly respected. Heizer became a

Figure 4.3. Mark Raymond Harrington holding two tule duck decoys, Lovelock Cave, Nevada, 1924.

professor at Berkeley in 1948 and taught there until his death in 1979. He was an energetic, disciplined, and devoted scholar with broad research interests who published a phenomenal 500 scholarly studies in several different fields during a distinguished career.

Heizer's work at Lovelock Cave established a chronology based on stratigraphy and radiocarbon dates. People first lived in the cave beginning about 4,600 years ago. The major human use of the shelter began about 3,500 years ago, and after that occupancy was intermittent. Later, dating by a new form of the radiocarbon method—accelerator mass spectrometry (AMS) dating, which requires that only a tiny amount of material be processed and therefore destroyed—demonstrated that the famous duck decoys excavated by Loud and Harrington were 2,000 years old. Heizer's careful analysis of baskets and other artifacts from Lovelock Cave demonstrated that the culture was indigenous to the Great Basin and did not derive from other Southwestern cultures.

Heizer's Great Basin work was wide ranging, but most importantly he brought attention to the overwhelming importance of lakeside and marsh resources in the lives of the Lovelock Cave people. Working with his student Lewis Napton in the early 1970s Heizer identified and analyzed the remains of meals preserved in dried human excrement left by the ancient Lovelock Cave dwellers. In doing so, he convincingly demonstrated the centrality of Great Basin marshlands to both the diet and the technology of Native people throughout the region. Research on the Native economics and uses of Great Basin marshlands continues to flourish today (see chapter 11).

Figure 4.4. Archaeologist Robert F. Heizer (left foreground) and students at Lovelock Cave, 1969. Left to right around Heizer: David Clement, Gary Encinas, Suzanne DeAtley, Monica Ley, Ethel Chang, Jennifer Scharteg, Mark Estis.

Fort Rock Cave, Oregon

Another founder of Great Basin archaeology was
Luther Sheeleigh Cressman (fig. 4.5), who was born
into a rural Pennsylvania doctor's family in 1897.
After graduating from Pennsylvania State University
in 1918, he completed training as a field artillery
officer just as World War I was drawing to a close.
He received his commission and an honorable discharge at the same ceremony. He entered Columbia
University General Theological Seminary in 1919 to
study for the Episcopal ministry. While at Columbia
he worked concurrently on a PhD in sociology, with
collateral course work in anthropology taken from
that early giant of the field, Franz Boas. From 1919
to 1929 Cressman was the first husband of the later
much-celebrated anthropologist Margaret Mead.
He earned and soon resigned his ordination as an
Episcopal minister, completed his PhD, and taught
sociology at City College of New York. After divorc-
ing Mead, he married Cecilia Loch and headed
west. He was hired as a professor of sociology at
the University of Oregon in 1929. He later founded
the anthropology department there and became the
"father of Oregon archaeology." He worked all over
the state, but the caves of the northern Great Basin
desert were his love. He retired from the university
in 1963 but continued research and writing for
two more decades. He died at
age 95 in 1992.

Cressman pioneered
interdisciplinary research in
Great Basin archaeology,
working closely with noted
specialists of the day such as
geochronologist Ernst
Antevs, geologist Howel
Williams, and palynologist
Henry P. Hansen, along with
other natural scientists.
Seeking the earliest traces of
humans in eastern Oregon,
Cressman excavated caves on
the high shorelines of now-
dry Ice Age lakes. He hoped
to find cultural materials in
beach sands and gravels or
associated with the bones

Figure 4.5. Archaeologist Luther Cressman, about 1938.

Figure 4.6. The Fort Rock Basin, Oregon, seen from inside Fort Rock Cave.

Figure 4.7. Portrait of Jesse D. Jennings painted by Alvin Gittins, 1975.

of extinct animals or other datable natural phenomena. At the bottoms of the Paisley Five-Mile Point caves in 1937 and 1938 he found bones of Ice Age horses and camels along with flaked stone artifacts. Colleagues were skeptical about whether the human tools were truly associated with the ancient bones, but renewed investigations almost 70 years later by one of Cressman's successors at the University of Oregon confirmed that both people and animals had been there around 14,000 years ago.

In Fort Rock Cave (fig. 4.6) Cressman found well-preserved fragments of more than 100 sandals, beautifully woven of sagebrush bark. They lay under a thick layer of volcanic ash from the cataclysmic eruption of Mount Mazama that left the caldera of famed Crater Lake in the Oregon Cascades. Howel Williams at the time estimated that the eruption had happened between 5,000 and 10,000 years earlier. It is now radiocarbon dated to about 7,600 years ago. Direct radiocarbon dating of Fort Rock sandals has yielded a range of

dates from 9,000 to more than 10,000 years ago. In other words, Cressman's work demonstrated that Great Basin cultures were far older than the Southwestern Basketmaker culture and indeed were in some part ancestral to that later culture. Today the interdisciplinary research approach so productively initiated by Cressman flourishes everywhere in the Great Basin.

3 Danger Cave, Utah

Jesse David Jennings was born in Oklahoma City in 1909 (fig. 4.7). He came west in 1919 with his parents and sister in their Model T Ford to establish a farm in the Estancia Valley southeast of Albuquerque, New Mexico. The farming was poor, and his father was often away working elsewhere. In 1925 his mother, determined that young Jesse go to college, abandoned the farm and loaded her son, daughter, and household goods in a covered wagon for a three-day trip to the town of Hot Springs (present-day Truth or Consequences), New Mexico.

Jennings attended Montezuma Baptist College in Hot Springs, paying his way by working in the campus heating plant and graduating in 1929. That summer he hitched a ride east with a Montezuma faculty member who was going to complete a degree at the University of Chicago Seminary. Jennings talked his way into the Chicago graduate program in anthropology. He paid his way by working on a campus construction gang, as an orderly in the university hospital, and as a campus policeman. After completing his course work, he found short-term jobs as a journeyman on archaeological projects throughout the Midwest, along with a stint in Guatemala. He joined the National Park Service in 1937 as a park ranger at Montezuma Castle in Arizona. During World War II he served as a naval officer in Iceland—and completed his PhD dissertation. He worked for the Park Service in the Southeast and the Great Plains until 1948, when he was hired by the University of Utah to establish an archaeology program. He directed many research programs all over Utah and in the South Pacific for four decades. He published prolifically, but his most famed work is that on the Desert Culture of the Great Basin.

In 1949–53 Jennings directed excavations at Danger Cave, in extreme western Utah on the edge of the Bonneville Salt Flats (fig. 4.8). His crews uncovered thousands of artifacts made of stone, bone, wood, and plant fiber, along with abundant plant remains and animal bones from some 10 feet of evenly stratified and very dry deposits (fig. 4.9). At the bottom were small hearths lying on clean beach sands and gravels left in the cave by a late low stand of Pleistocene Lake Bonneville. Radiocarbon dating—just then being made operational by University of Chicago physicist Willard Libby—established the age of this first human occupation at more than 10,000 years ago.

Figure 4.8. Danger Cave, western Utah, 2002. The site is on the National Register of Historic Places and is fenced to keep out unauthorized visitors.

Figure 4.9. Recording the stratigraphic profile in Danger Cave, a record of 10,000 years of human history, 1950. Jesse D. Jennings is at extreme right; Sarah Sue Price is standing; seated figure is unidentified.

Other dates confirmed that people had returned again and again throughout Holocene times. In his beautifully detailed report, Jennings integrated the radiocarbon, artifactual, floral, faunal, and other data from the unusually deep, well-stratified deposits. His report was a tour de force that stands as a first in Great Basin archaeology and some years later earned him the coveted Viking Medal in Anthropology.

Jennings's ecological interpretation of the excavated evidence, guided by ethnobotanical work on the area's nineteenth-century Gosiute people and other early ethnographic research in the Great Basin, was compelling. It described a Desert Culture lifeway characterized by nomadic movement and minute knowledge of the seasonal resources of local landscapes. This lifeway was documented in an archaeological record that had accumulated continuously from early Holocene times down to the early twentieth century. The Desert Culture concept is still a key reference point for archaeological research in the Great Basin.

Researchers did much important archaeology in the Great Basin during the foundational period anchored by Loud, Heizer, Cressman, Jennings, and their colleagues. I can do no more here than to introduce the flavor of those beginnings. Other chapters in this book reflect the hundreds of additional contributions made over many years by many scholars who followed in the footsteps of the early cave archaeology pioneers.

C. Melvin Aikens, a professor of anthropology emeritus at the University of Oregon, has been studying Great Basin archaeology since 1964 and is still at it.

Figure 5.1. The Paisley Five-Mile Point caves in south-central Oregon. In 2005 archaeologist Dennis Jenkins found human coprolites in one of the caves that were radiocarbon dated to 14,300 years ago.

The Early Peopling of the Great Basin

Bryan Hockett, Ted Goebel, and Kelly Graf

Who were the earliest inhabitants of the Great Basin, and how did they make a living? These are deceptively simple questions. In truth, we do not know precisely when the first people arrived and where they came from, although we do know they were hunter-gatherers. Many archaeologists have devoted their careers to answering these questions. Each generation has benefited from the knowledge and experience of previous researchers, steadily building a richer portrait of environments and the peoples who lived in them in the distant past.

The history of research on the earliest inhabitants of the Great Basin must be seen in relation to searches for the earliest human inhabitants of the Western Hemisphere. The first demonstrated relationship between ancient humans and late Ice Age animals came at the Folsom site in eastern New Mexico in the 1920s. An even earlier human occupation was found in the 1930s at the Clovis site, also in New Mexico. Radiocarbon dating later allowed archaeologists to define a Clovis "era" dating from about 13,100 to about 12,800 years ago. The Folsom interval was dated around 12,800 to 12,000 years ago.

The Clovis Era

For more than seven decades, from the 1930s until very recently, the earliest clearly documented archaeological artifacts and sites all across North America dated from the Clovis era, actually a brief span of about 400 years. The people of that time practiced a remarkably uniform set of lifeways continent-wide. They made distinctive spear points,

skillfully flaked on both sides with a long groove, or "flute," down the center (fig. 5.2), which they effectively used to hunt large game animals such as mammoths and bison. Some researchers theorize that the relatively sudden, widespread appearance of Clovis artifacts represents the rapid spread of people traveling from northeast Asia across the Bering land bridge into Alaska and down into what is today the continental United States. Others argue that it represents the spread of a new technology among small populations of hunter-gatherers who had already been in North America for a thousand years and perhaps longer. Given the current state of evidence, either interpretation might be valid.

Clovis points turn up in the Great Basin, but none has ever been found in a well-stratified, well-dated context, and none has ever been found with

Figure 5.2. A Clovis point made of white chert from north-eastern Nevada.

the bones of now-extinct animals. This lack of context means that we don't really know when or how people used them. Even surface finds are exceedingly rare. Only two Clovis points have been found in Elko County, northeast Nevada, an area roughly the size of Massachusetts, Connecticut, and Rhode Island combined, despite more than three decades of intensive archaeological survey.

The scattered, isolated spear points suggest that Clovis hunters were few and spent little time in the Great Basin. Only a few "hot spots" of Clovis activity have been found—China Lake in southeastern California, Lake Tonopah–Mud Lake in western Nevada, the Dietz locality in south-central Oregon, and the upland basins of Long Valley and Jakes Valley in east-central Nevada (map 3). Why Clovis hunters were drawn to these places remains a mystery. Perhaps they were staging areas of some sort, as David Anderson suggests, places from which bands of hunter-gatherer explorers could search surrounding uncharted lands for rapidly disappearing herds of mammoths and other big game or for high-quality stone for tool manufacture. Their exploration of the Great Basin might have been short-lived and encouraged them to seek greener grasslands elsewhere, for reasons yet unknown.

Further clues that only a few nomads traversed the Great Basin during the Clovis era come from tracking the tool stones used to make Clovis points back to their places of origin. If we know where a tool stone came from, we can trace the movements of the people who carried it to the place where they abandoned a spear point or other implement made from that stone. Obsidian and other fine-grained volcanic rocks are especially useful for this purpose.

At the Jakes Depression site in east-central Nevada, for example, Clovis people discarded two broken fluted points of obsidian that originated in two different volcanic flows in southwestern Utah—those in Modena Canyon and Wild Horse Canyon. Surprisingly, another Clovis point made of Wild Horse Canyon obsidian was found at Blackwater Draw, a famous Clovis site nearly 1,000 miles away in eastern New Mexico. Perhaps the point is evidence of a very early, widespread trade network. Perhaps the same Clovis hunters who visited Jakes Depression some 13,000 years ago also visited Blackwater Draw. Were they truly just passing through the Great Basin in search of mammoths and other big game animals, which they later found in abundance on the Llano Estacado of the southern Great Plains? We need to find more of their "calling cards," especially in buried contexts that can be radiocarbon dated, to answer these and other questions about Clovis people's transitory use of the Great Basin.

Buried Clovis sites likely do occur in the Great Basin, and archaeologists need to keep looking for them. The problem is that they may be so deeply buried under waterborne sediments that we cannot get at them with shovels and trowels, the conventional archaeological tools. Backhoes might solve the problem. At the Sunshine Well locality in east-central Nevada, Charlotte Beck and Tom Jones employed the services of a skilled backhoe operator to expose some late Pleistocene marsh sediments buried under many feet of gravel and sand. In one of the trenches they found a fluted point lying in stream gravels just below some wood charcoal that was radiocarbon dated to about 12,300 years ago. The point was not a typical Clovis fluted point. But the implication of the discovery is that the more we keep looking for and sifting through "old dirt," the better our chances of finding elusive, buried Clovis or even earlier sites that will tell us more about early peoples.

Seeking Earlier Great Basin Peoples

Archaeologists have sought clues to "pre-Clovis" people in North America for many decades. Many felt that the sophisticated stone tools of the Clovis culture should have had earlier, simpler precursors. In the Great Basin the search was coupled with a search for evidence of interactions between humans and big game animals. In the early 1930s Mark Harrington argued that artifacts uncovered in association with bones of extinct sloths at Gypsum Cave near Las Vegas and with bones of extinct horses and llamas at Smith Creek Cave in east-central Nevada suggested that early humans had hunted these long-gone animals. The Gypsum Cave artifacts, however, were later radiocarbon dated to about 3,000 years ago, eight or nine millennia after sloths had last entered the cave. Later work at Smith Creek Cave failed to make a convincing case for humans having killed ancient horses and llamas there.

XLuther Cressman conducted the first large-scale survey and excavation program in south-central Oregon between 1932 and 1940. He found stone tools and flakes beneath a thick layer of volcanic ash in Paisley Five-Mile Point Cave 3 (fig. 5.1). The ash came from the eruption of Mount Mazama, now dated to about 7,600 years ago but at the time thought to have been much earlier. Just as astonishing was the apparent association of the early stone artifacts with bones of extinct horses and camels. Cressman interpreted this association to mean that early humans at Paisley Five-Mile Point had hunted now-extinct big game. Analysts have recently reexamined the surface marks and breakage patterns of the bones and believe that some of them were left in the cave by carnivores rather than humans.

Cressman also excavated Fort Rock Cave. Again he found evidence of human habitation before the eruption of Mount Mazama. Most interesting were dozens of intacXsandals made of sagebrush bark. By 1951 one of these had been directly radiocarbon dated to about 11,000 years ago, establishing the Fort Rock sandals as the oldest footwear known anywhere in the world (see chapter 9).

Between 1949 and 1953, Jesse Jennings, of the University of Utah, led excavations at Danger Cave. The oldest occupation dates ranged between 12,000 and 13,000 years ago. Later research confirmed the date of the earliest hearths to be about 12,300 years ago. Although researchers found no bones of extinct animals in the cave, Jennings concluded from the other bones dug up that the hunting of large game, mainly bighorn sheep, was the principal subsistence activity in early times.

In the early 1950s Phil Orr dug at Fishbone XCave in western Nevada and uncovered bones of now-extinct camels and horses. Other items included a bone awl apparently manufactured from a piece of a lower leg bone of a horse, a human burial, fragments of netting, and a stone tool. Pieces of juniper roots and bark from the cave were dated to about 13,200 years ago, suggesting that the earliest human occupants of Fishbone Cave had lived there at a time when they could have hunted now-extinct big game. Later radiocarbon dating of a piece of the

netting proved it to be only about 9,000 years old. Other fiber artifacts were dated to less than 8,000 years ago. The bone awl was directly dated to only 3,100 years ago, and a careful reanalysis suggested that it was made not of horse bone but of bighorn sheep bone. Today most archaeologists agree that the human burial and artifacts are at least 3,000 years younger than the extinct large animal bones.

Archaeologists continued to search vigorously for early humans in the Great Basin in the 1960s and 1970s. Stephen Bedwell returned to Fort Rock Cave, Alan Bryan led several expeditions to Smith Creek Cave, and Richard Shutler led a large team of scientists in thorough investigations of Tule Springs near Las Vegas. At Fort Rock Cave, Bedwell reportedly found charcoal from campfires associated with artifacts lying on ancient lake gravelsXThe charcoal was an astonishing 15,200 years old. But Bedwell's excavation methods left little clear evidence that would allow experts to judge whether the charcoal and the artifacts were really closely associated with each other.

At Smith Creek Cave, Bryan uncovered charcoal and artifacts lying alongside llama hair. Charcoal from hearths was dated between 12,000 and 13,200 years ago, whereas the llama hair dated between 13,000 and 16,000 years ago. Bryan argued that humans might have hunted these small camels as early as 16,000 years ago, but most archaeologists think the hair and artifacts were mixed together by natural forces, perhaps by burrowing marmots. The human use of Smith Creek Cave probably dates more recently than 12,700 years ago, although it might have begun as early as 13,200 years ago.

In the 1930s Mark Harrington claimed to have found human artifacts and extinct animal bones at Tule Springs. Richard Shutler's later Tule Springs studies failed to produce clear evidence that humans lived along Las Vegas Wash before 12,000 years ago or were associated with any extinct forms of animals. But the project did yield much new information about the Pleistocene environments of the Great Basin.

After seven decades of searching for Clovis or earlier sites that could be dated, Great Basin archaeologists recently found what appears to be good evidence for aXpre-Clovis human population. Dennis

Figure 5.3. Typical stemmed projectile points dating to the Paleoarchaic period. Such points are found throughout the Great Basin.

Jenkins, of the University of Oregon, in 2005 unearthed human coprolites (dried feces) from Paisley Five-Mile Point Cave 5 in south-central Oregon that were dated by accelerator mass spectroscopy to about 14,300 years ago, at least a thousand years before Clovis times. DNA analysis suggests that the person who used the Paisley caves for a latrine so long ago had recently eaten bison meat—at last some evidence that ancient Great Basin residents preyed on big game.

The search for the earliest human inhabitants of the Great Basin has been long and frustrating. Excitement over new finds has repeatedly given way to disappointment once those finds received closer scrutiny. But that is the nature of scientific research. New data are collected, hypotheses are advanced to account for those data, and both are subjected to rigorous testing in light of current theories. In 2008 that process was under way for the Paisley find. Close scrutiny by Jenkins and his team and other archaeologists and specialists was intended to determine the scientific validity of the find. If validated, it would be the first clear evidence that people hunted big game in the Great Basin as much as 1,000 years before Clovis times.

A Picture Emerges: The Paleoarchaic Period

Despite the unanswered questions in pre-Clovis and Clovis archaeology, the past 70 years of research have produced a great deal of knowledge about the early inhabitants of the Great Basin after the Clovis era, between about 12,700 and 8,500 years ago. Most archaeologists refer to this time as the Paleoarchaic period.

Paleoarchaic people lived in a world very different from that of today. The Great Basin was considerably cooler and wetter then, and small lakes and shallow marshes covered many valley floors. Sagebrush was even more prevalent than it is now, and piñons and junipers grew at lower elevations. Cool-adapted small animals such as pikas and marmots lived in more places and at lower elevations than they do today.

Paleoarchaic people left many more clues about their lives than did those who came before them. They manufactured several styles of large, stemmed projectile points (fig. 5.3), quite unlike the earlier Clovis points. Archaeologists call these points by a number of different names, but most have a narrow leaf shape, distinct shoulders at the base end, and square to tongue-shaped stems—the part inserted

Mysterious Crescents
Eugene M. Hattori

Chipped stone artifacts called crescents (fig. 5.4) are relatively common in Great Basin archaeological sites older than 7,000 years ago, but we have no idea why. We lack convincing evidence for the crescents' function, despite some creative speculation.

Figure 5.5. "Winged" crescent. Maximum width 2.4 inches.

Figure 5.4. Crescents. Object on left is 2.5 inches long.

Crescents are found only in western North America, from central Washington to southeastern California and eastward to Arizona. Adding to the puzzle, they are found on the Channel Islands off California and near Santa Barbara along the Pacific Ocean. The greatest concentration by far is in the Great Basin, and the majority come from sites near former wetlands. Some sites, such as the Sunshine Well locality in Nevada, have yielded dozens of examples.

Some crescents are shaped roughly like a butterfly in outline (fig. 5.5), but most have a true crescent shape. The "wings" on either side are usually sharp, whereas the central "body" was intentionally dulled. People at the time frequently dulled the bases of projectile points to prevent

their edges from cutting the thong or cord that bound them to a spear or dart. So we are fairly certain that crescents were bound to another element, possibly a shaft or handle.

Crescent wing edges, however, were not clearly meant for cutting. We have no good evidence of edges being damaged from use or being resharpened. People often did resharpen projectile points during the Paleoarchaic period, so we know what that looks like. Faced with these puzzles, researchers have proposed that the crescents might have been any of a lot of things: projectile points mounted at an angle meant to stun water birds, knives for cutting tule stalks, scrapers for peeling roots, side blades mounted on sickles or throwing sticks, fish gouges, scalpels, and ornaments.

Crescents drop out of the archaeological record after about 7,000 years ago. Perhaps the drying of the marshes had something to do with their disappearance; possibly their makers left the region. Was the crescent replaced by another tool? Was its function no longer needed? Whatever the case, the utility of crescents was lost to later people, as it is to us today.

---

into a spear shaft for hafting (see fig. 6.2). The typical stone tool kit also included chipped stone scrapers for tasks such as hide working, sharp-pointed gravers for incising wood or bone, and knives, possibly including the enigmatic artifacts known as crescents. Dry caves and rockshelters have preserved a wealth of textiles dating to this

period, including mats made in a unique diamond-shaped plain weave, basketry, sandals, rabbit-skin blankets, cordage, rope, string, and netting fragments. Bone tools include awls, needles, and flakers, pointed tools used to push small flakes off stone implements. Obviously, Paleoarchaic residents of the Great Basin were well equipped to capture and collect a large variety of animals and plants and turn them into food, clothing, and tools.

In the 1970s Stephen Bedwell proposed a "Western Pluvial Lakes Tradition" to explain the hunting and gathering practices of Great Basin people living in caves near lakes and marshes, such as Fort Rock Cave. He envisioned people "tethered" to marsh habitats, exploiting a diversity of resources including waterfowl and fish for food. We now know that Bedwell's concept is too narrow to describe the subsistence practices of the earliest residents of the Great Basin. It is true that waterfowl and fish bones are found at several early sites, some dating to 11,000 years ago. According to David Madsen, as many as 500 ancient sites may lie alongside and near the terminus of the Old River Bed in the Bonneville Basin in Utah, where marshlands existed before 9,500 years ago and waterfowl and fish would have been abundant.

Figure 5.6. Entrance to Bonneville Estates Rockshelter, eastern Nevada.

But we also find Paleoarchaic stemmed points in upland habitats, where resources such as deer and bighorn sheep, chokecherries, currants, and rose hips were plentiful. Clearly people did not rely solely on the marshes for their survival. Recent excavations at Bonneville Estates Rockshelter in eastern Nevada (fig. 5.6), led by the three of us, have shown that people hunted deer, bighorn sheep, pronghorn, jackrabbit, and sage grouse and collected grasshoppers for food between 12,800 and 11,000 years ago. Open-air sites in Buffalo Flat in the greater Fort Rock Basin, Oregon, area also offer abundant evidence that people hunted jackrabbits before 9,500 years ago.

Plant remains do not preserve as well as animal bones, and their presence in early cave and rockshelter sites does not necessarily mean that humans consumed them. Charred seeds of rice grass and dropseed sandgrass were found in some of the

early hearths in Bonneville Estates Rockshelter. But none of the seeds appears to have been ground for meal, and indeed we find few grinding tools in Paleoarchaic sites. It is possible that pack rats brought these seeds into the shelter and they were later charred by fires built above them.

There is little reason to doubt, however, that humans played some role in collecting the plants whose remains are excavated from hearths at many open-air sites in the Great Basin. An open-air site far from any ancient marsh has produced such evidence. At the Paulina Lake site, 30 miles north of Fort Rock Cave, chokecherry pits, sedge seeds, and edible fruit tissues were extracted from a hearth dated to about 10,200 years ago. Like the Bonneville Estates animal remains, the Paulina Lake plant finds demonstrate that Paleoarchaic people frequented upland habitats and did not collect solely lowland marsh foods.

The concept of early people being "tethered" to marshes does not fit what we now know about Paleoarchaic settlement patterns. The people who left stemmed points here and there across the Great Basin were nomads who did not live at any one place for long. Most of their sites are small scatters of just a few stone tools and associated waste flakes. Even large sites with hundreds of stone

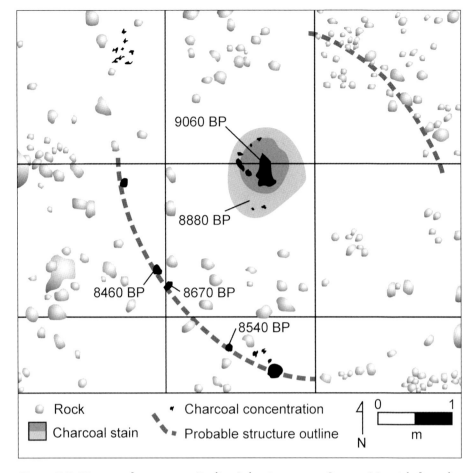

9060 BP

8880 BP

8460 BP   8670 BP

8540 BP

| ○ Rock | • Charcoal concentration |
| ▓ Charcoal stain | •• Probable structure outline |

0   1
m
N

Figure 5.7. Diagram of structure at Paulina Lake site, eastern Oregon. Materials from the structure were dated between 8,460 and 9,060 years ago.

The contents of the hearth—the seeds and fruit already mentioned—imply that people used it during the summer.

It seems clear that the Paleoarchaic people of the Great Basin before 8,500 years ago were mobile hunter-gatherers who used the many Great Basin environments and ate a wide variety of foods including marsh-related animals, large and small terrestrial animals, and plants. This far-ranging lifestyle based on a diverse diet did not last. Things were about to change dramatically.

The Transition to the Archaic Period

The climate of the Great Basin warmed steadily after about 12,000 years ago, and by about 9,500 years ago this warming significantly affected the basin's residents. Several important cave sites that contain thousands of bones of rodents, rabbits, hares, and pikas deposited by predatory birds such as owls record a dramatic shift in animal populations. Much of this shift was complete by 9,500 years ago. The shift from a cool, wet climate to a warm, indeed hot climate forced some types of animals out and made the region hospitable to others. Cool-loving small mammals had disappeared by 9,500 years ago from Homestead Cave in the vicinity of the Great Salt Lake. Similar evidence of change was found at Pintwater Cave, north of Las Vegas (fig. 5.8), where the hot climate was probably coupled with heavier summer rains. These warm but seasonally wet conditions led to the spread of modern Mojave Desert lizards such as the chuckwalla and the desert iguana into southern Nevada from their ranges to the south.

This warming trend lasted for more than 3,000

tools, such as the Sadmat, Coleman, and Parman localities in western Nevada, seem to be the results of repeated short stays, not of long-term residence. People made many of their tools well in advance of using them and carried them from place to place as they traveled long distances. In the central Great Basin, researchers have found that obsidian and chert tool stone was traded or carried for hundreds of miles along the region's north-south-trending valleys.

Although Paleoarchaic dwelling structures are extremely rare, one has been excavated at Paulina Lake. The structure had a hearth at its center and five charred posts that formed a semicircular outline (fig. 5.7). The living floor appeared to have been cleared of stones but was not dug into the ground. The structure probably was a simple windbreak or wickiup-style hut, lightly constructed.

years, although short periods of cooler or wetter climate developed at approximately thousand-year intervals, around 8,000, 7,000, and 6,000 years ago. Archaeologists are only now beginning to fully comprehend the complexities of this climatic phase, called the Altithermal, as well as its effects on humans.

We know that by 8,500 to 8,000 years ago, Great Basin people no longer made the large stemmed projectile points that characterized the early Paleoarchaic period. Instead, they made notched points—specifically, large side-notched varieties—for the first time (fig. 5.9). They largely abandoned the driest parts of the Great Basin, such as the central portions of Nevada. Other areas, such as the Fort Rock Basin of south-central Oregon, continued to be inhabited regularly. A few sites, such as Bonneville Estates Rockshelter, reflect intermittent, short-term occupations during times of relatively cooler or wetter climate, followed by long abandonments during warmer, drier times.

Figure 5.8. Pintwater Cave, southern Nevada.

Figure 5.9. Side-notched projectile points, characteristic of the early Archaic period in the Great Basin.

As would be expected in a time of climate change, people's diets became highly variable. The overall diversity of animals eaten diminished across the Great Basin. The widespread hunting and gathering of animals such as waterfowl, fish, and sage grouse dried up along with the lakes and streams. Jackrabbit hunting remained common at sites in south-central Oregon and north-central Utah. At Sudden Shelter, along the border between the southern Great Basin and the northern Colorado Plateau, large-game hunting dominated. At Bonneville Estates Rockshelter, two of the three occupations dating to this period show heavy reliance on large game, whereas one occupation shows greater reliance on small game.

After about 9,500 years ago, people throughout the Great Basin began to use milling stone technology—manos, or hand-held stones, and metates, or grinding slabs—to grind seeds. Milling stones are rarely found in Paleoarchaic sites but appear often in early Archaic sites and thereafter.

So far the evidence suggests that no one-size-fits-all description characterizes the way human groups contended with the difficulties of making a living during the trying times of drought and warmer climate in the early Archaic period of the Great Basin. But things were about to change drastically once again. The cooler and wetter climate of the late Holocene was right around the temporal corner.

Bryan Hockett is an archaeologist with the Bureau of Land Management, Elko Field Office, Nevada. Ted Goebel is the Endowed Professor of First Americans Studies, Department of Anthropology, Texas A&M University. Kelly Graf is a research associate with the Center for the Study of the First Americans, Texas A&M University. Eugene M. Hattori is curator of anthropology at the Nevada State Museum, Carson City.

Figure 6.1. The Bonneville Salt Flats, looking east from above Danger Cave, Utah.

Archaic Times

Charlotte Beck and George T. Jones

Contrary to popular views, the precipitous rise and calamitous collapse of civilizations was not a regular feature of the human past. True, in many places agricultural societies with densely packed cities experienced cycles of boom and bust. But where people lived by foraging, culture histories are marked by long periods of relative stability, which speaks to the flexibility and resilience of their lifeways. Most such peoples, certainly those living in desert regions, made use of many plant and animal foods, no one of them critical. When times were good they concentrated on a few preferred foods. When times were tough they had many others to fall back on. Such a stable way of life developed more than 8,000 years ago in the Great Basin and persisted until Euro-Americans arrived in the late 1770s. Archaeologists call this lifeway the Archaic.

The late Jesse Jennings defined a Great Basin lifeway that he first called the Desert Culture and later the Desert Archaic. In his 1957 study of Danger Cave he wrote that it was "difficult for modern man to conceive of a life so directly and continuously focused on sheer survival." He drew heavily on Julian Steward's earlier description of late-nineteenth- and early-twentieth-century Great Basin peoples and their lifeways, a study that had a profound effect on anthropological thinking in the region. Steward described a way of life in which small family bands were continually on the move, ever in search of food. They had a "broad-spectrum" diet centered on seeds of grasses and other desert plants. Jennings argued that this general lifeway had characterized Great Basin peoples for 10,000 years.

Jennings's view, however, was conditioned by what he saw in the desolate surroundings of Danger Cave. The cave looks out on the Bonneville Salt Flats, left by the drying of Pleistocene Lake Bonneville some 10,000 years ago (fig. 6.1). Others, particularly Robert Heizer and Martin Baumhoff, working in the much better watered western Great Basin, disagreed with Jennings's characterization. Steward, they argued, had written primarily about the Shoshones of the central Great Basin, whose lifestyle differed considerably from the lifestyles of other groups, such as the Northern Paiutes to the west. They agreed that most Great Basin peoples had always been foragers, but they believed lifeways had varied from place to place. In the end, Heizer and Baumhoff proved to be more on track than Jennings, but the concept of the Desert Culture or Desert Archaic anchored research and debate for the next 25 years.

Most researchers now agree that the Archaic lifeway emerged at least 8,500 years ago and diversified as people settled across the Great Basin. These people were mobile, timing their movements to coincide with the seasonal availability of food. They moved between valley floors and mountaintops and often across great distances to find sustenance. Life on the move offered little incentive to invest in building permanent houses. Indeed, these people left behind little for archaeologists to find, so we have few clues about Archaic social life.

New Technologies

New technologies appeared at the beginning of the Archaic period. About 8,000 years ago the large, stemmed projectile points common in Paleoarchaic times disappeared and were replaced by notched points. Notching is a more efficient way of hafting, or binding the point to a shaft, because it removes the binding from the sharp blade edges (fig. 6.2). More important, because damage to the hafted end of the point generally happens at the notches, the remaining blade can readily be reworked. This new point technology most likely reflected the introduction of the atlatl, or spear thrower (fig. 6.3).

The atlatl, the primary weapon propulsion system until the advent of the bow and arrow about 2,000 years ago, can deliver a stone-tipped spear with considerable accuracy and force over distances of 40 to 50 feet. It was an effective tool when used against animals such as mountain goats and pronghorn that had been herded into places where they could be ambushed. The most common "drive technology" was the antelope trap (fig. 6.4). It combined fences or spaced columns of juniper, sagebrush, or stone with natural features to form chutes that opened into large, often circular corrals, 450 to 1,500 feet in diameter.

Large-game drives are one example of a "mass capture" strategy that hunters developed in early

Archaic times. They also organized to drive rabbits into large, twined fiber nets, where the entangled animals were easily dispatched. To catch individual animals, hunters used traps and snares. These did

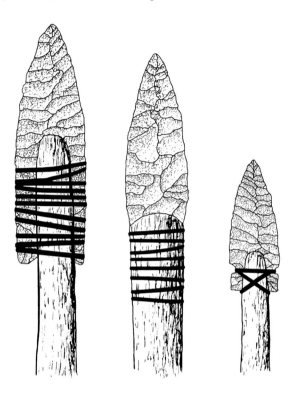

Figure 6.2. Methods of hafting early projectile points. Left, Clovis fluted point hafted in a split shaft; center, Paleoarchaic stemmed point hafted in a socketed shaft; right, early Archaic notched point hafted in a split shaft.

Figure 6.3. Throwing a dart using an atlatl.

not have to be watched vigilantly, so they eliminated the need for people to choose among resources that were available at the same time but in different places.

Jennings regarded baskets and grinding stones, used to gather seeds and roots and prepare them for eating or storage, as hallmarks of the Desert Archaic lifeway. Although they had existed earlier, they became widespread only in early Archaic times as people turned to previously unimportant plants for food. Archaic people used manos and metates to detach inedible husks from edible seeds, and mortars and pestles to grind seeds into meal (fig. 6.5). Baskets had many uses, including transport, storage, winnowing, and, when they were made watertight, cooking food in water boiled by heated stones (fig. 6.6).

Caching of foodstuffs and tools became more common during early Archaic times. People moved about the landscape frequently and could carry with them only a few multi-purpose tools. They cached special-purpose tools, often in caves and rockshelters, and retrieved them when needed. This practice explains why archaeologists have found remarkably well-preserved collections of baskets and other items made of wood, fiber, hide, and feathers in Great Basin caves and rockshelters. The implements reflect the ingenuity of the ancient people and provide a rich view of Archaic technologies and economic practices.

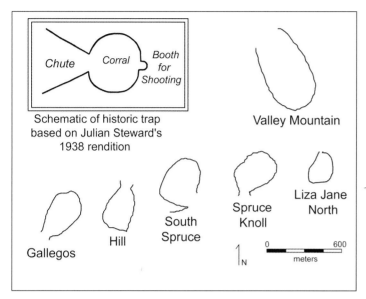

Figure 6.4. Schematic drawings of pronghorn corrals at Archaic Great Basin sites.

Figure 6.5. Late Archaic mortar and pestle (left) and metate and mano, used for grinding and hulling seeds. Western Great Basin.

Figure 6.6. Historic Numic Great Basin basket forms. Left, large carrying or burden basket; center, seed beater for gathering small seeds into collecting baskets; right, winnowing tray for separating seeds from chaff by tossing them. Similar forms were made and used during late Archaic times.

Responding to Climate Change

There is little doubt that the climatic drying of middle Holocene Altithermal times tested the resilience of Great Basin foragers. The geologist Ernst Antevs thought conditions roughly 7,000 to 4,000 years ago were so severe that people abandoned whole sections of the Great Basin. We now know that his scheme, although largely correct, oversimplified climatic changes during that time and that the Altithermal began about 1,500 years earlier than he proposed, at the beginning of the middle Holocene. Certainly many areas suffered periods of extremely hot, dry weather, but the timing and lengths of the intervals were not the same from place to place.

Yet Antevs seems generally to have been right about his "Altithermal abandonment." In 1993 Donald Grayson assembled a list of all dated Great Basin sites outside the Bonneville Basin that had

long records of continuous occupation. He identified 23 sites, 18 of which were rockshelters. Only seven of the sites had dates falling between 7,000 and 5,500 years ago—within the range of Antevs's original dates for the Altithermal period. New data collected since 1993 have not changed our view of the mid-Holocene interval, except perhaps in the northern Great Basin. There, Dennis Jenkins and his colleagues have excavated or reexcavated newly discovered and previously studied sites in the Fort Rock Basin. They find no breaks in the record from the earliest occupations to at least 6,500 years ago. This means people did not wholly abandon the region but simply changed the places where they lived and traveled. Elsewhere in the Great Basin, however, we still find little indication of human life during Altithermal times. This pattern may simply reflect the bias of relying only on dated sites. Few archaeo-

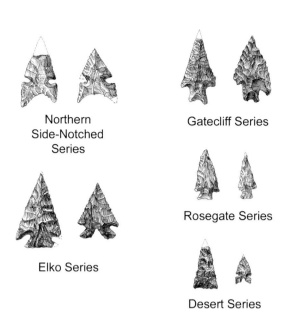

Date (years before present)			
Series	Western/ Central Great Basin	Northern Great Basin	Eastern Great Basin
Northern Side-Notched	5000–4500	7000–4500	8000–4500
Elko	3500–1300	7500–1300	8000–1000
Gatecliff	5000–3000	5000–3000	5000–1500
Rosegate	1300–700	1300–700	1700–1000
Desert	700–Historic	700–Historic	1000–Historic

Northern Side-Notched Series

Gatecliff Series

Rosegate Series

Elko Series

Desert Series

Great Basin Projectile Point Chronology

Figure 6.7. Great Basin Archaic projectile point chronology.

logical sites contain datable material, and that might be why we see so few middle Holocene sites. Maybe they exist but we simply cannot date them.

Time-Sensitive Artifacts

In the absence of radiocarbon dates we must turn to other ways to place sites in time, primarily by examining time-sensitive artifacts. Some types of artifacts changed in form and design over time, enabling researchers to pin examples of them to particular intervals. Think, for instance, of the tail fins that appeared on Cadillacs between 1950 and 1965, but not before or after. And no one who appreciates classic cars would ever confuse a 1956 and a 1957 Chevy. Some kinds of archaeological artifacts can be used in the same way. In the Great Basin, we use projectile points (fig. 6.7).

Projectile point forms, or types, are named for the area in which they were first defined and for something obvious about their shape. For simplicity, projectile point types that date to the same time period are combined into "series." The series, just like the tail fins on Cadillacs, are used as time markers, designating a certain interval, although the intervals differ depending on where the points are found. Elko Series points, for example, were used earlier in the northern and eastern Great Basin than in the west.

Both Elko and northern side-notched points appeared about 8,000 years ago in the Bonneville Basin, possibly marking the first use of the atlatl and dart there. Interestingly, both corner-notched and side-notched points came into use shortly after that time all along the eastern and northern peripheries of the Great Basin, but neither appeared in the central and western parts of the region until after about 5,000 years ago. This pattern suggests an answer to the question of whether people abandoned the Great Basin during the Altithermal period. The new notching technology was introduced just as the climate began to warm. If people were withdrawing from the central core of the basin at that time, we would not expect to see notched points there until people returned at the beginning of the late Holocene—and that is exactly what we see.

Good Times Ahead

Sites dating to around 4,500 years ago seem to appear suddenly in many parts of the Great Basin, marking the beginning of middle Archaic times. The human population began to grow, in tandem with changes in subsistence, mobility, and technology. Trade networks between the Great Basin and California developed at this time as well.

The people who moved into the region during middle and late Archaic times followed lifeways more diversified than those of their predecessors. Rivers, lakes, and marshes were reborn as the climate shifted to conditions more like those of the present. Large wetlands developed along the western, northern, and eastern margins of the basin, and as in Paleoarchaic times, people were drawn to them. Artifacts such as fishhooks, nets, and duck decoys from Lovelock Cave in western Nevada reflect the harvesting of the rich range of resources that wetlands provide. Relatively substantial dwellings, such as those at the Humboldt Lakebed site just a few miles from Lovelock Cave, show that people were living near marshes for substantial periods of time (chapter 11).

But marshes were only part of the economic picture. Robert Bettinger (chapter 12) believes people also began to hunt regularly in the high mountains in the middle Archaic, around 4,000 years ago. After 1,300 years ago they even established several high-altitude villages. They added a new food to their diet—pinyon nuts, which would become a staple for many Great Basin peoples. And in the eastern and southern Great Basin, so-called Formative-level cultures, the Fremont and Virgin Branch Puebloan peoples (chapters 14 and 17), developed maize-based horticulture between 350 and 500 CE. This horticulture-based lifeway, which lasted about 900 years, contrasted sharply with the Archaic-level foraging ways of life practiced throughout the rest of the Great Basin during that time.

In the central basin, which remained drier than the peripheries, people continued to travel from place to place, practicing a lifestyle similar to that of the Desert Culture. David Hurst Thomas demonstrated this similarity in his studies in the Reese River valley in the 1970s. He found that except for the introduction of pinyon nuts, life there had changed little over the past 4,000 years. The subsequent discovery of high-altitude villages by Thomas and Bettinger, however, substantially altered the view that little change took place during late Archaic times.

Late Archaic people continued to modify and use technologies that had been developed earlier. After about 1,500 years ago they devised new seed harvesting and processing tools such as the long grappling pole (used to dislodge pinyon cones from high branches), the sheep horn sickle, and the basketry seed beater (fig. 6.6).

The major new innovation in North America was the bow and arrow, which spread relatively quickly across the continent. Evidence of its arrival in the Great Basin between 2,000 and 1,500 years ago appears in the form of Rosegate Series projectile points, which are much smaller than points used to tip atlatl darts and spears. The use of the bow and arrow may have individualized the hunting of larger game and led to some changes in social dynamics. Robert Bettinger believes the new technology made it easier for hunters to kill both large and small animals. Meat from large animals is more easily shared than meat from small ones. The increased harvesting of large animals and sharing of the meat allowed meat from small animals, as well as plant foods, to be stored away for individuals or families. In this way the introduction of the bow and arrow might have changed some notions of food sharing. Communal hunts continued, however. Late Archaic antelope traps are found in upland areas, and large nets, some up to 300 feet long, were used for communal rabbit drives.

Earlier Great Basin people probably occasionally traded goods such as tool stone, hides, foodstuffs, and perhaps basketry with each other and with people outside the basin. But another innovation of middle and late Archaic times was the establishment of actual trade networks over which goods moved regularly and predictably. After about 4,000 years ago people in the western Great Basin began to import ornaments manufactured from ocean shells along the Pacific coast to decorate their clothing, shoes, and baskets (fig. 6.8). Coastal artisans fashioned beads and other ornaments from olive shells (*Olivella*), abalone (*Haliotis*), tooth shells (*Dentalium*), and various clamshells. People traded them widely across California to the Great Basin and beyond, following well-established routes. Traders probably engaged in transactions with trading partners in hand-to-hand, or "down-the-line," exchange, but probably no one trader traveled the entire route. Although styles of shell beads and ornaments came in and out of fashion over the years, the trade lasted until about 1500 CE,

Plate 1. *Prince's Plume*. View across sagebrush flat on the road to Blue Lakes in the Pine Forest Mountains, Humboldt County, Nevada.

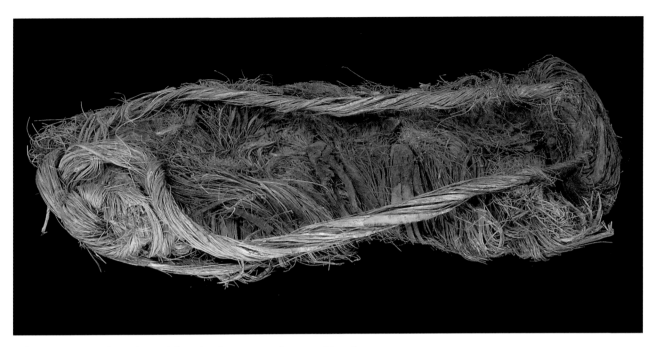

Plate 2. Figure-eight style sandal made of yucca, southeastern Nevada.

Plate 3. Bag from the Winnemucca Lake basin, western Nevada.

Plate 4. Tule duck decoy from Lovelock Cave, Nevada.

Plate 5. Bristlecone pine tree, White Mountains, California.

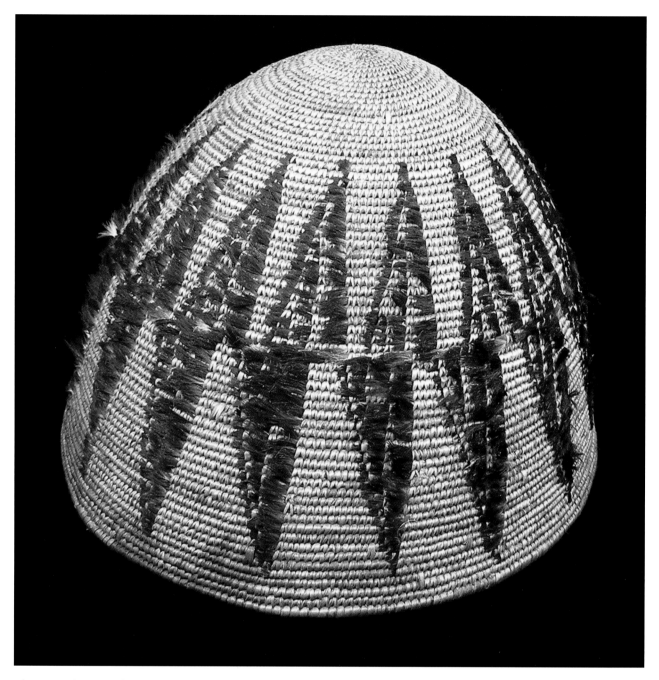

Plate 6. Basketry hat from Charlie Brown Cave, Nevada, decorated with interwoven feathers. Maximum diameter 8.5 inches, height 5 inches.

Plate 7. Basketry bowl from Charlie Brown Cave, Nevada, decorated with earthen pigments and waterbird feathers. Diameter 8.4 inches, height 4 inches.

Plate 8. Basketry tray from Charlie Brown Cave, Nevada. Diameter 27 inches, depth 3 inches.

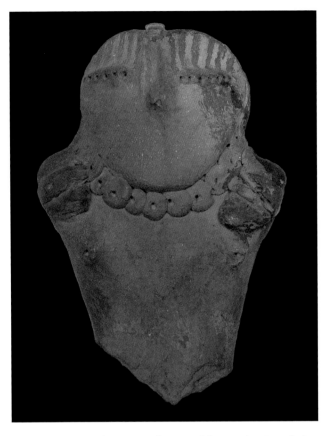

Plate 9. Fremont figurine with painted face and red "sash," Nine Mile Canyon region, Utah.

Plate 10. A big-eyed Barrier Canyon–style anthropomorph bordered by unnatural beings. Overhead is a lifelike snake. San Rafael Reef area (head of Sinbad Canyon), eastern Utah.

Plate 11. *Desert Ponds*. Ponds on sagebrush flat east of Denio, Nevada, Bilk Creek Mountains in background, Humboldt County, Nevada.

Plate 12. *Summit Lake Mesas*. Looking northeast from top of Summit Lake Mountain toward Denio, Nevada. Note Ice Age terraces in middle distance.

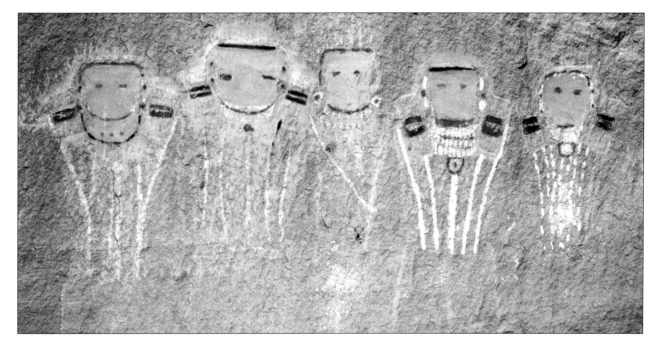

Plate 13. Figurine-like anthropomorphs, Canyonlands National Park, Utah. The "Five Faces" shown here are painted and abraded and have heavy hanks of hair bundled on each shoulder. They wear a variety of necklaces typical of these figures.

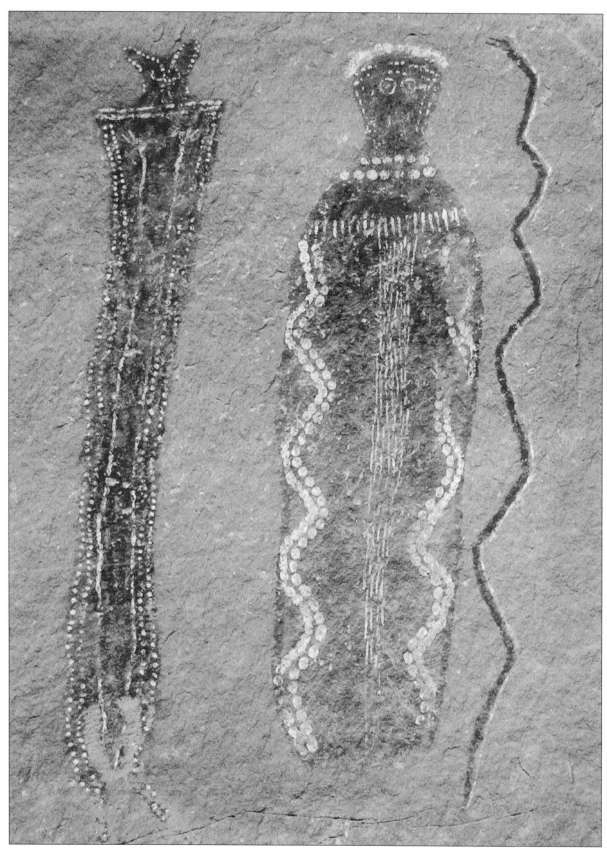

Plate 14. Barrier Canyon–style paintings with dot decorations and supernatural snakes. Clear Water Canyon, eastern Utah.

Plate 15. *Mountains of Blue*. Photograph taken from top of Granite Mountain north of Gerlach, Washoe County, northwestern Nevada. Six mountain ranges are in photograph, with valleys or basins in between.

Plate 16. *Black Rock Blues*. Looking across a playa of the Black Rock Desert toward the Jackson Mountains, Humboldt County, Nevada. During the Ice Age, the playa was covered by Lake Lahontan.

Plate 17. Rectilinear and curvilinear motifs on a panel in Lagomarsino Canyon, northern Nevada.

Plate 18. Rectilinear and stick figure ("snowman") motifs on a panel in Lagomarsino Canyon, north-western Nevada.

Plate 19. Fremont ceramic pitcher with coffee-bean appliqué, from the Round Springs site, central Utah.

Plate 20. Flicker feather headdress from the Fremont site of Mantles Cave near Dinosaur National Monument, northeastern Utah.

Plate 21. Range Creek Canyon, looking south from the top of the dugway into the canyon.

Plate 22. Excavation of Hidden Cave, Churchill County, Nevada.

Plate 23. *Low Tide in the Desert*. Looking across a playa toward Black Rock Point, Humboldt County, Nevada.

Plate 24. Rainbow over the Pueblo Mountains. Scene from Long Hollow west of Fields, Oregon, looking back toward Pueblo Mountains, Harney County, southeastern Oregon.

Plate 25. *Icy Winter.*

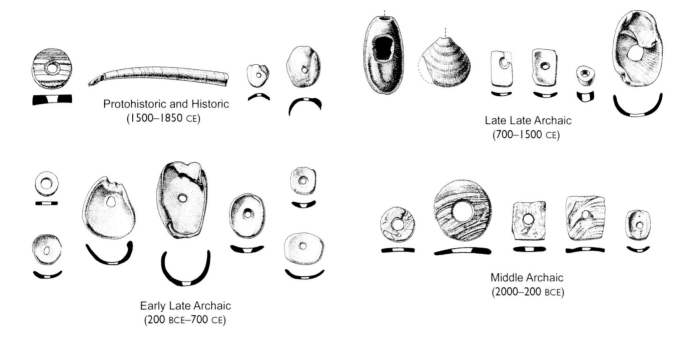

Protohistoric and Historic
(1500–1850 CE)

Late Late Archaic
(700–1500 CE)

Early Late Archaic
(200 BCE–700 CE)

Middle Archaic
(2000–200 BCE)

Figure 6.8. Late Archaic shell beads and ornaments.

when it fell off sharply for unknown reasons.

Some evidence exists for trade in obsidian, too, after about 4,000 years ago. At Hidden Cave in western Nevada, for example, the discovery of obsidian and shells together suggests that the two traveled the same network. But people probably also continued to acquire some obsidian directly from its sources, both local and distant. Certainly this was the case in historic times.

The "Numic Expansion"

Two of the most hotly debated questions relating to late Archaic times are, When did the Native people who lived in the Great Basin historically, particularly speakers of Numic languages, arrive there, and where did they come from? The three Numic language groups were distributed in a peculiar geographic pattern, fanning out from a small area in southeastern California. Each of the three groups subsumed two languages. Western Numic included the Mono and Northern Paiute tongues; Central Numic, the Panamint and Shoshone; and Southern Numic, the Kawaiisu and Ute (fig. 6.9). Mono, Panamint, and Kawaiisu were spoken only in a small area of southeastern California. Northern

Paiute, Shoshone, and Ute speakers covered much larger areas.

This pattern puzzled researchers for many years. In 1954 the linguist Sidney Lamb suggested that Numic-speaking people had expanded from around Death Valley into the Great Basin about 1,000 years ago. The great diversity of Numic languages in the vicinity of Death Valley indicated to Lamb that those languages had been spoken there for much longer than those spoken in the rest of the Great Basin. He used a method called glottochronology to estimate dates at which the Numic languages diverged from their larger language family, Uto-Aztecan. His results suggested that the Numic branch of Uto-Aztecan was becoming distinct about 3,000 years ago, with Mono, Panamint, and Kawaiisu separating about 2,000 years ago. Then, about 1,000 years ago, each of these three languages began to diversify internally as the ultimate speakers of Northern Paiute, Shoshone, and Ute expanded outward across the Great Basin.

In 1982 Robert Bettinger and Martin Baumhoff presented an archaeological version of this suggestion in which they explored the economic patterns of "Numa" and "pre-Numa" peoples in southeastern

California. They argued that pre-Numa people depended on a few high-energy resources such as mountain sheep, whereas the Numa relied on a broader range of foods. When the two groups came into competition, the Numa won because their diet was more diverse. About 1,000 years ago, as population density increased in southeastern California, the Numa began to move outward across the Great Basin, driving out or possibly absorbing other peoples.

Other researchers promptly challenged this suggestion. Most agreed that the ancestors of Numic-speaking peoples originated in southeastern California, but they disagreed over the timing of Numic language divergence and its causes. Correlating language distributions, populations, and archaeological cultures has been found to be notoriously difficult all over the world. In the Great Basin, a major conference was held in the early 1990s to explore the complexities of such correlations relating to the Numic expansion. No consensus answer was reached, but several alternative models were proposed, and archaeologists continue to explore them.

Some hope for an answer arose after a series of wet years during the 1980s caused lake levels to rise in several parts of the Great Basin. The waters then retreated, exposing large numbers of ancient burials along Malheur Lake in southern Oregon, Stillwater Marsh in western Nevada, and the Great Salt Lake in northern Utah—in other words, at places around the periphery of the Great Basin. Although of deep concern for both Indian people and archaeologists, the exposure of so many burials provided a rare opportunity for study. Through negotiations with the tribes of each area, researchers reached agreements to conduct certain types of analyses on the exhumed skeletons, one of which was DNA analysis. The majority of burials in all three places dated between 600 and 1300 CE, reaching back into late Archaic times

Although inconclusive, the DNA analyses suggested that the populations of those centuries were genetically different from modern Numa, adding support for a late migration of Numic-speaking

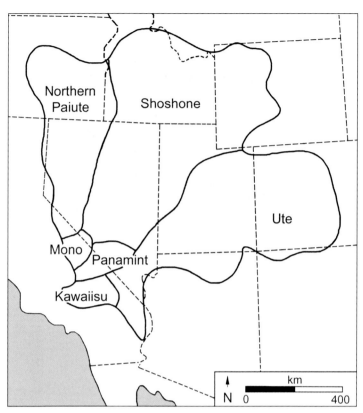

Figure 6.9. Distribution of Great Basin Numic languages.

peoples into the peripheries of the Great Basin. But there are no comparable skeletal data from the central Great Basin to provide crucial information about continuity, absorption, or replacement of one or more populations by Numic-speaking peoples in that region. Thus several key questions about the Numic expansion remain open and continue to be investigated.

Late Archaic Cultures in Transition
Spanish Americans met the easternmost Great Basin people, the Southern Numic Utes, soon after 1600 CE. Farther west, Native people had met Spanish Americans and Euro-Americans by 1750, and the newcomers became a flood tide soon after 1800. Euro-Americans brought new technologies (metal, firearms), animals (horses, pigs, cattle), and other material goods. Great Basin peoples rapidly adopted metal tools, firearms, and Euro-American clothing into their existing lifestyles. Horses had been adopted in the easternmost parts of the cultural Great Basin, within the range

of bison, by the early 1700s but came to be used farther west more slowly, in some instances only after the 1850s. Euro-Americans also brought European diseases—smallpox, influenza, measles, and cholera. The spread of such diseases after 1500, often preceding Indians' actually meeting Euro-Americans, had devastating results for Native people throughout the Western Hemisphere.

Researchers generally agree that the period just before Euro-Americans arrived in the Great Basin is poorly understood, but some evidence does exist. The high-altitude sites in the White and Toquima Ranges were probably established because of population pressure in the valleys below (chapter 12). These sites were used until the mid-eighteenth century and then suddenly abandoned, suggesting that the population pressure no longer existed. The most obvious explanation is depopulation due to

European diseases. Unfortunately for scholars, few introduced diseases leave evidence on bones, so they are difficult to document.

As Euro-Americans flooded into the Great Basin after the 1820s, Native people continued as best they could to live on the land using the complex Archaic lifestyles that had served them and their ancestors so well for millennia. But by the 1860s almost all Native groups in the Great Basin had been forced onto reservations. Their descendants continue to live on reservations, as well as in cities. The older, late Archaic lifeways, however, are remembered and cherished.

Charlotte Beck and George T. Jones are both professors of anthropology at Hamilton College, Clinton, New York.

Figure 7.1. Big Butte Valley, at the base of Big Butte, northeastern Nevada, site of the Tosawihi stone quarries.

Tosawihi Quarries and Sacred Sites

Robert Elston

Near the northern margin of the Great Basin, west of the Tuscarora Mountains, lies a broad, south-tilted upland, highest on the northeast side. There, a group of small volcanic formations is known as the Santa Renia Mountains. One of these is cone-shaped Big Butte, looming 1,000 feet above a crescent-shaped valley on its south and east (fig. 7.1). The valley floor, at about 6,000 feet above sea level, is drained by Little Antelope Creek, which has cut a narrow bedrock gorge known as Velvet Canyon through the basin rim.

During volcanic eruptions in the middle Miocene, at about 16.5 million and 14.9 million years ago, volcanic ash, or tuff, fell into a lake where this upland now stands. Rhyolite domes, including Big Butte, were produced during the final volcanic eruptions. Heavy faulting and the horizontal subsurface circulation of hot, mineral-laden water replaced some of the tuff layers with a form of chalcedony, commonly known as chert. Erosion then exposed layers of chert and tuff on the south rim of Big Butte Valley and in the canyon walls where Little Antelope Creek cuts Velvet Canyon. These geological processes created a tool stone bonanza that Native people visited for about 12,000 years (fig. 7.2). The chert beds make up one of the largest bedrock quarries in North America (map 3).

Today these quarries are on land managed by the US Bureau of Land Management. They are known as the Tosawihi quarries, after the Tosawihi Shoshones, who live on reservations at Owyhee and Battle Mountain, Nevada. Their ancestors collected the quarries' distinctive white chert, which gave the tribe its name, meaning "white knife."

The same geological events that created the chert beds also left deposits of mercury, gold, and silver around Big Butte, which attracted mining development in the 1980s. Under federal laws and regulations, the mining companies had to support archaeological research to help prevent the destruction of the Tosawihis' cultural heritage. Between 1987 and 1992 I directed for Intermountain Research an intensive archaeological investigation of the Tosawihi quarries, focusing on the economics of stone tool production. Ancient people expended a great deal of time and effort extracting raw chert from the earth, turning it into tools, and transporting those tools to places where they were used. Our surveys, surface collections, and excavations helped us explore how ancient quarriers solved technological and logistical problems. We conducted experiments to estimate how much time, effort,

Figure 7.2. Abandoned pit quarries and quarrying debris at the Tosawihi quarries.

and raw material were needed to produce a tool. Ethnographers Richard Clemmer, of the University of Denver, and Mary Rusco and Shelly Raven, of Archaeological Research Services, Inc., interviewed Tosawihi Shoshone consultants about the cultural and religious significance of the quarries. The following is what we discovered.

The Tosawihi Western Shoshones

Richard Clemmer parses the Shoshone word *tosawi-hi* as "white [*tosa*] knife [*wihi*]." Before metal tools became available, stone tools were a basic component of Native technology in the Great Basin, providing projectile points and edges and surfaces for cutting, scraping, piercing, and grinding other materials. High-quality obsidian and chert tool stone were so important that the Tosawihi people identified themselves with the white chert of Big Butte Valley, 20 to 30 miles north of their winter camps. This chert also possessed spiritual qualities, providing protection, healing, and power in hunting and war.

Tosawihi people lived in small, nomadic kin groups who made their winter camps along Rock Creek and the Humboldt River around Battle Mountain, Nevada. Their annual round could take them as far west as Golconda, east to the Independence Mountains, south to the Toiyabi Range, and as far north as the upper reaches of the Owyhee and Snake Rivers. In Tosawihi oral tradition, the area surrounding the quarries offered insufficient food or shelter for long-term residence—and indeed, we found no residential structures or constructed hearths there. People on spring foraging trips scheduled stops at the quarries to "tool up" and obtain medicinal minerals. Food and stone tools were cached there for the return trip to the winter camp.

Tosawihi oral tradition is unclear about whether only Tosawihi people had use of the quarries or whether anyone could go there. Families probably had claims to particular quarry places, but absent permanent residence, ownership could not be defended. The Tosawihis and neighboring groups frequently intermarried and granted each other hunting and gathering privileges, perhaps extending to quarry access as well. With white chert tools as currency, Tosawihis traded with neighboring

Northern Paiute and Western Shoshone people for foodstuffs and implements, with Snake River Plain Shoshones for salmon fishing rights, with Bannocks for elk and salmon, and with Nez Perce people for horses. Archaeologists found Tosawihi chert in a late bison kill site near Malheur Lake, Oregon, nearly 200 miles from the quarry.

Mining Chert and Gathering Medicine

The Tosawihi quarries provided several minerals in addition to chert. Powdered red tuff (*pisappih* or *tempisa* in the Shoshone language) mixed with grease was used as paint. Chalky white tuff (*aipiri*) also served as paint but primarily as medicine for power or healing. People used small green stones to purify springs. These minerals could be gathered from surface outcrops.

The goal of the Tosawihi chert quarriers was to extract large pieces of stone with which to make "blanks," or unfinished starts of tools that would eventually be flaked on each of two relatively flat faces, becoming what archaeologists call "bifaces" (fig. 7.3). Their best prospects were mines that were already productive, which explains why we find clusters of quarry pits in the same locality and why people repeatedly expanded existing pits. Tosawihi consultants said that both men and women worked in the quarries except when the women were menstruating. Young men probably did most of the prospecting and quarrying. Tool caches—unlike food caches, which others might use in times of need—were owned by their makers and could not be taken by others. Indeed, people avoided picking up intact tools and projectile points because *someone* owned them, perhaps a doctor (shaman) or Coyote the Trickster.

The Tosawihis quarried the bedrock with muscle, simple hand tools, and fire (fig. 7.4). Hammerstones up to the size of basketballs are common on the ground surface and in quarry and workshop debris. We found a few elk antler wedges, small antler hammers, and bison shoulder blade scoops in our quarry pit excavations, and we assume that people also used wooden wedges and digging sticks. The quarriers used fire to help break up bedrock, leaving deposits of charcoal and burned rock as evidence.

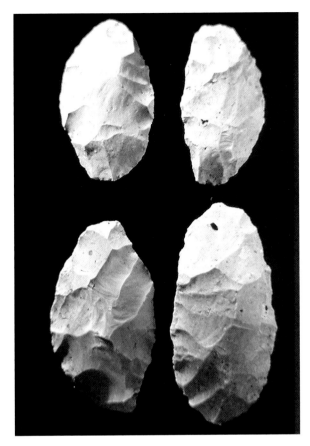

Figure 7.3. Bifacial artifacts from Tosawihi quarries. The implement at lower left is approximately 5 inches long.

Figure 7.4. Experimental quarrying in a pit quarry at Tosawihi.

Tosawihi quarriers often worked faces and ledges of bedrock exposed in stream cuts and on slopes. They undermined blocks of chert by pounding the softer tuff with stone hammers and picks and then broke up the blocks by hammering them or heating them with a small fire. Most of the talus deposits in Velvet Canyon consist of quarry waste. Pit quarries, the most common type, were excavated into horizontal beds of chert just below or protruding through the surface in flat areas. Pit quarries range from one pit to complexes of as many 55 in an area 18 by 25 feet, with each pit from 1 to 5 feet deep.

Pit quarriers usually had first to remove covering soil with digging sticks. Our experiments suggested that removing half a foot to 4 feet of soil to expose 10 to 12 square feet of bedrock would take one person roughly one and a half to two and a half hours. We also found that pounding on massive chert blocks with heavy hammerstones yielded little but dust and angular chunks. We got better results

by using natural fissures in the chert, opening cracks by tapping repeatedly with a small hammerstone, driving in wedges, and enlarging the cracks with more tapping. We extracted 60 blocks of tool stone weighing altogether 180 pounds. We rejected half the blocks, weighing a total of 60 pounds, for size or poor quality. Our quarrying work took about 13.5 person hours. We estimated that in places with more overlying soil, one quarrier could have done the work in about 16 hours.

Making White Knives

The white knives made by Tosawihi stone knappers are technically bifacial cores—roughly oval pieces of tool stone with flakes removed on both sides, which would later be refined into tools by additional chipping and flaking. The sharp-edged flakes removed from the cores could themselves be used as tools or further modified. Bifaces were the ultimate goal of quarrying at Tosawihi. We uncovered thousands,

Figure 7.5. Experimental chert knapping using stone and bone tools to manufacture bifaces.

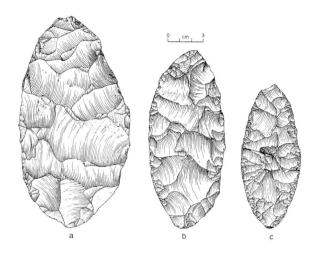

Figure 7.6. Major reduction stages of Tosawihi bifaces. The product of each stage could be used as a tool. Stage C bifaces were carried away from the quarries for later use to make other forms of stone tools, such as knives, scrapers, and projectile points.

most of them broken, misshapen, or containing flaws. In Tosawihi oral tradition, both men and women were knappers and made the tools they used from quarry bifaces. Knapping was a highly valued skill, and knappers sometimes competed while onlookers bet on the outcome. Consultants explained that women were highly skilled knappers because they were more competitive than men, more dependent on the use of knives and other tools, and had to know how to make and maintain them when men were absent. One consultant said that women knappers were important because of female destructive power while menstruating.

Knappers began with chert blocks and large flakes (fig. 7.5). As they first trimmed the edges of the core and then removed flakes from both sides, it became thinner, symmetrical, and smaller (fig. 7.6). Knappers used stone hammers for the initial shaping and probably switched to softer antler hammers for the later stages, when more control was needed. They may have finished using pressure applied with pointed antler tools. Thinned and resharpened throughout its life as a tool, a biface was used for different tasks, perhaps beginning as a heavy chopping and cutting tool and ending as a small knife, projectile point, or scraper. Of the 29 experimental blocks we kept for processing, 18 failed or broke apart as we worked them. We successfully produced

15 bifaces from the remaining 11 blocks. Chipping them to the point of final shaping took about 2.5 person hours.

Altogether, 77 percent of the raw material, by weight, that we extracted in our experimental quarrying we discarded at the quarry pit or found to fail during manufacturing. We were probably less skilled than Native quarriers and knappers, but the waste fraction in quarrying and processing tool stone is large and accounts in part for the astounding quantities of waste flakes and quarry debris that blanket the landscape around the Tosawihi quarries (see fig. 7.2).

Both archaeological and ethnographic evidence suggests that people chipped the blanks into roughly finished tools right at the quarry, because they needed to prove the material's quality and because it was costly in labor to transport large pieces of stone. Later, to refine the pieces into smaller, sharper tools, they often treated them with heat to make the tough chert glassier and easier to work. They buried bifaces just beneath a campfire to heat them slowly to between 450 and 650 degrees Fahrenheit and then let them cool. Tellingly, Tosawihi consultants referred to early-stage bifaces by a term meaning "I am making this into a knife." Late-stage bifaces they called simply *tosawihi*, white knife. Knappers sometimes made more bifaces than they could carry away, caching the excess at the quarries for later retrieval.

Figure 7.7. Cache of Tosawihi bifaces in various stages of reduction.

We discovered five biface caches at the quarries, each containing 6 to 38 shaped pieces (fig. 7.7).

The Sacred and the Secular

Several Tosawihi Shoshone consultants and their families still used the quarries to gather chert and materials for paint. They regarded the quarries and the area around them as places where *ofbu*, spiritual power, was concentrated. The summit of Big Butte is an important power spot where people fast, pray, and leave offerings. Another is at the springs on the west slope of Big Butte.

The quarries, as an important source of tool stone, once played a critical role in the secular, economic, and practical life of Tosawihi Shoshones. What distinguished the secular from the sacred uses of the quarries were the goals and talents of the users. The intrinsic power of Tosawihi chert remains dormant unless brought out by someone gifted in working the stone. Doctors could release the special protective and healing powers of the chert, whereas ordinary people could employ it for making ordinary tools. Pointed tools, however, were perhaps always a little dangerous. People found that white chert projectile points were particularly powerful in hunting and deadly in warfare, especially if the hunter prayed to the spirit within. Tosawihi doctors still use pointed tools in curative bloodletting, and Sun Dancers use them to pierce their skin. Although the Sun Dance originated among Great Plains tribes in the late 1800s, in recent times many other tribes, including the Tosawihis, also participate. Some dancers make a "flesh offering" by piercing their chests or backs with pointed tools of white chert, inserting a long thong attached to a pole, and dancing until it is torn out.

The Tosawihi Shoshones were probably not the first people to use the chert quarries. Several lines of evidence suggest that people drew on their riches as early as Clovis times, some 12,000 years ago. The vast piles of flakes and quarry debris and the myriad pits we find today are the results of innumerable short-term quarrying episodes over a dozen millennia. Archaeological evidence also suggests that use of the quarries became more intense about 1,500 years ago, but we do not know why. Perhaps the expansion of people speaking Numic languages into the Great Basin about then (chapter 6) created reciprocal social networks that promoted access to, and trade in, Tosawihi chert. Trade networks between Tosawihi people and their neighbors have yet to be archaeologically traced.

About 150 years separate living Tosawihi Shoshones from the last people to work the quarries as part of their seasonal round, yet the people preserve much quarry information in their oral tradition and still obtain tool stone and spiritual benefits there.

Our five-year study of the Tosawihi quarries made a good start at understanding this remarkable archaeological site. Yet most of our work took place in areas directly affected by contemporary mining, and these were not, unfortunately, in what the late Mary Rusco called "the heart of the quarries." There is much more to be learned about the economics and technology of quarrying and toolmaking at Tosawihi and how these changed through time.

Robert Elston works in the Great Basin and western China, where he applies theory from economics and behavioral ecology to problems in stone tool technology.

Figure 8.1. Plain weave bag from Spirit Cave, western Nevada, dated at 10,600 years old. Note the three vertical leather strips incorporated into the weave and the column of dark bulrush spots just to the right of center.

The Great Basin's Oldest Textiles

Catherine S. Fowler and Eugene M. Hattori

More than 10,000 years old! As we stared at the beautifully woven fiber bag (fig. 8.1) on the table in front of us in the basement of the Nevada State Museum, we could hardly believe it was that ancient. It was tightly woven, obviously in a complex technique, and it appeared to be decorated with small spots of a dark material and with leather strips. One of humankind's oldest known skills is making useful items such as string, bags, footwear, and even clothing out of plant fibers. But very old textiles are rare in the Great Basin. Decorated textiles older than 7,000 years are even rarer. In addition, this bag had an undulating pattern of dark and light across its surface that made it even more intriguing. But the most amazing thing about it was that it was complete and so flexible that it might have been woven yesterday.

Complex fiber artifacts, including sandals, nets, baskets, bags, mats, hats, and aprons, as well as various types of string and rope and the prepared materials used to make them, have been found in many dry sites in the Great Basin. We had often marveled at the excellent preservation of these fragile artifacts, but only rarely had any been discovered in such mint condition as the woven bag on the table. Although we had long admired the complex weave structures of the textiles that Great Basin people created 2,000 and even 5,000 years ago, we had not considered the possibility of such sophisticated traditions dating to 10,000 years ago or even more. But here was this beautiful fiber bag, 10,600 years old.

As we continued to stare, we asked ourselves, exactly how was it made? How widespread was this weaving tradition? Have we overlooked other textiles that might be this old? Who was the weaver and under what circumstances did she or he work? Thus began our odyssey into ancient Great Basin textiles. Our methods for answering these questions would be both old and new. We used standard descriptive techniques of textile analysis along with the newer means of radiocarbon dating, accelerator mass spectrometry (AMS).

Old Textiles

Why are ancient textiles useful to archaeologists? In the 1940s and 1950s, Robert Heizer, Luther Cressman, and Jesse Jennings recognized the unique opportunities that the remarkable textiles preserved in Great Basin dry caves and rockshelters afforded for interpreting early Great Basin history (chapter 4). James Adovasio, who studied many textiles and fragments in museum collections in the 1970s and 1980s, pioneered the development of chronologies based on changes in textile techniques, styles, and forms. Other researchers used fiber artifacts from archaeological sites to describe intriguing cultural patterns and possible intercultural connections. But for various reasons, the 10,600-year-old bag and others associated with it at Spirit Cave in the Carson Desert of western Nevada (map 2) had not previously been analyzed or dated. Our examination of them in 1998 broke new ground.

Until the 1980s archaeologists occasionally but unwillingly had to sacrifice large pieces of textiles and often entire items in order to date them by the older radiocarbon method. Fiber artifacts of any kind are not so abundant that they are readily expendable. Rather, archaeologists used less culturally significant finds such as charcoal, wood, and animal bone for radiocarbon dating, choosing pieces that were likely associated with the textiles to get some idea of the time when people might have used the textiles in a particular site. This approach is not fully satisfactory. In dry caves, people walking around or digging into the surface to bury things, animal activity such as rodent burrowing, and vandalism can mix items that people have left behind at different times. The development of AMS dating in the 1980s was as revolutionary for archaeologists —and certainly for textile analysts—as the original development of radiocarbon dating was in the late 1940s. AMS uses only tiny fragments of organic materials, less than 0.1 gram, so it preserves the integrity of significant objects such as textiles. And the dates are determined directly from the specimens, which yields much more accurate information about their true ages.

Nevada State Museum personnel used AMS to date the bag and other remarkable woven artifacts from Spirit Cave. The researchers who originally discovered the bag and two others in the 1940s thought they were no more than 2,000 to 3,000 years old. The AMS dates were a real surprise. Perhaps it was time to reassess our assumptions about the earliest textiles in the Great Basin.

Analyzing Weave Structure

The first step to understanding ancient textiles is to figure out exactly how the weavers made each piece. Researchers do this by carefully examining the way the fibers interlace to form the *fabric*, or weave structure. They also look at the way the weavers started and finished their pieces and attempt to identify the materials used to make them. Along the way they make other important observations, but these are the primary starting points.

One determines weave structure by first identifying which fiber element acts as the *warp*, or passive element, and which acts as the *weft*, or active element. In *plain weave*, the over-one, under-one weave most familiar to people today, the warps

remain more or less stationary while the weaver passes the weft over and under the warps from one side to the other and then back again. We looked at the first bag, the one that intrigued us in the beginning, with hand lenses and a microscope to see whether we could tell the warp from the weft.

The bag was so tightly woven that we had to carefully separate the elements to see which was doing what. The bag turned out to be plain weave, but with a unique feature that we first suspected by looking at the edges of the bag. They showed that after each two rows had been woven, the two weft threads were twisted together along the edge before the weaver started the next two rows (fig. 8.2). This implies that the rows were being woven across the warps at roughly the same time, but basically in pairs. Once the maker had completed the mat, weaving roughly 20 inches of weft rows, it was folded in half, parallel with the warps, and the warps were trimmed flush to the weft rows at either end. The two trimmed edges were then overcast stitched to form a bag roughly 15 inches wide by 10 inches high. The open weft edges at the top of the bag required no further finishing.

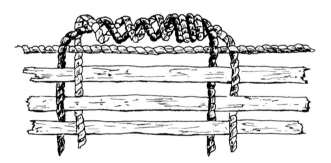

Figure 8.2. Schematic of edge finishes on the plain weave bag.

This method of weaving might have been time saving, but considering the tightness of the weave and the materials used in the bag, it also added some complications. The warps were made of relatively stiff, split pieces of bulrush (*Scirpus* species), whereas the wefts were a much thinner and more flexible twisted string made of strands of dogbane (*Appocynum cannabinum*) mixed with sage (*Artemisia tridentata*) or juniper (*Juniperus* species). Because of the difference in pliability between these fibers, the weaver would have had difficulty controlling them while weaving. To produce a weave this tight, the weaver would have had to pull hard on the string wefts, either singly or the pairs together, after the weft strings were interlaced with the warps. How was this done? Some other textiles from Spirit Cave would eventually answer the question, but first we continued to study this bag and two others.

The decoration on the bag was equally interest-ing. On one side the maker had inlaid short lengths of dark pieces of bulrush stem to form a column of "spots." The weaver did so while making the bag, not as an afterthought. In addition, the maker incor-porated three leather strips into the weave, perhaps to form the bases for handles or ties. Both additions indicated that the weaver planned from the begin-ning to make a bag and decorate it on only one face.

The dark-to-light color changes across the bag's surface were more difficult to explain, because they apparently were not the result of changes in materi-al. Rather, it appeared that the practice of weaving the two wefts at a time, pulling them tight, and then twisting the strings together at the edge before starting another two rows somehow created a spac-ing of the warp rows that gave peculiar highlights to the natural colors of the bulrushes.

Two other bags from the site (figs. 8.3, 8.4) were of comparable age but made in a different

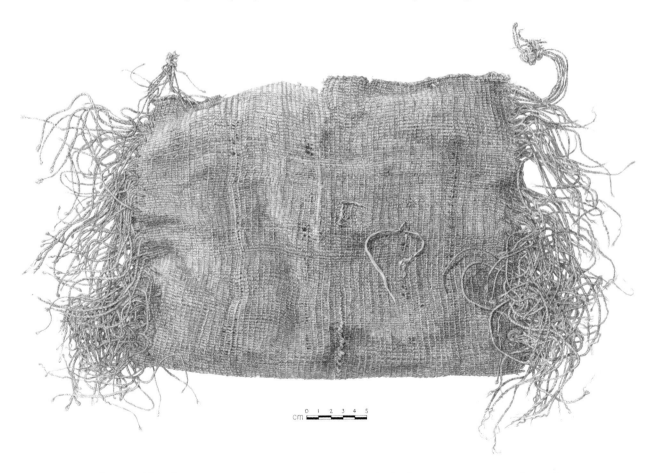

Figure 8.3. Loosely twined bag from Spirit Cave, western Nevada. Note the leather pieces incorporated into the weave as decoration in the lower center, center, and right. The two small black spots are duck feathers. Approximately 10 inches deep (to fold) by 15.5 inches long, plus fringe.

Figure 8.4. Closely twined bag from Spirit Cave, western Nevada. The dark spots left of center are duck feathers. Approximately 10 inches (to fold) by 16 inches long, plus fringe.

technique. In both, the passive elements, the warps, consisted of strings like the wefts of the first bag, but much thicker. The wefts were also string. In both bags the wefts were *twined*, or twisted around each warp string as they formed each row. Nevertheless, the weaver created one bag in a very tight structure, with rows of twining closely spaced, and the other in a looser weave, with rows of twining more widely spaced. The top and bottom ends of the warps were then left dangling, so that when the flat fabric was finished, folded in half, and stitched together, these ends became fringe on either side of each bag.

While carefully checking our observations of the bags, we noticed something else tucked into the weave structure and creating a vague pattern—duck feathers. The weaver had placed short brown and white feathers into the weave to create diagonal lines across the face of one of the bags (fig 8.3) and to make isolated "spots" on one surface of the other (fig. 8.4). The second bag was also made half in dark and half in light weft fibers, giving it a distinctive look. These bags, along with the plain weave

bag, are certainly among the oldest, if not *the* oldest, decorated textiles yet collected in North America.

In addition to the three bags, we looked at other textiles from this site. Two were large mats, one 30 and the other 40 inches square, made in the same technique and materials as the first bag but without decoration. The smaller one was folded and stitched to make a large bag; the other was left flat. They were equally finely and tightly woven, but their large sizes made us wonder even more how the weavers had been able to control the materials and achieve such a tight fabric. The maker would have had to handle literally hundreds of bulrush warp ends while hand manipulating the two weft threads over and under them and then pulling the wefts tightly across the entire fabric. We needed to think more carefully about to how this might have been done.

First, we made a small model to get a feel for the difficulty of the task. Armed with 30 split, wet bulrush strips and two small balls of string, one for each row, we wove about 12 inches of a mat, trying various techniques for pulling the strings tight to

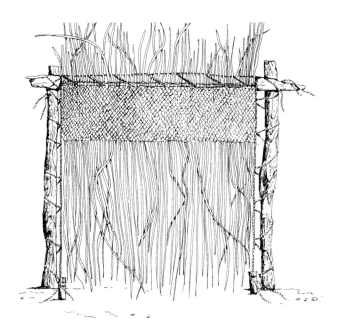

Figure 8.5. Model of a possible upright frame for weaving large, plain weave mats.

The only way it seemed feasible to work with this much material was to use some type of controlling device, such as an upright frame from which to suspend the warp and help control the weft or some type of ground frame that might do the same job (figs. 8.5, 8.6). An alternative might be for more than one person at a time to work on such a piece while sitting on the ground, but this would not likely result in the control needed to pull the materials tight. Even on our small piece we found it difficult to get the mat as tight as the originals by weaving one weft string for more than a few inches without following it with the other. Both wefts had to be woven for a few inches and then pulled together to achieve a tightness close to that of the original weave.

This finding reinforced our conclusion that the ancient weavers must have been exceedingly skilled and had some type of controlling frame—in other words, a loom. It also made sense that given the amount of string needed to weave a large mat in this technique—several *miles* of it—and the total absence of knots in the string of the mats and bags, the weaver would have had to splice in new string frequently. Furthermore, our model developed some peculiar color changes similar to the ones on the first bag we examined, the result of the tensioning of the weft or of weaving from first one side and then the other. Our appreciation for the weavers of these ancient textiles, their skill, and their ingenuity in developing some type of loom or frame with which to weave these pieces grew steadily.

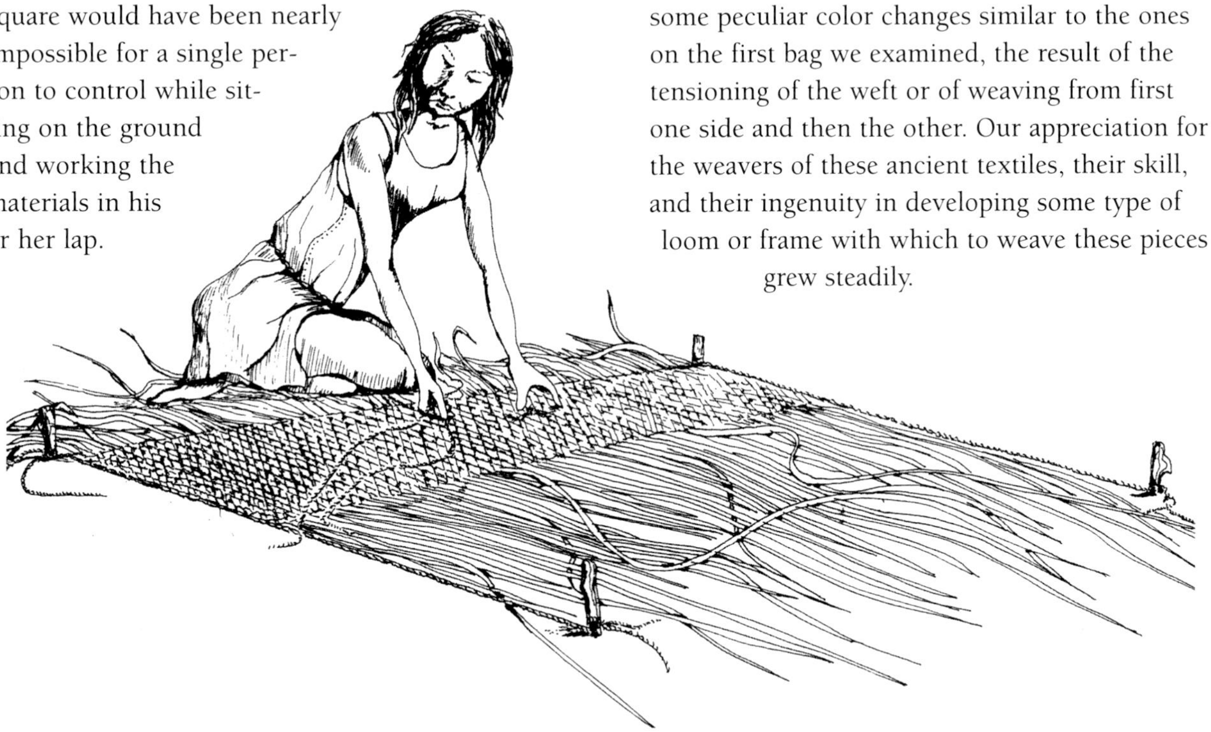

get the same appearance as the original weave. Even on this small piece it was difficult to keep the materials tight and in place. The roughly 700 split bulrush stems required to make a mat 40 inches square would have been nearly impossible for a single person to control while sitting on the ground and working the materials in his or her lap.

Figure 8.6. Model of a possible ground frame for weaving large, plain weave mats.

Figure 8.7. A large Catlow twine mat, 32 by more than 28 inches, from the Winnemucca Lake basin, western Nevada.

Other Old Textiles

Once we felt we understood how ancient weavers had made the oldest Spirit Cave pieces, we began looking at collections from other Great Basin sites for examples of these or similar weaves, in order to analyze and date them by the AMS technique. We found examples of the plain weave with paired wefts technique from other cave sites in the Carson Desert (Hidden Cave, Grimes Point Cave), in the Winnemucca Lake basin (Crypt Cave, Chimney Cave), and nearly 200 miles northeast (Elephant Mountain Cave) (map 2). We submitted samples for AMS dating and received nearly identical results. They all dated between 10,600 and 9,500

years old. After that time, this weaving technique vanishes from the textile record in the Great Basin, although it has been reported for peoples of the Columbia Plateau, the upper Midwest, and the Northeast some 8,000 to 9,000 years later—an observation not easily explained.

The two twined bags have no exact duplicates elsewhere in the region, although bags similar in technique are known. Two bags from the Winnemucca Lake basin display a slightly coarser but otherwise comparable weave and less fringe; one has some feather decoration, not visible in the illustration (plate 3). The two bags were dated to more than 9,000 years ago. An incomplete,

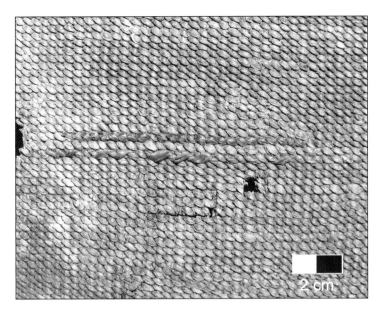

Figure 8.8. Detail of the mat in figure 8.7, showing decoration using techniques known as overlay (top row) and false embroidery (bottom row).

coarsely twined bag from Hogup Cave in western Utah proved to be roughly 7,000 years old.

As we began looking for additional weaving techniques and forms that might date to this oldest period of Great Basin textile history, we were in for more surprises. In the northern Great Basin, especially in southeastern Oregon, archaeologists had unearthed textiles made in a unique form of twining called Catlow twine, after Catlow Cave, where researchers found the first examples. Small fragments of Catlow twine from Fort Rock Cave and the Paisley Five-Mile Point caves were dated in the 1950s by conventional radiocarbon methods to at most about 8,000 years ago, and the oldest dates were controversial. A large Catlow twine mat from a cave in the Winnemucca Lake basin (fig. 8.7) has now been AMS dated at more than 9,000 years old. It is decorated with dark bars made by sophisticated techniques that required strips of decorative material to be laced on top of the wefts as the piece was being woven (fig. 8.8). Working with archaeologists, museum personnel, and other textile analysts, we have obtained more than 150 AMS dates on baskets, sandals, and other fiber artifacts in

Great Basin collections, nearly all of them older than anyone expected.

Who Were the Weavers?

The hardest question to answer about these ancient textiles is who might have made them. Weaving has traditionally been women's work in many societies around the world, but we cannot assume that it was always so. Trying to decide the ethnic identity of the Great Basin weavers is even more difficult, because the pieces are so old. But whoever made these early pieces, they were no strangers to weaving. They knew well which materials to gather, how to evaluate their quality, and when and how to prepare them. From the weavers' choices of materials such as bulrush and dogbane, as well as the locations of many of the cave sites, we know that these people lived near marshes, where such plants were readily available. Because weaving is much easier if the materials are kept wet while they are worked, we know that the people had sources from which to carry water or did their weaving near the shore of a lake or marsh.

Other chapters introduce some of the woven items that make up such an important part of the archaeological record in the Great Basin and reveal so much about its early peoples and their knowledge of their world. Some woven pieces were useful, such as footwear (chapter 9) and baskets (chapter 16). Others made artistic statements, such as the beautiful feathered caps and bowls described in chapter 10. Along with the mats and bags we have described, they survive as documents for textile analysts to decipher, as well as elegant testimonies to the abilities of many generations of weavers.

Catherine S. Fowler is UNR Foundation Professor of Anthropology Emerita at the University of Nevada, Reno. Eugene M. Hattori is curator of anthropology at the Nevada State Museum, Carson City.

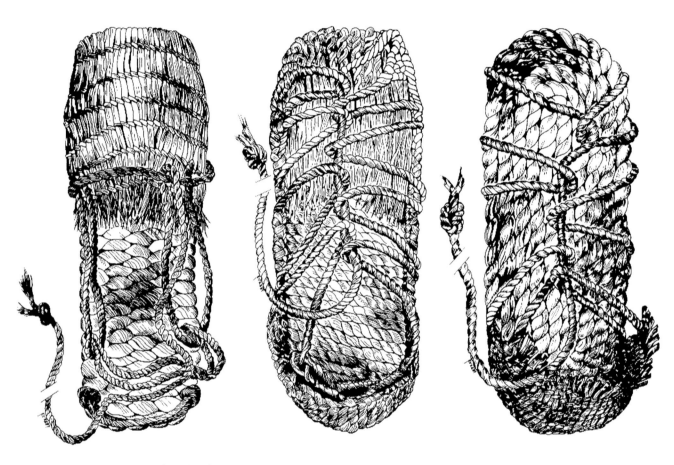

Figure 9.1. Major types of sandals from the northern Great Basin. Left to right: Fort Rock style, multiple warp style, spiral weft style.

Great Basin Sandals

Thomas J. Connolly and Pat Barker

In the 1880s, Otis T. Mason, curator of ethnology at the US National Museum, described the Native peoples of the far West as "basket Indians." The label recognized not only the fine quality of the baskets those peoples produced but also their use of plant fibers to make so many of the other things they needed in their daily lives—bedding, clothing, shoes, ropes, nets, shelters, even watercraft. Basketry, in this broad sense, is a relatively plastic medium that allows much variation in structure and style. People learn how to make basketry products using certain techniques, materials, and styles, and they pass that knowledge down across generations. Closely examining those products is a useful way to learn about the continuity and discontinuity of traditions over time.

Throughout much of the Great Basin in ancient times, people wore sandals woven from plant fibers, to the near exclusion of hide shoes. Thanks to the region's dry climate, many of these fragile items have been preserved in dry caves and rockshelters. They are found commonly enough that archaeologists can determine how fashions changed over the centuries and identify the territories of cultural groups distinguishable by their techniques or styles. Archaeologists have collected many sandals under circumstances that made it difficult to know how old they were, but the development of AMS dating has remedied that problem.

Early residents of the northern and western Great Basin left behind sandals of three distinct styles: spiral weft, multiple warp, and Fort Rock

(fig. 9.1). The first two got their names because of the way they were made. The Fort Rock style is named for Fort Rock Cave, which Luther Cressman excavated in 1938. Other, rarer types include V-twined sandals, known from Lovelock Cave in western Nevada, and open-twined sandals, reminiscent of footwear collected from historic-era Klamath weavers in southeastern Oregon.

Fort Rock Cave yielded more than a hundred sandals, all similar and many of them tied in pairs, buried beneath 7,600-year-old Mount Mazama volcanic ash. This style has a flat, closely twined sole with five rope warps formed into an arc at the heel and extended to the toe. A few examples have six or eight warps. Weft twining proceeded back and forth across the sole from heel to toe, tightly enough to cover the warps. At the toe the thick warps were subdivided into finer cords and turned back to form an open-twined toe flap. The tie system has a series of interlocking loops fixed to one edge of the sole and at the heel; these were then looped with a tie rope attached to the other edge and cinched tight around the ankle.

Fort Rock–type sandals are the oldest style in the northern Great Basin. They have been found in several other caves in the region (fig. 9.2). Most of them are made of sagebrush bark, but two from Cougar Mountain Cave, including one dating to about 9,600 years ago, and one example from Horse Cave near Winnemucca Lake in Nevada, dated to about 9,200 years ago, are of tule, or bulrush. There are 14 radiocarbon dates on Fort

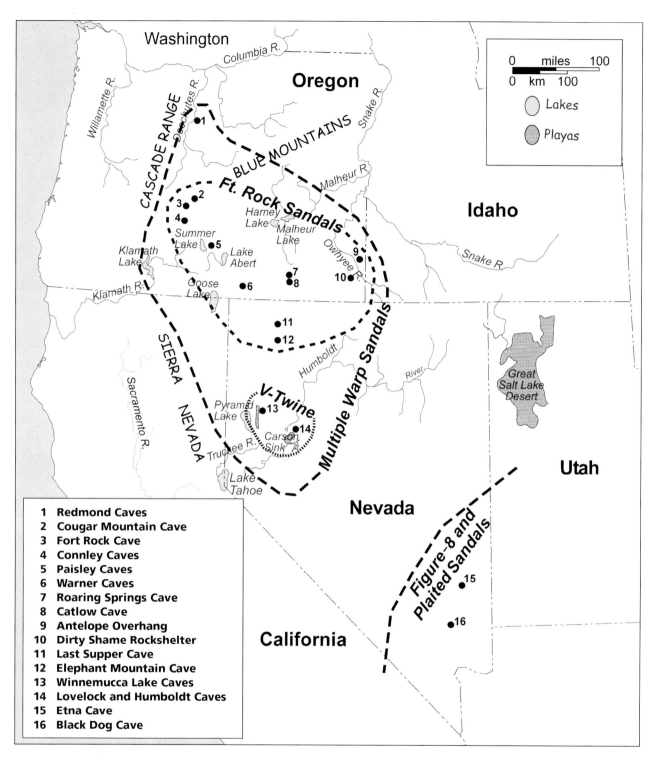

Figure 9.2. Distribution of northern Great Basin sandal types.

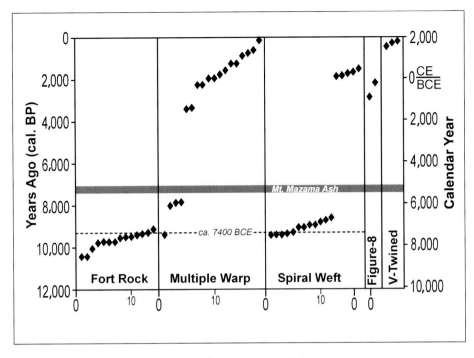

Figure 9.3. Radiocarbon chronology of Great Basin sandal styles.

Rock–style sandals from six northern Great Basin sites, ranging from 10,500 to about 9,200 years ago. The sandals disappeared about the time that multiple warp and spiral weft sandals first appeared, between 9,200 and 9,000 years ago.

Multiple warp sandals have from eight to more than a dozen warps, a few of which were brought around the heel to form a pocket and then the sole. Weft rows of twining were closely spaced from heel pocket to toe, again covering the warps. Loose warps were then bent back from the toe as a toe cover but were rarely twined. Tie loops were built into the sole, typically by extending wefts beyond the last warp, twisting them into a cord loop, and then returning them as sole wefts. A separate cord was then run through the loops and tied across the top of the foot.

This sort of sandal protected people's feet over a larger territory than any of the other types (fig. 9.2) and for an extremely long time—from about 9,500 years ago to just 130 years ago. Four of the 18 known examples from caves in southern Oregon and northern Nevada date between 9,500 and 7,900 years ago. Fourteen others are later, from about 3,800 to about 200 years ago. One sandal from

Catlow Cave, dated to about 2,300 years ago, was made like a multiple warp sandal but has more loosely twined wefts, like those of late-nineteenth- and early-twentieth-century Klamath sandals from Oregon. Other examples in museum collections from Winnemucca Lake are about 3,400 to 1,200 years old.

Younger examples of multiple warp tule sandals, dating between 730 and 600 years ago, come from Warner Valley, Oregon. A child-size sandal from near-by Catlow Cave is 850 years old, and an example from more distant Elephant Mountain Cave is less than 300 years old. What do all these dates tell us? The style appeared about 9,000 years ago and was made until perhaps 200 years ago—surely a fashion record. But there is a troubling gap of some 3,000 to 4,000 years' duration for which we have no sandals of this kind. There is no clear explanation for this gap, nor for a similar one in the dates of spiral weft sandals (fig. 9.3).

Spiral weft sandals were made with warps running at right angles to the axis of the foot. The weft was then twined in a spiral pattern, like a circular basket start, beginning along the centerline of the foot and continuing around the warps to form the oblong sole. Tie loops were formed by extending the warps beyond the edge of the sole. Spiral weft sandals, which in shape resemble small braided rugs, have been found in several caves along the Oregon-Nevada border.

Seventeen spiral weft sandals from sites in southeastern Oregon, northern Nevada, and western Idaho have been radiocarbon dated. Most of them range from about 9,500 to 8,400 years old, but five are between about 1,900 and 1,500 years old. In general, spiral weft sandals were contemporaneous with multiple warp sandals and were worn

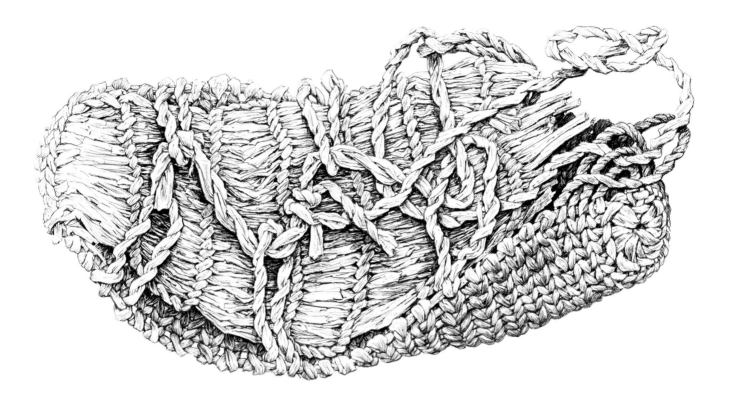

Figure 9.4. V-twined sandal.

by people across much the same territory. But a gap of more than 6,000 years separates the older from the younger set of spiral weft examples.

People in the western Great Basin made V-twined sandals from grasses or reeds (juncus, tule, or bulrush) by first twining a heel pocket around a circular start. Then they alternated rows of clockwise and counterclockwise weft twists from side to side to produce a V pattern, finishing with an untwined toe flap (fig. 9.4). These sandals have been found only in Lovelock Cave in western Nevada. Two of the Lovelock Cave examples date more recently than 500 years ago.

The sandal styles described so far do not exhaust the fashion repertoire of early Great Basin footwear. In the southern Great Basin, archaeologists excavated three different types of sandal from Black Dog Cave near Moapa in southeastern Nevada. One type is a twined yucca style with the square toe and square heel usually associated with the early ancestral Pueblo culture of northeastern

Arizona and southeastern Utah between about 2,000 and 500 years ago (see fig. 17.4). The second, found throughout the Southwest, is a weft-faced plain weave style—that is, its makers used simple over-one, under-one plain weaving in which the weft completely covers the warp. The third is a plain weave form made of yucca known as the figure-eight style (plate 2).

Figure-eight sandals from Black Dog Cave have four, six, or more warp elements that were made mostly of flat yucca leaves knotted together at the heel and toe. The leaves were bundled to form two warps, around which a weft of partly shredded yucca leaves was woven in a figure-eight pattern. The sandals were fastened to the foot by extending the two warp ends between the toes, thong fashion, and tying them behind the ankle. Archaeologists have collected similar sandals from Etna Cave in southeastern Nevada and other sites in the southwestern Great Basin. In the US Southwest, figure-eight style sandals date from roughly 2,300 to 700 years ago. Two of the Black Dog Cave sandals are about 1,500 years old.

Whatever the sandal style, archaeological sites in the Great Basin hold a unique record extending over the past 10,000 years. During those millennia, hundreds of generations of American Indian men, women, and children walked untold miles wearing ingeniously designed and well-made woven sandals. Both well-worn and nearly new archaeological examples attest to the skill and patience of their weavers.

Thomas J. Connolly has served as research division director for the University of Oregon Museum of Natural and Cultural History and the Oregon State Museum of Anthropology since 1986. Pat Barker is a research associate at the Nevada State Museum who studies Great Basin textiles, political evolution among hunter-gatherers, and prehistoric landscape manipulation.

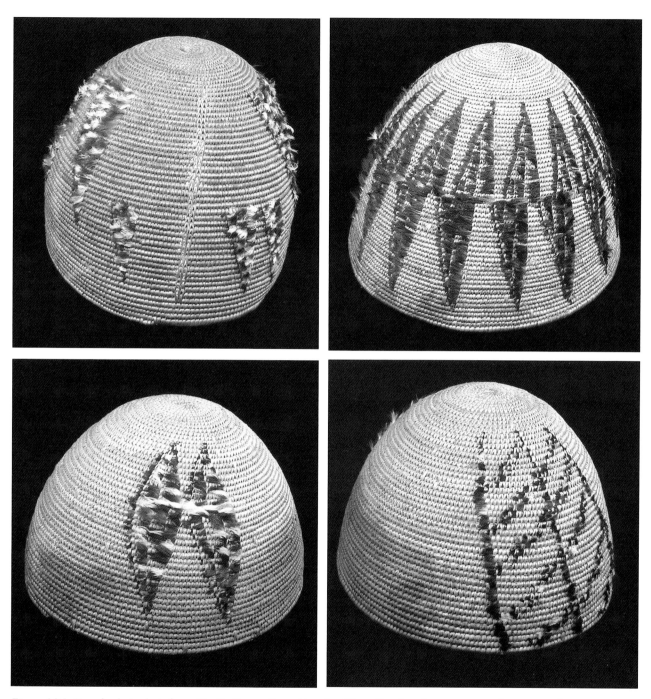

Figure 10.1. Four basketry hats from Charlie Brown Cave, Nevada. All are 8 to 9 inches in greatest diameter and 5 to 6 inches tall.

Hats, Baskets, and Trays from Charlie Brown Cave

Edward A. Jolie and Ruth Burgett Jolie

Dry caves and rockshelters in the Great Basin have yielded some of the oldest and best-preserved textiles in the world. Among them are hundreds of fragmentary and complete baskets, many with intricate, multicolored designs. Some weavers added mineral paint and bird feathers to create lively patterns. Many of the baskets archaeologists find are in pieces and provide little information about how ancient people made and used them in daily life. For this reason, we were delighted to study a spectacular collection of complete, finely woven, and elaborately decorated baskets from a cave in western Nevada. What we learned sheds new light on the significance of basketry to people in the western Great Basin 1,300 years ago.

In the late 1960s, two avocational archaeologists uncovered 20 baskets in a single cache in a cave site on the eastern edge of the Winnemucca Lake playa, about 40 miles north of Reno. They donated the collection to the Nevada State Museum. The extreme dryness of the site, named Charlie Brown Cave after one of its excavators, had helped preserve the baskets in almost pristine condition. The cache contained six bowl-shaped hats nested together and, stacked nearby, three large, shallow trays and 11 wide-mouthed bowls. The baskets were unearthed just as they had been stored centuries before. Five AMS radiocarbon dates on individual baskets tell us they were all woven around 1,300 years ago.

We examined the baskets to learn what we could about them and their makers. What we found underscores the importance of basketry to ancient people of the region and highlights their aesthetic tastes and artistic achievements. All the baskets were woven by coiling, a technique in which a horizontal element or set of elements, called the foundation or warp, is coiled around itself and sewn together, row upon row, with a vertical element called the stitch, or weft. The resulting basket spirals up and outward from the center starting point. The striking similarities in the baskets' construction suggest that perhaps three weavers made all 20 of them. Some of them are so alike technically and stylistically that the weavers might have been family members or, if unrelated, students and teachers.

We distinguished the hats from the bowls by their depth, wear patterns, and the way they were shaped to fit a human head (fig. 10.1, plate 6). The small size of one suggested that a young adult or child had worn it. In recent times, women in California and Nevada wore basketry hats to keep pitch out of their hair while they gathered piñon nuts or to protect themselves from the bands they wore around their foreheads to support heavy burden baskets. The Charlie Brown hats were perhaps leisure wear or worn as finery on special occasions.

The 11 bowls are too large to be hats and show heavy wear (fig. 10.2, plate 7). One bowl has a gruel-like food residue and small seeds stuck to its interior, indicating its use for processing or serving food. The other bowls may have been used for the same purpose or other utilitarian tasks, including serving as basins during gathering and processing small plant seeds for food.

The three trays average 27 inches in diameter

(fig. 10.3, plate 8). We found small marsh plant seeds stuck to the interior surfaces of two trays. Perhaps they were feasting trays, brought out for serving food on special occasions. It is also possible that the trays, like the bowls, were used as basins in which to catch seeds beaten or stripped from plants during harvesting. The baskets might even have served as gambling trays onto which players threw dice. All these uses for trays were common among people in California and Nevada over the last few centuries, so it is reasonable to think that ancient people practiced them, too.

The large trays and possibly the hats might have served other purposes on special occasions. Perhaps they were cached to be used seasonally, at the time people harvested certain food plants and conducted accompanying ceremonies.

The beautiful designs on the baskets and the ways they were created offer a glimpse into the artistic skills and aesthetic concerns of the weavers. These artisans preferred young willow shoots as their weaving material. They created geometric designs by alternating lengths of buff-colored and reddish brown willow. They painted two baskets with white and blue mineral pigments in amorphous designs; one of these is shown in plate 7. They wove feathers into walls of the hats and some baskets to produce curving designs. They used brown, white, and iridescent green feathers from water birds, including the common merganser, the green-winged teal, and the cinnamon teal. There are golden feathers from the eared grebe, and the few contrastive reds and yellows came from red-wing and yellow-wing blackbirds. Using feathers to decorate mats and bags is a technique of more than 10,000 years' antiquity in western North America and is still favored by some contemporary weavers.

The skilled weavers whose work found its way

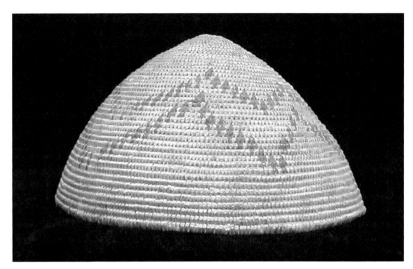

Figure 10.2. Two basketry bowls from Charlie Brown Cave. Both are about 9 inches in diameter and 5 inches deep.

into Charlie Brown Cave created dynamic designs that give a great sense of movement. Each design is well positioned on the basket, sometimes growing as the basket itself grew during weaving. Some designs are asymmetrical, but they are never placed haphazardly. The weavers balanced background space with decorated space. They used diverse design elements, including triangles, stars, zigzags, diamonds, and crowns. The designs on all but one of the hats were accomplished with variations of triangles, and triangles often appear on trays as well. Stars and zigzags are almost always restricted to bowls.

We know from studies of contemporary Native American weavers that they readily borrow designs

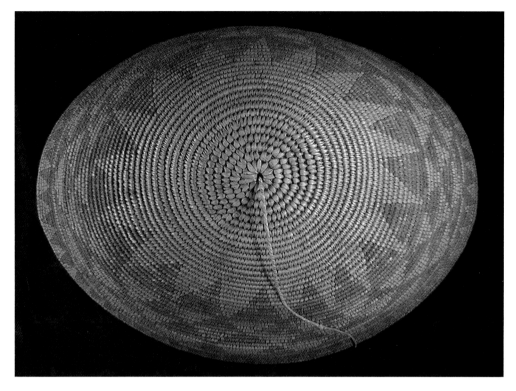

Figure 10.3. A basketry tray from Charlie Brown Cave, about 27 inches in diameter and 3 inches deep.

from others. Not surprisingly, the Charlie Brown designs are much like those on fragments of baskets from other archaeological sites around Winnemucca Lake. Diamond design elements also appear on baskets from Lovelock and Humboldt Caves, about 100 miles to the east. This suggests that the makers of the Charlie Brown baskets were linked to their immediate neighbors and to other people some distance beyond.

Although 1,300 years have passed since the Charlie Brown baskets were made, they most closely resemble baskets produced over the last few centuries by Maidu, Konkow, and Nisenan people, who live just west of the Sierra Nevada in central California. Indeed, when early archaeologists examined baskets similar to the Charlie Brown examples from other western Great Basin sites, they thought they were exotic imports, because contemporaneous baskets from the region looked very different. Our comparison of the Charlie Brown baskets with those from nearby sites demonstrates that they were part of a long regional tradition of basketry production with origins in western Nevada dating back at least

4,000 years. Between 1,000 and 700 years ago this tradition was gradually replaced by one in which people made and decorated baskets differently. The new style corresponds strongly to the style of contemporary Great Basin baskets, suggesting that the ancestors of modern Native peoples moved into the area sometime in the last millennium.

Basket styles changed over time, but baskets themselves remained a vital part of people's daily lives. They were used in food preparation, storage, ritual, and recreation. The Charlie Brown Cave baskets allow us to fully appreciate the significance of their utility and beauty to people of the past. Some of the Charlie Brown baskets are on display at the Nevada State Museum in Carson City for everyone to learn from and enjoy.

Edward A. Jolie is an Oglala Lakota–Hodulgee Muscogee Indian doctoral student at the University of New Mexico studying textiles from archaeological contexts in the American Southwest. Ruth Burgett Jolie is a doctoral student at the University of New Mexico interested in textile arts, urban ethnography, and gender.

Figure 11.1. The Ruby Marshes with the Ruby Mountains in the background, northeastern Nevada.

The "Good Sweet Water" of Great Basin Marshes

David B. Madsen and Robert L. Kelly

The most striking thing about the Great Basin is not the neon lights of Las Vegas but the land's stark contrasts. Traveling from south to north, you begin your journey in the hot, dry Mojave Desert and end it in the cold sagebrush deserts of the Snake River plain. Traveling from east to west, you repeatedly cross high ranges, some with snow-clad peaks, that tower over valley bottoms covered with sagebrush and greasewood. And if the Great Basin is a "sagebrush ocean," as some call it, then as you travel it you will come across some "islands" of marshes and lakes.

You would not be the first to welcome these wetlands. In June 1859, as Captain James H. Simpson charted a wagon route across the Great Basin, he described the land as "thirsty-looking" and "ashy." When at last he reached Carson Lake near present-day Fallon, Nevada, he exclaimed in his journal, "O the luxury of good sweet water to a thoroughly thirsty traveler! How little do we value the daily common bounties of Providence!" Carson Lake, he wrote, "presents at sunset a very pretty landscape," one "quite extensive and rich.… Curlew, pelican, and ducks, and other aquatic birds frequent the locality, and the lake is filled with fish…the water of Carson Lake beautifully blue, lake margined with rushes; the shores are covered with mussel shells."

What are wetlands and lakes doing in a landscape that is otherwise so "thirsty-looking"? The answer lies in the Great Basin's geography. If we could slice the basin in half from east to west, we would see three striking characteristics. First, the region is rimmed by high mountains, the Sierra Nevada on the west and the Wasatch Range on the east. Second, it contains a series of north-south-trending fault-block mountains reaching several thousand feet above the valley floors, all formed by tectonic forces stretching the earth's crust. And third, the Great Basin in east-west section is dome shaped, meaning that the valley floors in the middle are higher than those at the margins, and many of the peaks of the interior ranges reach significant heights. Mount Jefferson in central Nevada, for example, tops 11,000 feet.

This geographic structure affects the distribution of water. Westerly winds push warm, moisture-laden air in from the Pacific Ocean. As this air rises over the Sierra Nevada, it cools, and rain or snow falls in the high mountains—leaving little for the Great Basin. This rain shadow effect continues across the Great Basin, favoring the high elevations with moisture while leaving the valleys dry. For example, the ski town of Brighton, Utah, in the Wasatch Range, receives about 144 inches of precipitation each year, but Wendover, to the west on the salt flats near the Utah-Nevada border, receives only 7 inches. The region's split personality led the geomorphologist Donald Currey to label the Great Basin "hemi-arid," meaning half wet and half dry.

Most of the mountain precipitation falls as snow during the winter. As the snowpack gradually melts, it creates lakes and wetlands in the valley bottoms. Because of the basin's domelike structure and the mountain ranges on its margins, these wetlands concentrate along the western and eastern sides of the basin. Marshes in the Bonneville Basin, adjacent to the Wasatch Range, and those in the Lahontan Basin on the west, adjacent to the Sierra Nevada, are larger than those bordering the interior ranges. This geography creates a paradox: some of the otherwise driest parts of the Great Basin contain most of its lakes and wetlands.

During the last Ice Age, up until about 14,000 years ago, 80 percent of the Great Basin's 187 separate drainage basins contained lakes (see fig. 2.7). Captain Simpson might not have thought the land so thirsty-looking back then; instead, he would have found it difficult to travel without a boat. The largest of these lakes were Lake Lahontan, which covered 9,000 square miles in eastern Nevada, and Lake Bonneville, an enormous lake covering 20,000 square miles. But as the Ice Age ended in global warming, these vast lakes shrank, leaving behind much smaller, shallower lakes and marshes. Walker, Carson, Pyramid, and Honey Lakes are remnants of Lahontan, and Utah, Sevier, and the Great Salt Lake are remnants of Bonneville. Other remnant wetlands, such as Ruby Marsh in northeastern Nevada (fig. 11.1), exist at the bases of particularly high interior ranges. Marshes and lakes are also found in the northwestern Great Basin, including the Harney-Malheur Basin, Lake Abert, Warner Valley, and Goose Lake (map 1).

Over the last 10,000 years, millennial-scale climate changes have caused even the larger lakes and marshes to expand and contract. Unfortunately for researchers today, such changes erased or mixed much of the archaeological evidence as rising water eroded sites left by earlier inhabitants. As a result, except in a few unique cases, much of what we know about how humans adapted to living in and near marshes in the Great Basin is based on descriptions of the way historic-period people lived and on archaeological sites dating to the last 2,000 to 3,000 years.

Life in Great Basin Wetlands

At the time of Euro-American contact, Great Basin people used one of two major survival strategies. Both revolved around the need to store food for the winter. Great Basin summers can be unbearably hot, but winters can be long and cold, with heavy snow shutting people out of higher elevations. In the winter, plant foods were not abundantly available, and snow could make hunting difficult. People not only had to find food to eat daily during the warmer months but also had to collect and store food to last through the winter.

One of their strategies for doing so was to live as nomads. In the drier parts of the Great Basin, people moved around to find foods that were available in different seasons at widely scattered places. For example, a family might winter in the piñon-juniper forests of the uplands, relying on stored pine nuts and dried pronghorn meat. Come spring they moved to the lowlands, where they foraged in the valley bottom and foothills through the summer, collecting seeds, bulbs, and tubers, hunting pronghorn, and trapping small game. Late summer and early fall found them back in the uplands, collecting pine nuts and hunting mountain sheep. No single place harbored an abundance of food, and so people moved, eating much of what they foraged and storing and caching the rest.

The other strategy was to live "tethered"—as the archaeological jargon has it—to large, stable marshes. People living in these wetlands were not sedentary in the strict sense. Rather, they moved around within the marsh, collecting an array of seeds, tubers, and small animals throughout the year. Much of the food collection fell to the women, while men fished and traveled longer distances to hunt in the mountains.

This tethered settlement system helped people meet their need for winter food. Wetlands offered a diversity of foods more or less in one place. It is true that many wetland foods return relatively few calories per hour of work, but they have the advantage of being sequentially available throughout the year. Cattail tubers, for example, yield relatively small returns in the summer, but they can be dug up year-round. In fact they provide a better return in winter, after they have stored energy for the following spring. The particular suite of foods people collected might change from year to year as lake and marsh levels rose and fell with the vagaries of desert climate. A year of high runoff might see an abundance of fish, and a drier year might see a bumper crop of bulrushes or pickleweed. Sometimes marshes dried up or flooded so severely that

Figure 11.2. Paiute house at Stillwater Marsh, Carson Sink, about 1900.

then tied the mats to the willow frame, beginning at the bottom with successively overlapping layers, to form a weatherproof roof and walls. One mat was reserved as a door, and another to cover the smoke hole in inclement weather.

The Toedökadö usually erected these houses half a mile or so from the wetlands to avoid the hordes of mosquitoes. Smoky fires also helped keep the insects at bay. People carried water in basketry jugs made watertight by their fine, tight weave and a covering of pitch. They drew their water from the center of the marsh, where it was fresher, although in dry years even that water could be alkaline and bitter. Mark Twain once wrote that the Carson Sink's water tasted "like lye, and not weak lye, either." Even after adding whiskey and molasses, he declared it "too technical" to drink.

But these problems were minor relative to the abundance of food the wetlands offered to the Toedökadö. In the spring they gathered the corms, or underground stems, of sago pondweed and water plantain, bulrush shoots, the eggs of birds and waterfowl, and freshwater mussels. Some families traveled a short distance into the foothills and collected greens, bulbs, and tubers from carved seed, wild onion, and sego lily. Others traveled west to the Truckee River to take advantage of spawning runs of cutthroat trout. Later in the summer people collected cattail pollen, the seeds of bulrushes, sago pondweed, pickleweed, and saltgrass while some families returned to the hills to collect seeds and tubers. As fall approached, people continued to collect seeds such as those of bulrush and spikerush, but they added to the menu the tubers and roots of cattail, bulrush, and nutgrass. Others traveled into the hills again to collect berries, bulbs, and especially piñon nuts. Men traveled throughout the year, sometimes considerable distances, to trap wood rats and to hunt bighorn sheep and pronghorn.

In the rare years when the piñon trees produced bumper crops of nuts, the Toedökadö

food plants and game were destroyed. But usually a knowledgeable person could find something to eat in the wetlands at any season, including winter.

What was life like in these marshes? Two of the best descriptions we have are those for the Utes of Utah Lake and the historic-era Northern Paiutes of the lowland known as the Carson Sink (map 1). These cases describe two ends of the range of wetland habitats, for the Carson Sink contained a shallow, alkaline marsh, whereas Utah Lake is a deep, freshwater lake.

The Toedökadö of the Carson Sink

The Northern Paiutes who lived in the Carson Sink were known as the Toedökadö, "cattail eaters." They lived in small clusters of related families scattered throughout the Carson Sink's Stillwater Marsh. During the warm months their homes were little more than windbreaks or shade structures made of cattail or bulrush mats and branches. As colder weather approached they built more substantial houses (fig. 11.2). After making a domed framework of willow, perhaps 10 to 15 feet in diameter, women gathered dried cattail or tule leaves and stalks and made 15 or more mats. Each of the mats was about 5 feet square and ended up sandwiched between several willow cross-poles. The women wintered in the mountains. But they passed most winters in the marshes, gathering some persistent seeds such as pickleweed, harvesting cattail and bulrush tubers, and fishing.

✗ The lakes and marshes of the Carson Sink were home to several species of small fish—tui-chub, Tahoe sucker, redside shiner, and speckled dace. People took fish year-round, by several means. Women gathered minnows by quietly sieving the water with their burden baskets or winnowing trays. People also used dip nets and fine-mesh gill nets. The latter they strung through the water and had waders drive fish into them.

Throughout the year, but especially during the spring and fall migrations, people hunted birds and waterfowl, including the pintail, teal, redhead, canvasback, northern shoveler, mallard, and American coot. They attracted these birds using duck decoys, beautifully formed from tule and covered with feathers or even the entire skin of a duck. Captain Simpson found them to be "perfect in form and fabric." We know that this practice extends far back in time, because researchers found a 2,000-year-old cache of a dozen such decoys at Lovelock Cave, just north of the Carson Sink (plate 4).

Hunters took ducks in several clever ways. Ducks attracted to the decoys were shot with arrows tipped either with blunted heads, to stun the ducks, or with sharp obsidian points. Shooting at the water just in front of the duck caused the arrow to skip and strike the duck in the breast. Hunters also netted ducks with nets strung at a 45-degree angle across an open channel. Once a flock was in position, waders would startle them, and the birds would ensnare themselves on takeoff. People used this technique mostly at night, so that the ducks could not avoid the nets. During the molting season, late summer and early fall, coots could not fly, and waders could herd them ashore with a long net stretched across open water. Those coots not netted could be captured as they hid in the rushes.

People stored many of these foods for the winter. They gutted, split open, and dried waterfowl and fish. They kept seeds in tightly woven baskets or skin bags and stored them in pits. Although some food species could be taken throughout the year, especially fish and waterfowl, the stored foods

were critical for winter survival. Direct evidence for storage comes from a 1,700-year-old human coprolite from Hidden Cave, near the Carson Sink (plate 22). These ancient feces contained cattail pollen and seeds, which had to have been gathered in the summer, as well as fragments of piñon nuts, which must have been gathered in the fall. Most likely the pine nuts were stored from the previous fall harvest and eaten ten months later, mixed with cattail pollen.

The Utes of Utah Lake

At the time of Euro-American contact, the Timpanogots (the name refers to "those who live at the mouth of a rocky canyon," perhaps meaning Provo Canyon) lived along the shores of Utah Lake, at the eastern edge of the Great Basin. If you could travel back in time to visit these people around 1800, what might you see? You might first notice domed or conical structures covered with reed mats or other brush, similar to those of the Carson Sink but perhaps larger. Next to them are simple windbreaks used as summer homes and winter cook houses. Drying racks stand nearby, bearing fish or waterfowl, skinned, gutted, and split, drying in the sun. Seeds fill burden baskets set beside the house, waiting to be ground into flour with a nearby stone metate and mano. Tubers collected from cattails, bulrushes, and other marsh plants lie drying in the sun.

✗ If you visit in the fall, you might see someone placing packages of dried fish, roots, or chokecherries or bags of bulrush seeds in a pit, to be stored for the winter. Parfleches—folded bags or pouches made of untanned leather—containing dried, pulverized meat mixed with fat and berries might sit on top of a platform, stored for winter where the ever-hungry dogs cannot reach them. If you arrive in late morning you might see someone remove his or her jackrabbit fur robe as the morning's chill wears off. Others might wear fringed deerskin shirts and leggings or skirts fashioned from shredded sagebrush bark or tules, with sagebrush sandals on their feet.

A pottery vessel might be on the fire, a fish broth simmering inside, along with a roasting muskrat. You might see men returning from the hills with dried meat from a bighorn sheep hunt

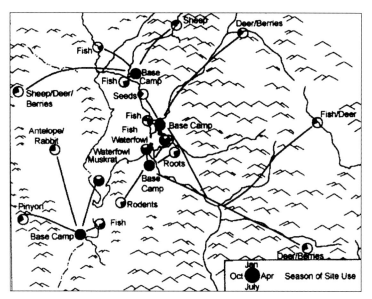

Figure 11.3. The annual round of Timpanogots people, Utah Lake, Utah, around 1800.

and others returning from a morning spent on the lake, carrying strings of fish and the limp bodies of waterfowl hanging from sagebrush bark belts.

Later in the day you might see women and children returning with basket loads of grasshoppers. As grasshoppers fly out over the lake, they tire, fall, and drown. Their bodies eventually wash up on shore, forming long windrows—sometimes tens of thousands of grasshoppers that anyone can simply scoop up. In other times or places, people got together to drive grasshoppers or crickets through the grass, forcing them into a brush-filled pit that was then torched. Early Euro-American explorers who ate these roasted grasshoppers thought them quite tasty. And of course there are fish. Great Basin deepwater lakes were home to varieties of cutthroat trout, among other species. They provided an ample food supply, especially during the spring spawning run, when the trout ran from Utah Lake up their feeder rivers.

The Timpanogots used hooks and gorgets strung on lines, fishing arrows, and spears tipped with greasewood points to catch these fish. In spawning season they built weirs and dams across the mouths of streams, channeling the fish through narrow defiles so they could be scooped out with dip nets. In other places people strung gill nets across streams or through shallows, holding them

in place with net-sinker stones tied along the bottom. Men also fished with arrows and spears from tule rafts, and in winter they took fish with hooks and lines or spears through holes cut in the ice.

Whereas the Toedökadö lived in small family settlements, the Timpanogots lived in larger communities of some 20 to 30 families. One reason might have been the fish. The fish of deepwater lakes, because they are larger and more abundant than fish in marshes, enabled people living near Utah Lake to gather in larger and perhaps more permanent villages than was possible in the Carson Sink.

This greater reliance on fish does not mean that the Timpanogots ignored the uplands. Men and women traveled into the hills to hunt pronghorn and deer and to gather serviceberries, chokecherries, currants, and tubers. But they always returned to the lake, its fish, and its supply of winter and stored foods (fig. 11.3).

Earlier Great Basin Marsh Dwellers

Considering the picture we have of marsh use from historic data, we might expect that wetlands were always good places to live and that ancient people used them in much the same fashion over the centuries. But earlier groups decided how to incorporate a wetland into their annual round by balancing the foods the wetland offered against those they could acquire in the surrounding uplands. Like all of us, they weighed the costs and benefits of the choices that lay before them. In this case they had to balance living in a wetland or the surrounding uplands against the need to move foods acquired in one of those areas to the other. How did they make this decision?

In general, people located their homes close to foods that women collected. Why? Among people who forage, children breast-feed for the first four to six years of their lives. This custom means that throughout most of their adult lives, women must attend to their daily chores while accompanied by a breast-feeding child. Having a small child in tow means that a woman cannot travel far from camp to seek foodstuffs, so camp must be located near the foods that women collect. As a result, men must make longer forays to hunt large game, which is profitable to acquire even when trips require several days.

Ancient human skeletal remains from the Carson Sink, when analyzed, showed evidence of this division of labor. Men's skeletons showed more pathologies associated with long-distance walking, such as osteoarthritis in the hip and ankle, than did women's. Women's skeletons showed high rates of osteoarthritis in the lower back, evidence of a lifetime of carrying children and grinding seeds.

We know that wetlands and lakes were important to people from the very moment they set foot in the Great Basin some 13,000 years ago. Some of the earliest evidence of human presence in the Great Basin comes from the fossil shores of Ice Age lakes and from ancient stream courses, such as the Old River Bed southwest of the Great Salt Lake, that used to feed the lakes. Direct evidence that ancient people fished in the lakes comes from the bones of tui-chub, Tahoe sucker, and other fish in 9,400-year-old human coprolites unearthed at Spirit Cave, a site overlooking the Carson Sink. But these lakes shrank rapidly after 10,000 years ago. And from about 7,000 to 4,200 years ago, the Great Basin saw generally more arid conditions. Many wetlands, such as Ruby Marsh, disappeared, and some of the deepwater lakes became saline and undrinkable. During this time only the largest marshes, such as those in the western Bonneville Basin, might have supported human populations year-round. Lake Bonneville itself may have vanished for a time about 7,300 years ago.

With the return of wetter times about 4,200 years ago, people came back to the lakes and wetlands. How they used them depended in part on what foods they offered and what was available in the surrounding uplands. For example, piñons, which today are ubiquitous throughout much of the Great Basin, were absent from many places until quite late. They arrived in the Stillwater Mountains bordering the Carson Sink only about 1,500 years ago and in the Reno area about 500 years ago. Also, people's needs varied. Those who lived in the northern Great Basin experienced harsher winters and had greater need to store food or

to live near a steady winter supply than those living to the south.

Because the Great Basin is a desert, drought was an ever-present danger. Drought affects shallow wetlands like those in the Carson Sink more heavily than deepwater lakes like Utah Lake. Sometimes large climatic changes caused droughts, but in other instances the cause was local. For example, Walker Lake in western Nevada was dry from 1,500 to 1,000 years ago and from 500 to 300 years ago because at those times the Walker River cut through the Adrian Valley and ran northward, diverting its flow to the Carson Sink. These were bad times for Walker Lake but good times for the Carson Sink.

What is the evidence for heavy use of the wetlands in ancient times? While nomadic people may call a windbreak, a wickiup, or a simple hearth under the open sky home, sedentary people invest in houses, which leave distinct archaeological traces. Archaeologists mostly find evidence for houses around Great Basin lakes and wetlands. Large, semisubterranean houses appeared about 5,600 years ago in Surprise Valley in the northwestern Great Basin. Some 25 feet across and two and a half feet deep, the houses had log roofs held aloft by several substantial posts and covered with mats and sod. They were soon replaced, for several millennia, by simpler houses, suggestive of a somewhat more seasonally nomadic but still tethered

Figure 11.4. Excavation of a house floor in the Carson Sink, Churchill County, Nevada.

population. Shallow pit houses appeared near Harney and Malheur Lakes in the northwestern Great Basin about 4,700 years ago and at Lake Abert about 4,000 years ago. But such houses appeared only 1,500 years ago in the Carson Sink (fig. 11.4) and about 2,000 years ago around the lakes and wetlands of the eastern Great Basin. It is possible that in these cases we simply have not found the earlier homes or that erosion caused by the rise and fall of wide, shallow lakes destroyed the evidence long ago.

Something else is different about the Carson and Humboldt Sinks. Great Basin people used caves and rockshelters as temporary residences, overnight hunting camps, and simply places to wait out the heat of the day while collecting seeds and tubers. But in the Carson and Humboldt Sinks, caves such as Lovelock, Hidden, and Humboldt Caves were used primarily as places to cache gear, often in pits lined with grass or basketry. In one, someone stored a basket maker's tool kit, and in another, dried fish and a field-mouse-fur blanket that required months to make. Many of the pits contained the mundane tools used to exploit wet-lands—duck decoys and their repair kits, nets, and fishing lines with hooks.

Why were these tools, so useful for getting food from the wetlands, stored in caves? Most like-ly people made the caches during times of drought, when the wetlands dried up, and they found that the benefits of moving to the uplands or to other valleys exceeded the benefits of remaining in the Carson or Humboldt Sink.

Although people used the caves into historic times—one cache contained a steel arrowhead, canvas ore sacks, and trousers—most of the caches were made between 3,800 and 1,500 years ago. In other words, caching stopped just when houses appeared, signaling that people had become more tethered to the wetlands after 1,500 years ago. One reason may be that the climate became drier and more volatile after that time. The Great Basin suf-fered several severe droughts—from 1,010 to 940, from 864 to 830, and from 725 to 700 years ago. These droughts lessened the productivity of wet-lands, but imagine their effect on the desert. At the same time, the Walker River ran into the Carson

Sink, making the latter all the more attractive (though in drought years the river also ran dry). There was no need to cache gear in caves. People were not leaving the security of the wetlands.

The severity of the droughts between 1,000 and 700 years ago eventually took its toll. We do not know exactly when the Paiutes and Shoshones spread throughout the Great Basin, but it was probably sometime in the last 2,000 years. They displaced whoever lived in the region before them, and it is possible that the periodic droughts encouraged those others to leave. With a niche left open, and with the improved climate of the Little Ice Age, a global cold phase that saw renewed growth of mountain glaciers, the Paiutes and Shoshones might have moved in with a some-what different lifeway, the "tethered" strategy exemplified by people such as the Toedökadö and Timpanogots.

It is no surprise that in a land as "thirsty-looking" as the Great Basin, wetlands and lakes figured prominently in the lives of ancient people. But it is also clear that the way Great Basin people used wetlands was a product not only of what foods the wetlands offered but also of what was available elsewhere, as well as changes in the wet-lands produced by local and regional climatic and environmental conditions. Still, the wetlands may well turn out to have been the engine of Great Basin prehistory, as changes in their character drove shifts in regional and local population den-sities. It may even be that wetlands played a key role in the final "changing of the guard" in Great Basin prehistory—the displacement of earlier pop-ulations by the Numic-speaking peoples.

David B. Madsen, formerly the Utah state archaeologist and director of the Paleontological and Paleoenviron-mental Program of the Utah Geological Survey, is affili-ated with the Texas Archaeological Research Laboratory and the Mercyhurst Archaeological Institute, Mercyhurst College, Erie, Pennsylvania. Robert L. Kelly, author of *The Foraging Spectrum: Diversity in Hunter-Gatherer Lifeways*, is professor and head of the Department of Anthropology at the University of Wyoming.

Figure 12.1. Alpine plateaus in the White Mountains, California. White Mountain Peak (14,246 feet) dominates the background. The highest known Great Basin alpine village sits near the small dome just to the right of center.

High Altitude Sites in the Great Basin

Robert L. Bettinger

Visitors to the Great Basin stick mostly to the bottom of the basin, driving across vast sagebrush expanses, over low, piñon-and-juniper-covered mountain passes, from one valley to the next, stopping at the occasional scenic viewpoint or historical landmark along the way, without venturing higher. Death Valley, the lowest point in the continental United States at 282 feet below sea level, and Mount Whitney, the highest, at 14,491 feet above sea level, are equally spectacular, world-famous tourist attractions in the Great Basin—only 75 miles apart. But Death Valley is visited about 40 times more often than Mount Whitney. The reason is obvious: the higher places are harder for tourists to get to, especially the alpine mountain meadows and peaks above the tree line, which is usually between 11,000 and 11,500 feet.

Ancient people, perhaps less interested than modern tourists in scenic views, found the alpine zone just as difficult to get to and the effort harder to justify, because resources there were so scarce.

Yet we find clear archaeological evidence that early people used the alpine zone. They left a record of land use that stretches back thousands of years. This record mostly takes the form of hunting blinds, kill sites, and the short-term hunting camps that go with them, but there are also rare instances of longer residence in the form of full-blown villages —the highest villages in aboriginal North America. Why would people choose to live at such high altitudes amid scarce resources?

The Great Basin Alpine Zone

Excluding the Wasatch Range and the Sierra Nevada on the margins of the Great Basin, the region holds well over 200 separate mountain ranges. Twenty-eight of them reach elevations in excess of 10,000 feet, and peaks in the five highest—the White and Spring Mountains and the Snake, Deep Creek, and Toquima Ranges—reach from 12,000 to more than 14,000 feet.

The severely exposed crest lines of all the 10,000-foot ranges are generally treeless, but two Great Basin conifers, the bristlecone pine (*Pinus longaeva*) and the limber pine (*P. flexilis*), can grow at elevations as high as 11,500 feet in sheltered areas. Only in Great Basin mountain ranges reaching well over 11,500 feet was the treeless alpine zone, or alpine tundra as it is sometimes called, large enough to provide significant food and other resources to early people, although they made some use of smaller alpine tracts in the lower ranges.

The Great Basin alpine tundra is really a desert. It receives little snow and even less rain. Permanent sources of drinking water—creeks, springs, and seeps—are few and far between. The famously dry cities of Denver, Salt Lake City, and Santa Fe each receive more yearly precipitation, 12.9 inches on average, than falls at 10,000 feet in the White Mountains of California.

Scarce water is not the alpine zone's only challenge. As anyone who has traveled above 10,000 feet knows, breathing is difficult. Along with a host of subtler physiological side effects including temporarily impaired vision, the oxygen-depleted air makes routine chores difficult and even moderately strenuous activity, such as running and hauling loads of firewood, exhausting. Breathing deeper and faster helps but also promotes dehydration, making scarce drinking water that much more valuable.

And the alpine zone is cold. Nighttime temperatures hover near freezing year-round, and even in summer incessantly gusting winds can put the daytime chill factor well below that. Clad not in microfleece and down parkas but in rabbit-skin blankets, ancient people could not escape the wind and cold while hunting and gathering. They did gain some measure of nighttime relief by setting their camps in wind-protected spots near stunted growths of dwarf sagebrush (*Artemisia arbuscula*) and wax currant (*Ribes cereum*) or near living or relict stands of trees that provided firewood.

The austerity of the alpine tundra mirrors the harshness of the alpine climate. The tundra is treeless, of course. Little moisture, low temperatures, and short growing seasons stymie the growth of even the hardiest bristlecone and limber pine, which are confined to the slopes farther below. Warm spells in the past sometimes permitted these pines to grow higher than they do today, but only briefly. When conditions inevitably grew colder again, they died, leaving "fossil tree lines," littered with dead stumps, trunks, and limbs that were important sources of firewood for early people. The plants—mainly herbs—that are tough enough to live in the alpine zone produce little fruit and few seeds. Most seek protection from the wind and cold by growing close to the ground and developing more plant mass beneath the surface than above it. This made edible roots like the dwarf bitterroot (*Lewisia pygmaea*) much more impor-

tant to early people than alpine seeds or berries.

Thin air, tough climate, few edible plants: Why would any self-respecting ancient forager venture into this high-altitude desert? The main attraction was a comparatively rich array of mammals, chief among them the mountain sheep (*Ovis canadensis*). Weighing up to 200 pounds, it was the largest animal that most Great Basin people regularly saw. Mountain sheep use the alpine zone seasonally, arriving as the growing season begins in late spring and leaving as it ends with the first heavy snows of late fall. In between they inhabit this zone and the rugged canyons and slopes just below it almost exclusively. Hunting them always entailed long trips and overnight stays in or near the alpine zone.

The only other large-bodied alpine game of any significance was the pronghorn (*Antilocapra americana*), which made occasional summer visits to mountain ranges with relatively large, flat alpine plateaus. Deer (*Odocoileus hemionus*) were virtually absent until recently. Today they are more common in the alpine zone than mountain sheep, whose numbers have dwindled because of competition with domestic cattle and sheep and their intolerance of almost any form of human activity. Deer, on the other hand, have increased, because livestock grazing has shifted the composition of alpine vegetation from herbs favored by cattle, domestic sheep, and mountain sheep to shrubs (mainly sagebrush) favored by deer. The deer have brought with them their traditional predators, mountain lions (*Felis concolor*), which have further reduced mountain sheep populations.

The alpine zone is also home to a variety of smaller mammals, none large or abundant enough to warrant a special trip but many worth hunting or trapping if a hunter happened to be there on other business. The yellow-bellied marmot (*Marmota flaviventris*), weighing 5 to 10 pounds, was among the largest and most abundant of these and the one early hunters pursued most often. Emerging from hibernation in early May, marmots become increasingly attractive targets as the summer progresses, adding more than a pound of body weight each month until they return underground in late August. Hunters could shoot or club the relatively slow animals, but trapping them was more productive because it freed time for other tasks. Traps were equally effective for white-tailed hare (*Lepus townsendii*), cottontail (*Sylvilagus* species), golden-mantled ground squirrels (*Spermophilis lateralis*), and chipmunks (*Eutamias* species). Hunters also shot or clubbed these animals if the opportunity presented itself.

The alpine zone offered resources other than food that ancient people valued. Open terrain and relatively abundant small mammals made the zone particularly attractive to the golden eagle (*Aquila chrysaetos*), a bird that people prized highly for its plumage and talons, which they used in ritual garb, as talismans, and in shamanic performances. Hunters caught adult eagles or took flightless young birds from nests, then raised and later reverently killed them. Although historically known people of the Great Basin never pursued eagle hunting on a large scale, it was evidently worth a good deal of risk-taking—Native eagle hunters are known to have fallen to their deaths in the White Mountains—probably enough to warrant an occasional visit to the alpine zone mainly for that purpose.

Like eagle feathers, parts of the mountain sheep, notably its horns and fat, were believed by many Great Basin Natives in historic times, and likely in ancient times as well, to be magical or medicinal. Although mountain sheep provided a great deal of meat, people also made the decision to hunt them to obtain these scarce and valuable materials. Mountain sheep meat itself may have been valued more highly than meat of other game, simply because it was so difficult to obtain.

Alpine Hunting Camps

As the list of high alpine resources suggests, hunting was one of the main reasons ancient people climbed the heights. Hunting trips involved short-term stays by small groups of men. The hallmark of early hunting is the hunting blind, typically a ∪-shaped (less commonly circular) low rock wall just large enough to afford a single hunter concealment and some protection from the wind while waiting for game. Hunters often erected blinds at canyon heads, where they waited for sheep to pass by on their way to graze on the alpine plateau above, or next to seeps and shaded snowbanks where sheep might linger to drink or graze. Not surprisingly, historic-period shepherds built their taller, square-cornered windbreaks at many of these same vantage points, overlooking areas with good grazing. We occasionally find aboriginal blinds strung out in a line, often in combination with long rock walls and cairns of stacked rocks evidently meant to direct mountain sheep, perhaps a small herd, along a route that would expose them to several hunters in succession.

The hunters normally left few artifacts in or near blinds—a few bits of stone chipping waste and maybe a broken stone projectile point or knife. These fragments were perhaps the remains of hasty repairs made after a missed shot or while butchering a kill, but certainly not of craft work filling long hours while men waited for game. Mountain sheep have acute vision and hearing, and the sounds of flint knapping would have frightened them away. In rare instances hunters left behind objects that are harder to interpret, like the seven naturally polished beach pebbles found tucked into a White Mountains blind. These might have been hunting talismans or perhaps "sucking stones" kept in the mouth to fight thirst, a trick used by ancient and modern desert dwellers nearly everywhere.

Alpine hunters almost never camped near where they expected to hunt, because the simple presence of their camps would have driven sheep to more remote pastures. They usually camped in sheltered canyons below the alpine plateau and crest, venturing up daily to hunt and returning nightly to camp. We have no evidence that they built shelters of any consequence. The surfaces of hunting camps excavated in the White Mountains, however, are often burned and littered with charcoal and ash, suggesting that hunters kept warm by building sleeping fires. Perhaps they used an arrangement like that employed by parties of traveling males in aboriginal Australia, who slept side by side with small fires between them and at either end.

The archaeological remains found in camps that archaeologists have excavated are exactly what one would expect: a lot of mountain sheep bones, broken hunting and butchering equipment (points and knives), and small quantities of chipping waste from resharpening and repairing these implements.

Figure 12.2. A house ring in an alpine village at 12,640 feet in the White Mountains. A dark midden inside the stone foundation is clearly apparent. Many of the small stones surrounding the foundation are plant processing tools. An unusually deep snowpack from the previous winter had not melted when the photograph was taken in early July.

Although mountain sheep were the primary targets, we also find the remains of smaller mammals because, like all big game hunting, the pursuit of bighorn sheep is notoriously chancy, even if game is abundant. Native bighorn sheep hunters usually did at least some small game trapping on the side to provide a modest but reliable supply of camp meat without taking time away from sheep hunting, the main order of business.

Evidence of alpine hunting appears in nearly every Great Basin mountain range high enough to have an alpine zone, but it is abundant only in the highest ranges—those with perennial alpine springs and expanses of alpine tundra large enough to support mountain sheep in sizable numbers. Great Basin projectile points made during different periods differ in style, and those found near blinds and camps show that hunters have likely pursued mountain sheep in the alpine zone since humans first entered the Great Basin more than 10,000 years ago—although they began to hunt regularly at high altitudes only about 4,000 years ago. In most of the Great Basin, alpine hunting evidently persisted right up until the influx of Euro-American miners, ranchers, and settlers finally drove Native peoples out of the adjacent valleys or so changed their lives that they had to abandon alpine hunting, along with many other practices.

Alpine Villages

In two of the highest ranges in the Great Basin—the White Mountains on the California-Nevada border and the Toquima Range in central Nevada—the alpine hunting pattern ended about 1,500 years ago, but people replaced it with a very different kind of land use. This one centered as much on gathering as on hunting and encompassed whole families who stayed in the alpine zone long enough to need to build substantial houses. Archaeologists call the sites these people left alpine villages, each a site with one or more well-built houses, a debris-rich midden, or refuse deposit, and a diverse collection

Figure 12.3. Alpine village house rings in a high meadow in the White Mountains. House in foreground is approximately 12 feet long.

Figure 12.4. Alpine village house ring at the Alta Toquima site on Mount Jefferson in the Toquima Range, central Nevada. Stacy Goodman takes notes, July 1981.

of artifacts including both chipped stone tools such as projectile points, knives, and drills and ground stone implements such as milling stones and hand stones (fig. 12.2). These artifacts indicate that families who engaged heavily in both gathering and hunting lived in the sites seasonally. As expected, alpine villages invariably lie close to a reliable and permanent source of water. In the alpine zone of the White Mountains, the square houses built by

historic shepherds are telltale signs that an aboriginal village is likely nearby, because the shepherds, too, were tethered to water.

We identify the aboriginal houses by their circular rock wall foundations, two or three courses high, which enclose an area from 6 to 10 feet in diameter—large enough to accommodate a family of about five (fig. 12.3). Their builders probably set several poles just inside or directly into this foundation, fastening them together overhead in the center to form a dome- or cone-shaped framework. This they reinforced by attaching shorter horizontal members, and then they thatched the frame with brush or grass. These houses usually had a rock-filled hearth for cooking and warmth in the center of the enclosed floor. Once heated, the stones would have kept the house more safely warm at night than would a fire, which might have set the house aflame while its occupants slept. Most house foundations have no obvious doorways. Openings that might represent them point in no consistent direction but seem oriented to take advantage of local conditions of wind, slope, and sunlight.

The largest alpine village, Alta Toquima, situated at 11,000 feet on Mount Jefferson in the Toquima Range (fig. 12.4)—and the only such village outside the White Mountains—has more than 20 stone houses, many more than any of the several villages in the White Mountains. This concentration of land use was likely a response to the relatively small size of the alpine zone on Mount Jefferson. In the White Mountains people had much more room and many more water sources, so they spread out in smaller groups.

The array of artifacts we find in alpine villages in both the Toquima Range and the White Mountains shows that plants were a major part of the diet. The milling stones and hand stones used to grind plants are as well represented among the tools there as they are in sites on the adjacent valley floors, where we know that plant foods were critically important. Because seed-bearing plants fare poorly at high elevations, berries and seeds were much less important than root plants. Greater dependence on roots in the alpine villages probably explains the abundance of crudely battered stone cobbles, which people likely used both to pulp roots and to sharpen the digging sticks used to obtain them. The importance of plant procurement makes it clear that many alpine villagers were women, and with them came their children and husbands. The basic social units were families—mothers, fathers, and children.

Bones from excavated sites indicate that animals were as important as plants and likely a major attraction. As in the hunting camps, we find the bones of both mountain sheep and small mammals, especially marmots. But although the range of species is about the same in both hunting camps and villages, in the latter we uncover proportionally more bones of small mammals. Whereas alpine hunters preferred mountain sheep and took smaller mammals only when needed, the alpine villagers squeezed the environment for all the animals it could provide, large and small.

The plant remains uncovered in village middens show that the heavy use of alpine plants was an extension of the same principle: use virtually every possible food source. These trash dumps are rich not only in charcoal but also in the discarded remains of meals and in debris reflecting many other activities. For example, alpine hunters spent most of their craft time repairing gear they brought with them, and villagers brought along the raw materials necessary to work skins, shape points, and craft baskets. They left all the by-products of these tasks in their middens.

Archaeologists can date the villages, like the hunting camps, by the styles of projectile points they contain, nearly all of which are arrow points made sometime in the last 1,300 years. Radiocarbon dates for midden charcoal, too, almost always fall in the last 1,300 years. Other methods used to date the villages, including obsidian hydration, which measures the thickness of a "rind" of hydrated water that accumulates on the surface of an obsidian artifact at a constant rate over time, and lichenometry, a method of determining the rate of accumulation of lichens on rocks, confirm that the sites were inhabited only in the last 1,300 years. This uniformity naturally raises a question. If people had been living in the Great Basin for at least 10,000 years and regularly hunting in the alpine zone for the last 4,000 years, then why were alpine villages first established so late—why didn't they appear earlier? For that matter, if people had been living in the Great Basin for at least 10,000 years, why did they begin hunting regularly in the alpine zone only in the last 4,000 years?

One answer is that climate change made the alpine zone more inviting. It is conceivable that just as warmer conditions in the past allowed bristlecone and limber pines to grow much higher on the mountainsides than they do today, so those conditions had the same effect on people, encouraging them to use the alpine zone more frequently. An alternative climatic explanation is that widespread regional drought forced Native people from their normal haunts on the valley floors and adjacent uplands to the higher, better-watered mountains.

There are problems with both explanations. In the case of alpine warming, the timing is wrong. Great Basin climate was warmest in the middle Holocene, about 7,500 to 4,000 years ago—before humans first began hunting regularly in the alpine zone. The second explanation, that of alpine zone as drought refuge, is likely wrong, too, because water is scarce in the alpine zone even under normal conditions. With few permanent springs, it would likely have been just as severely affected by drought as lowland environments, and perhaps more so.

What is missing from these and other climatic explanations is the human element—specifically, population size. Among hunter-gatherers, climate determines resource supply, but population determines resource demand. Even if the climate stays constant, human populations tend to grow and seek new sources of food. It is this propensity for population growth that likely explains the archaeological record of alpine land use in the Great Basin.

When one thinks about it this way, it is easy to understand why regular alpine hunting began when it did. It takes more effort to hunt in the alpine zone, so the net benefit would have been smaller than the benefit gained from the same kind of hunting on the valley floor, *until* hunters had so greatly reduced the game, or until there were so many competing hunters, that valley floor kills became infrequent. Alpine hunting made good sense as soon as its returns (with their greater costs) matched those of valley floor hunting (with its lower frequency of kills). Evidently people living in the Great Basin reached this point about 4,000 years ago.

The same logic explains the appearance of alpine villages. These made sense as soon as returns from hunting and gathering from valley floor villages fell enough from resource depletion or competition to make hunting *and* gathering from alpine villages a reasonable alternative. Alpine village chronologies suggest that Great Basin people reached this point about 1,300 years ago.

Climate change might still be part of the equation, because it might have triggered the growth in population that accounts for the surge in alpine hunting around 4,000 years ago. We know that climate began to improve about 5,000 years ago (chapter 2) and that population, likely very low before that, began to increase. It is probably no coincidence that hunters first began to visit the alpine zone regularly about the same time. Most likely populations quickly grew too large to support themselves solely with valley floor resources, so people turned to alpine hunting to make up the difference.

The initial use of alpine villages coincided with a second observed rise in population, for which we have several possible explanations. One is continued intrinsic population growth. Like interest on an unpaid credit card, population increases not 1-2-3 but 1-2-4: that is, more rapidly over time. The population increase associated with the initial occupation of Great Basin alpine villages might simply represent this kind of acceleration.

Another possibility is that new technology triggered an adaptive change. The earliest alpine villages coincided roughly with the appearance of the bow and arrow in the Great Basin. The bow is a much more effective hunting weapon than the

older spear-thrower, or atlatl. Its use seems to have encouraged larger bands of foragers to split into smaller social units centered on the nuclear family, units that were independent and mobile enough to be extremely efficient hunters and gatherers. When food plants or animals were concentrated in abundance—for example, when piñon nuts ripened in the fall—these fast-moving family units could come together to take advantage of them. When such resources grew scarce, they could strike out independently in search of more ephemeral concentrations of food too small to sustain more than a single family. This intensified form of hunting and gathering might have nurtured the population growth that coincided with the initial occupation of alpine villages.

Some archaeologists think this new adaptation first developed in eastern California, not far from the White Mountains, and proved so successful that groups originally living there were able to spread north and east into the rest of the Great Basin. These eastern California groups are thought to have spoken languages ancestral to the Numic languages spoken in the Great Basin today. The spread of their successful adaptation might account for the fanlike distribution of Numic languages radiating out from eastern California (see fig. 6.9). If that is what happened, then the initial occupation of alpine villages in the White Mountains would represent the early development of this novel adaptation in the Numic homeland. The occupation of Alta Toquima in central Nevada, the only other alpine village in the whole of the Great Basin, would have come later, coinciding with the later spread of Numic-speaking peoples out of eastern California into the central Great Basin.

However we explain them, alpine villages are among the most remarkable sites in the Great Basin. Native people did not merely visit this spectacular but challenging environment, they also made it their summer home, creating the highest aboriginal villages in all of North America.

Robert L. Bettinger works on hunter-gatherers and evolutionary theory, has conducted field research in California, Nevada, and China, and is a professor of anthropology at the University of California, Davis.

Figure 13.1. Pronghorn antelope trap near Montello, Nevada. The juniper branches are remnants of the trap.

Making a Living in the Desert West

Steven R. Simms

Our 15-passenger van rolled to a stop on a small rise overlooking a sage-covered plain. This place looked like all the others we had jostled past for the last hour on the seemingly endless dirt roads of northeastern Nevada. We were part of a university course titled "Archaeology and Paleoenvironments Field Trip," but this was no arrowhead hunting trip. We wanted to see how people lived in the ancient Great Basin. People craned their necks and their eyes searched when I declared, "We're here! Can you see it?" The students tumbled out of the van as I began walking a line of broken juniper branches made gray by three centuries of cold, dry desert air. The branches lay jumbled upon one another, but together they marched through the sagebrush in a long, gently curving line (fig. 13.1).

The branches were the remnants of a toppled fence—a pronghorn trap, a place where Shoshones hunted the misnamed antelope by driving them into large enclosures. We walked a third of a mile along the discontinuous alignments of branches forming the length of the trap and traced the quarter mile of its width. From the air the trap looks like a giant keyhole. It opens below the small knoll where we parked, and the collapsed fence curves around the base of the knoll to create a natural funnel that surely once steered animals to their deaths (fig. 13.2).

This pronghorn trap is about 300 years old. Like most others, it takes advantage of the terrain and the natural behavior of the animals, demonstrating that hunters of the past knew their prey well. Pronghorn typically escape their predators by following the lowest ground, sometimes even

appearing to skulk a bit to be less visible. This trap was built around a subtle swale at the bottom of a long, shallow slope down a valley. Hunters drove the animals here from miles away, probably steering them with piles of brush festooned with strips of bark that fluttered in the breeze and an occasional human "beater" to keep them on the right path.

The hunt likely started the day before the actual kill, with people moving the animals naturally but deliberately. A pronghorn headdress worn by a shaman helped charm the animals into proximity by playing on their natural curiosity. As the pronghorn neared the trap, the hunters closed in, causing their prey to accelerate into their characteristic high-speed run. The animals hugged the swale and unknowingly entered the enclosure, only to be surprised by people hiding around its perimeter. The fence of branches was only waist high, but the

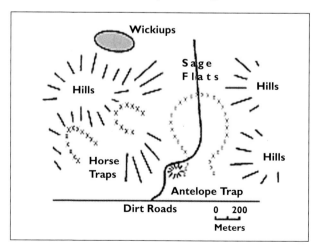

Figure 13.2. Sketch of the antelope trap north of Montello, Nevada.

Figure 13.3. A wickiup, or log and brush shelter, at the Bustos site near Ely, Nevada. This was one of five wickiups at the site, a pine nut–gathering camp used in the fall. Eight circular, rock-lined storage bins were found nearby.

builders knew that instead of leaping the fence, the pronghorn would obligingly turn in order to maintain full tilt. (This response to barriers is one reason pronghorn suffered so much as fences parceled out the American West for cattle.) Once hunters surrounded the animals, they forced them into a small herd on the lowest ground near the middle of the corral. Hunters took several dozen in a hunt like this, picking them off one by one with arrows or forcing them to run until they collapsed from exhaustion and could be clubbed.

The remnants of a small village of log and brush houses, or wickiups (fig. 13.3), stand about a quarter mile from the pronghorn trap. Easily refurbished whenever hunters wanted to use the trap, the village served as home base during the hunt. For days or even weeks afterward, people remained in the village to process the animals for dried meat, hides, and sinews. They boiled the bones for grease or fashioned them into awls and

fishhooks or pendants and beads. When people departed, they left behind some of the things they had needed for the hunt. They always carried stone from the best quarries, to be flaked into tool blanks and perhaps cached at a village for the next hunting trip. People also cached fiber for ropes and string, extra arrows and tips, and perhaps even snares that could be set and left to work while people hunted the pronghorn.

People used the village to prepare for the hunt and repair their equipment afterward. One such place near a pronghorn trap in eastern California yielded the broken base of an arrowhead that fit perfectly with a tip archaeologists found inside the trap. The tip must have lodged inside a slaughtered animal, and when the hunter returned to camp, the broken base was removed from the arrow shaft and discarded.

Several years or even a decade might have passed before hunters used this trap again, but it was only one of many traps placed strategically across the landscape. Archaeologists have records of dozens of pronghorn traps in northeastern Nevada alone. They were common features of the "built environment" of the indigenous peoples of the Great Basin.

A Full and Rich Life

The Great Basin is a land so harsh that many modern people passing through it seem reluctant to get out of their cars. US Highway 50 across central Nevada is billed as "the loneliest road in America" on bumper stickers sold at gas stations and rock shops. In our modern world of comfort and insulation from nature, which extends even to the outdoorsy among us, it is difficult to imagine people living in such a place, let alone living well. But the ancients were no mere survivalists wandering desperately in search of food. Their 13,000-year history, spanning more than 400 human generations, testifies to their success at living in the Great Basin. The reason they thrived there is that they knew the region intimately. It was a human landscape.

The people had a geographically expansive sense of place. They envisioned the land in terms of homelands rather than of single, fixed homesites. The landscape was socially full, enveloped by a network that cycled people among kin and place. The sizes of their groups pulsed according to circumstances, and broad notions of kinship assured connections even in a land with some of the lowest population densities ever recorded.

People were nomadic, but their movements were not aimless. Where they lived and moved was structured by the seasonal scheduling of activities, social expectations, religious rules, and an intimate knowledge of nature, all of which formed a seamless whole. For instance, the sequence of ripening plants had to be followed, but an opportunity to harvest a sagebrush flat rich in cottontail rabbits would not be passed up. Much of what people did in the summer was in anticipation of winter, when stored food supplies were essential. They lived in some places for months and in others for only weeks or days. Such decisions depended as much on kin and other social dynamics as they did on where the food was—but then those things, too, were inextricably connected.

Ancient people did not have the same notions of private property as modern Americans, and they defined territoriality largely by use, not by permanent residence. Most resources and property were public goods that people shared. During their lifetimes people might weave many territories into their lived experiences. Relations of kinship and social obligations hovered over the land like a net. Where fences now divide the land into private parcels, the landscape then was a stage on which interactions of cooperation, but also competition and even conflict, shaped who lived where and who decided what would happen. A built environment specialized to fit many places and uses complemented this pliable social fabric and means of making a living.

The Built Environment

The built environment of our modern world is so much a part of life that we give it scarcely any thought. Imagine life without our homes, roads, churches, baseball fields, and schools. Where would we be without sewers, fiber optic cables, electrical generating plants, and factories? We rely on our infrastructure.

The early peoples of the Great Basin also had built environments. They did not have to carry all their worldly possessions on their backs. Instead, they cached gear and supplies in places they knew they would return to. When it was time to hunt in the marshes, they could swing by a cache containing net bags and snares to capture small animals, as well as fishing lines, hooks, and weights. They might have left in storage bone tubes for snorkels and duck decoys like those woven from cattail stalks 2,000 years ago and left in Lovelock Cave, Nevada (plate 4).

When it was time for the fall pine nut harvest, the log or pole frames of wickiup houses like those at Bustos Wickiup Village (fig. 13.3) awaited refurbishment. The Bustos site sat in a mature piñon forest but also in an area where a winter village might be nearby so that the stored nuts could easily be retrieved. Besides leaving houses there, people cached long hooked poles for pulling down cone-laden branches and big grinding stones and hullers for cracking open the nut meats. Even the circular rock storage facilities where people cached the harvested nuts had only to be refurbished and filled once again.

A cave or rocky ledge near a favored mountain hunting ground might shelter caches of arrow shafts made from the giant cane grass that grows in valley wetlands. A farmer in Willard, Utah, once found a storage pit on his land that contained more than 600 small arrow points ready for use. They had been placed in a bag and buried in a small pit perhaps hundreds of years earlier. Ancient people also kept snare bundles in many places, along with baskets, bags, woven mats, stone axes, and digging sticks—just about anything that allowed them to go to work as soon as they arrived.

Tools for getting food were not the only items people cached. Archaeologists have found shaman's bundles, too, such as those from Humboldt Cave near Lovelock, Nevada. The bundles were little pouches holding pine pitch, ocher (iron oxide pigment), vegetal cakes that might have been medicines or prayer offerings, a stuffed weasel pelt with feathers in its mouth, and a host of other small objects. The so-called Patterson bundle, found in eastern Utah, is a shaman's curing kit with leather pouches containing individual doses of herbs as well as a ball of pine pitch, pouches of stones, red ocher, a strand of deer dew claws, and much more.

As people used the landscape more and more fully, an inventory of metates and manos, the grinding stones used to mill plant foods, accumulated on the ground. Sometimes people stored them in the crotches of juniper and piñon trees or leaned them against tree trunks so that they could be easily spotted. In other instances the coveted grinders were buried so that other people could not take them. Demonstrating the value of these tools, Southern Paiute consultants told the anthropologist Isabel Kelly in 1932 that they would make a new grinding stone only if an old one could not be found.

Not all early Great Basin people shared the same built environment. During the earliest times, when Paleoarchaic people first explored and perhaps colonized the land more than 13,000 years ago, few structures or caches existed, because people moved much longer distances in those days. But even then they cached valuable things such as the spectacular hoards of stone tool blanks uncovered in the Fenn cache near the intersection of Utah, Idaho, and Wyoming. This cache held 18 pounds of superbly flaked blanks made of high-quality stone from quarries in all three states.

During the time archaeologists call the Archaic period, beginning about 9,000 years ago, people spread across the Great Basin and became more tethered to particular landscapes. The redundant use of places, relative to Paleoarchaic practices, stimulated greater use of a built environment. People constructed houses intended to be used again and again and invested in food storage facilities and animal traps. They made caches in caves and crevices as well as on ledges—places they could easily describe, remember, and locate.

By 2,000 years ago, some parts of the Great Basin had literally become land filled with people. Distinctions between territories were strengthened. Where larger villages sprang up in some of the rich wetlands, some places and their resources became more exclusive. In a landscape with more neighbors, people exercised greater control over the built environment and began to hide caches of equipment and food from prying eyes.

What to Eat and How to Get It

The cuisine of the ancient Great Basin was for the most part simple but probably less strange than the grislier stereotypes lead us to believe. On one hand, the Native diet strikes modern Americans as strong and bitter, yet on the other, its lack of fat and sugar makes it seem bland to modern sensibilities. Daily fare came mainly out of the stewpot. For most of antiquity this pot was not ceramic but a tightly woven, coiled basket whose contents were heated with hot stones from the campfire (fig. 13.4). One could boil a basketful of water this way in less than five minutes. Ingredients varied by season, but the stew often began with a base of flour made from seeds such as Indian rice grass, blazing star, saltbush, and native bluegrass, to name just a few. The cook might lace this mush with bits of meat, typically rabbit. Greens and seasonings such as thistle, peppergrass, and tansy mustard added spiciness. In the fall and winter, stews might be based on pine nut meal, one of the delicacies of the year. The basketry stewpot embraced the fruits of a landscape

Figure 13.4. Great Basin people preparing roots and bulbs for cooking. Most ancient meals were stews cooked by placing food and water together with hot rocks—here heated in the fire in the center of the group—in watertight baskets.

Figure 13.5. A party in the northern Great Basin harvests bitterroot in the early summer. Roots were dug with digging sticks made of hardwoods such as mountain mahogany. Chipped stone tools known as crescents may have served to scrape the skin from the roots.

that offered a variety of fresh foods rivaling that found in many modern supermarkets.

People also collected and processed starchy roots such as biscuit root, bitterroot, bulrush, cattail, and camas (fig. 13.5), which might be baked in the sand at the bottom of a campfire or in a

Figure 13.6. Situated at 7,600 feet in the Jarbidge Mountains of northern Nevada, this spectacular mountain sheep corral was used for thousands of years. Blinds were dug into the slopes near the top center of the photograph, and a flattened butchering area can be seen inside the corral at the lower left.

rock-lined earth oven. Left in their skins or peeled with a stone tool with a concave sharp edge, roots could be wrapped in leaves and steamed. Many foods were best eaten raw, and people ate as they picked, nibbling throughout the day. Travelers might string dozens of bulrush and cattail roots the size of human fingers on a line that could be thrown over the shoulder or wrapped around the waist. This ancient gorp provided sustenance and served as tiny canteens, because starchy water made up three-fourths of the roots' weight.

Bread as we know it did not exist, but we have some evidence that people baked roots to a bread-like consistency. Curly dock seeds were sometimes pounded, soaked, and made into dough, then baked on coals. Cattail pollen was formed into

cakes and cooked like tortillas on a stone slab.

Not all cooking was for immediate consumption. Desert fruitcake is a concoction made of whatever dried berries, meat, and seeds were available, mixed with animal fat to form long-lasting loaves. Roasted larvae of the pandora moth or the brine fly could also compose the base of desert fruitcake, preserving the superabundance of a highly nutritious food that was available only a few weeks a year. Desert fruitcake in all its variety provided a portable and concentrated form of energy and protein—an early version of the energy bars of today.

After stewing, roasting was the most common way of preparing meat. Bighorn sheep, mule deer, and of course pronghorn were common sources of roasted meats. Ancient people knew other prey animals as well as they knew the pronghorn for which they designed such clever traps. To attract bighorn sheep during the rut, hunters bashed two hollow logs together to simulate the sound of the rams' horns slamming together in mating contests.

Hunters also constructed traps. One such trap in the Jarbidge Mountains of northern Nevada (fig. 13.6) was made of wood and stone fences built on a steep talus slope. Bighorn fleeing up rocky slopes easily outpaced their pursuers. But humans positioned above the trap could block the sheep's escape and force them to descend, where hunters popping up from blinds dug into the rocky slopes promptly shot them. These fences changed over time as hunters acquired new technology, shifting from the dart and atlatl to the bow and arrow. The adoption of guns did not make the trap obsolete; we find nineteenth-century shell casings from Henry rifles in the blinds. In one section of this mountain death trap, hunters even arranged the jagged stones to create a flat area for butchering their kills.

Despite thrilling images of big game hunts, small and medium-size mammals were the staples of the meat larder. Archaeological research shows that even before modern habitat encroachment, the supply of large animals was not endless. During some periods of antiquity, hunting kept their populations low enough that large game alone could not supply people's needs. The most commonly eaten desert meat in all of antiquity was rabbit, from both cottontails and jackrabbits, stewed or roasted on hot coals after the fur had been singed off. At a marmot roast in the summer of 1995 at Fish Lake, Utah, the Kanosh Band of Paiutes cooked the animals this way. The meat was dark and a bit greasy, but it was rich and filling. Ancient cooks gutted smaller animals such as squirrels, voles, and pikas by squeezing them and then made them into kebabs of a kind by inserting a stick into the body. Pieces of meat from larger animals were barbecued much as they are today. People made jerky to preserve meat.

Unlike most of us today, ancient people had to seek fat. Despite the variety of meats and the relatively high fat content of wild seeds and pine nuts, their diet was so low in fat that people actively sought this essential nutrient. Meat from wild game is almost completely lean except for fat under the skin and in the bones. Fat scraped from the skin bound together the ingredients of desert fruitcake. Fat skimmed from a boiling pot of bones might get a person through the worst days of winter. Left in, it certainly richened the stew.

Few people think fish and deserts go together, but large wetlands exist in many Great Basin valleys, fed by mountain snowpacks and desert springs. They form mazes of contrasting habitats, from open ponds and spacious meadows to narrow channels lined by walls of rushes. The ponds and lakes offer a variety of sucker-type fish that people caught with nets or drove into schools that could be scooped out onto the banks during the spring spawn. Streams flowing from the mountains offered trout. Archaeology shows that people ate all kinds of fish, and in some places, such as Utah Lake and Pyramid Lake, Nevada (chapter 11), fish were a culinary cornerstone (fig. 13.7).

Perhaps the epitome of culinary opportunism and thoroughness appears in Lakeside Cave, on the edge of the Bonneville Salt Flats in Utah. For more than 4,000 years the ancient beaches outside the cave became occasional spectacles of superabundance. Whenever it rained, and during particularly wet centuries, water covered the salt flats. In the summer, when the winds were right, untold millions of drowned grasshoppers washed onto the beaches in ankle-deep windrows that could stretch for 10 miles. People could collect tens of thousands of calories' worth of grasshoppers in a single hour, and each insect was 60 percent protein. This was a harvest no prudent forager would pass up. People carried the naturally dried and salted grasshoppers from the beaches and processed them in the cave. Coprolites, the dried human feces found in the cave, bristle with grasshopper parts. People must have known when conditions were right for these occasional jackpots and traveled to Lakeside Cave for the event.

Roasting and eating grasshoppers at Lakeside Cave in the early 1980s, my graduate student friends and I found the strip of white meat along

Figure 13.7. Fishers use nets anchored by stone weights to capture fish that will be dried and stored for future use. Fish taken during spawning season were a resource that could firmly tether people to a place. The tule boat on the water was used for harvesting a variety of marsh resources.

their backs reminiscent of shellfish. We dubbed them "desert lobster."

The traditional diet was short on sweets, and one of the few sugars reported was aphid honey, deposited by the insects on plants such as cattails. People scraped it off with a flattened stick and ate it. Although this diet may seem strange to contemporary Americans, people accustomed to it found the food rich and satisfying.

Maude Moon, a Goshiute Shoshone born in the late nineteenth century somewhere south of Wendover, Nevada, reported the change in her people's eating habits in the story "The Pickleweed Winter." Long ago, she said, "Indians had everything they needed. They ate these things which grew on this earth…all kinds of seeds. This pickleweed, and also ones such as sunflower seeds, bunch grass seeds, rye grass, and just any kind, like *keppisappeh*, like wild onions, like Indian bal-

sam, like carrots, like wild potatoes, like thistle.… During the winter, one ate all he wanted. It was over there at Big Springs, they called it the pickleweed winter. They ate it with pine nuts, they say. They ate it with jackrabbits. Times were good, they say.… But now you modern people, girls and other modern Indians: they don't know anything. If they were gathered, they wouldn't eat them. They taste bad, they say. The sweetness has killed their mouths. They eat and drink canned sweet things. Only these taste good [to them today]. Indian food doesn't taste good anymore. It tastes too strong. It just tastes bad. It can't be swallowed. This is how it is."

A Human Wilderness

The ancients lived in the desert West with the nimbleness of long familiarity. They needed no street signs or maps because everything and every place had names and stories. Their languages held no word for "wilderness." The people marked no separation between humanity and nature, nor did they pose humanity against nature. The notion of "making a living" involved no distinction between work and play. There was harmony and balance, but these things were not static. The ancient people shaped their wilderness. They used it and sometimes even used it up. The balance they achieved was not a final state but an unsteady relationship between human needs, beliefs, and the tyranny of circumstance.

The deserts and mountains of the Great Basin remain the last large wilderness in the lower forty-eight of the United States. Many of us can find a wilderness sense of place in the Great Basin, but in the ancient past it was a human landscape, a human wilderness.

Steven R. Simms is a professor of anthropology at Utah State University.

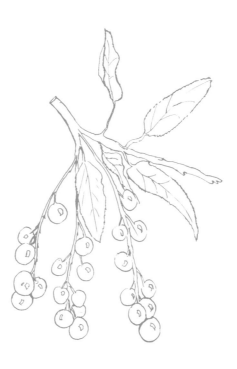

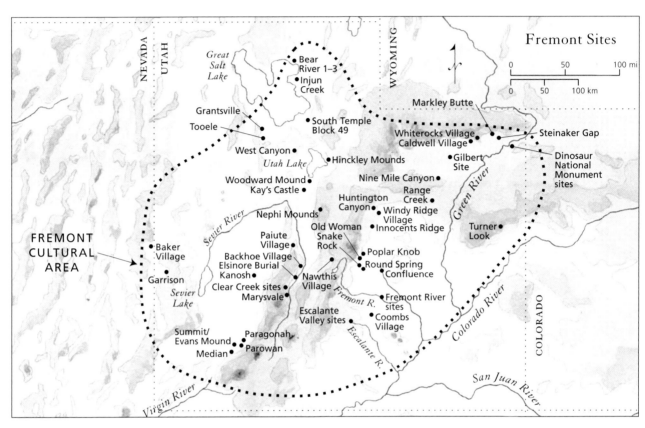

Figure 14.1. The Fremont culture area at its greatest extent. Horizontal scale is exaggerated.

The Enigmatic Fremont

Joel C. Janetski

Noel Morss, a budding archaeologist on a 1929–31 Harvard-sponsored expedition into Utah, explored caves and alcoves in the picturesque canyons of the Fremont River and its tributaries in south-central Utah. He dubbed the "partly or predominantly agricultural" people whose remains he excavated the Fremont, after the river. Morss recognized that these people showed many similarities to ancestral Pueblo Indians. The Fremont people grew corn, beans, and squash, made pottery, and constructed adobe and masonry storage features, just like the ancestral Pueblos. Yet they were different from those more southerly peoples—they wore moccasins, not sandals, made basketry in a different way, crafted large numbers of clay figurines, and seemed to rely more on wild foods.

Although Morss first used the term *Fremont* and recognized that this distinctive culture was widespread, he followed in the footsteps of several pioneers of research into these people. Edward Palmer had explored what he called Puebloan sites in Utah in the late 1800s and sent collections from them to eastern museums. Henry Montgomery, a professor at the University of Utah, had brought a more systematic approach to investigating Fremont mounds in the 1890s. Morss also acknowledged earlier work by Neil Judd in the 1910s at mounds in central Utah along the westward-facing Wasatch Front.

Julian H. Steward followed Judd and Morss in exploring Fremont culture while teaching at the University of Utah in the early 1930s. Like Judd, Steward mostly dug in mounds along the Wasatch Front and labeled the sites Puebloan, focusing on similarities in ceramics, architecture, and corn farming with ancestral Pueblo sites to the south.

Morss's term and the idea that these sites represented a distinct culture won the day, thanks to the research of Jesse Jennings and his students. Jennings arrived at the University of Utah in 1947 and started an aggressive program of archaeological research that included caves and rockshelters as well as mounds. Working closely with graduate students in the 1960s and 1970s, he defined the geographical extent of Fremont culture (fig. 14.1) and, through radiocarbon dating, placed it in time. This work led to abandoning "Puebloan" in favor of Morss's "Fremont," in recognition of the latter culture's uniqueness.

Fremont, then, refers to a cultural tradition whose practitioners farmed, hunted, fished, and gathered across most of present-day Utah between 2,000 and 700 years ago. All scholars of the Fremont from Morss to Jennings noted differences in material goods, architecture, and diet across the region. But they also believed the commonalities they saw justified subsuming these peoples under the rubric Fremont. Some cultural differences certainly arose from the contrasting landscapes people lived in. Wetlands lie along the northern rim of the eastern Great Basin; arid and dissected canyons and plateaus dominate the land to the southeast; the Uinta Basin has a colder climate; and fertile, well-watered soils are present along the Wasatch Front. Each of these landscapes offered certain advantages and posed certain problems for Fremont people in making a living and creating the things of their world.

Other differences stemmed from unique local historical trajectories, including interactions with neighbors. Fremont farming and village life was clearly an expression of the general Southwest farming tradition. But the Fremont people developed their own distinctive basketry, rock art, clay figurines, pottery, and ornaments.

Research on the Fremont people continues today, addressing old questions and raising new ones. In addition to environmental and historical differences among recognizably Fremont groups, researchers have found less visible sites away from larger villages and questioned whether some Fremont groups were farmers at all. When retreating floodwaters in the Great Salt Lake wetlands during the 1980s revealed ancient burials, analyses of them yielded unexpected insights into dietary diversity. This information led to a new understanding of the complexity of Fremont strategies for producing and gathering food.

Brigham Young University archaeologists excavated in Clear Creek Canyon in central Utah and at Baker Village on the Utah-Nevada border in the 1980s and early 1990s. Their work aroused renewed interest in Fremont communities and social life. More recently they looked at sites in the Escalante River drainage to explore issues of ethnicity in the dynamic borderland between Fremont and ancestral Pueblo peoples.

Fremont Origins

What has all this research told us about Fremont people? The genesis of Fremont society got under way 2,000 years ago. Inklings of a shift from reliance on hunting and gathering wild foods to farming come from several deeply buried sites including the Elsinore Burial in the Sevier River valley, the Steinaker Gap site in the Uinta Basin, and the Confluence site on Muddy Creek in central Utah. House floors at the Confluence and Steinaker Gap sites were shallow ovals, some with central fire pits. Deep, bell-shaped storage pits containing corn lay adjacent to the houses. At Steinaker Gap, researchers found irrigation ditches and a check dam, a clear sign of the importance of farming. They found no pottery, but both sites had evidence of bows and arrows. Archaeologists working at the

Steinaker and Elsinore sites discovered burials in the bell-shaped pits. In the former site they found infants swathed in bone and shell beads, demonstrating how highly these communities valued children.

These findings tell us that by 500 CE people were farming on the floodplains across much of present-day Utah. They lived near their irrigated fields, stored corn in deep pits, and used bows and arrows for weapons. Perhaps a hundred years later they began making plain gray pottery. These practices sharply distinguished these people from foragers elsewhere in the Great Basin.

The Fremont culture reached its greatest geographical extent about 1050 CE. At that time Fremont settlements ranged from present-day Brigham City on the north to Cedar City on the south. Many Fremont communities existed in the Uinta Basin and along the eastern flanks of the Wasatch Plateau, but they tended to be smaller than those found elsewhere. In all cases Fremont people situated their villages near arable, well-drained land and water with which to irrigate crops. Many modern Utah towns, originally based on irrigation agriculture, overlie these old villages. Later sites along the Wasatch Front tend to be larger and located on ridges and knolls. More ephemeral sites are common, too. Some people camped at high elevations in the Uinta Mountains and on the Wasatch Plateau, and others set up temporary lodgings in the arid lowlands of western Utah. There they collected seasonal foodstuffs and other critical resources such as tool stone.

Shelter

The Fremont people invested in architecture in keeping with their intentions: long-term residence required greater investment than temporary stays. With the materials available they built pit houses and adobe-walled storage facilities along the Wasatch Front and at the Baker Village and Garrison sites on the Utah-Nevada border. They excavated pit structures up to 3 feet deep and 12 to 15 feet across, usually making them circular in plan with vertical walls and flat bottoms. They roofed the houses with timbers reaching from the perimeter of the pit toward the center, covered the larger beams with

Figure 14.2. An adobe-walled granary with stone paving, Nawthis Village, central Utah.

smaller thatch or branches, and sealed it all with as much as a foot of dirt. In most cases they climbed in and out of these houses via a ladder through a central roof hole. Shallow, roofed ventilator tunnels typically reached 10 to 15 feet south from the house perimeter, facilitating air circulation to move smoke out through the center entry. Sometimes residents plastered the pit house walls to hold rocks and dirt at bay. House floors were hard-packed dirt, perhaps cushioned with mats. A circular hearth with a clay rim in the center of the floor provided warmth and a place for cooking.

The Fremont also built large surface residences and granaries made of adobe blocks, each roughly a foot square and half a foot thick, laid like bricks to construct walls up to several feet high (no evidence remains of what completed the walls above that height). The best example of an adobe house and its associated granaries is at Nawthis Village in central Utah (fig. 14.2), but others exist at Baker Village, Nephi Mounds, and Bradshaw Mounds near Beaver, Utah. Some researchers consider these to be more than residences—perhaps community gathering places.

Eastern Utah houses varied considerably. Some were shallow and edged with large basalt boulders. In Nine Mile Canyon, Fremont people built both storage structures and living quarters of stone masonry laid with mud mortar. Pit houses in the Escalante River drainage reflect influence from

Figure 14.3. A slab-lined Fremont pit house with wing walls at the Dos Casas site in the Escalante Valley.

ancestral Puebloan neighbors. Similarities to Puebloan architecture include large flat slabs set vertically against walls to line pit houses and entry ramps (fig. 14.3) and the defining of hearths and wing walls with stones set into adobe.

For temporary or seasonal use Fremont people built brush houses. First they cleared and smoothed an area and edged it with large rocks to support a tipi-like superstructure of poles joined in the center. They covered this frame with brush or perhaps hides. Such houses, referred to as wickiups, are most common in relatively remote areas and represent special-use camps associated with farming villages, although some might have been residences of non-Fremont people who farmed little or not at all. Archaeologists find wickiups in the Utah western desert and at high altitudes. These ephemeral structures might actually have been more common than the labor-intensive pit houses, but evidence of wickiups is less visible than remains of the more elaborate pit and surface houses.

The Fremont and other peoples who farmed in the Great Basin (see chapter 17) needed storage structures and granaries to store food, tools, and raw materials for future use. Early on, from about 100 to 400 CE, Fremont people kept such goods in bell-shaped pits. Later, as in Range Creek Canyon (chapter 15), they tucked granaries built of stone, adobe, and timbers into protected niches in cliffs, often well away from residences. In other areas they built adobe-walled granaries of one or two rooms adjacent to their pit houses (fig. 14.2). Miscellaneous pits inside and around the edges of houses also served to store food and gear.

Making a Living

What went into Fremont people's meals depended on the farming potential of the locale and the availability of wild foods. Cultivated crops such as corn, squash, and beans were important for everyone. Even those who might not have farmed had access to these foods through trade or perhaps raiding.

Archaeologists find burned corncobs and kernels in most sites, regardless of location. But how much corn people ate varied widely, as researchers learned from analyzing human bones from Fremont-age burials in the Great Salt Lake marshes.

Fremont people also ate meat, as attested by the abundant animal bones left in trash dumps. Deer and cottontail rabbit bones outnumber all others in most sites along the Wasatch Front; mountain sheep replace deer in the more arid valleys and canyons to the east. Marshes adjacent to the Great Salt Lake and Utah Lake attracted waterfowl, muskrats, and beavers and supported vast stands of bulrushes and cattails. The opportunistic Fremont made good use of these and other wild resources. Thousands of trout, sucker, and chub bones come from sites in Utah Valley, and near the Bear River marshes sites have yielded abundant waterfowl remains.

The Fremont people used bows to shoot their prey, and arrow points are plentiful in some sites. Rock art depicts groups of hunters driving mountain sheep and other large game into nets, showing that the hunt was a communal pursuit. Drives and nets no doubt served for smaller game, too, such as molting waterfowl and speedy black-tailed jackrabbits. Snares would have targeted ground squirrels, cottontails, and perhaps grouse. Bone harpoons found in sites alongside lakes and streams are evidence of one fishing technique. Basketry traps, perhaps bows and arrows, and even people's hands were other effective ways to harvest spawning fish.

Wild plants, especially nourishing pine nuts and small seeds from rice grass, goosefoot, bulrush, and cattail, were important in Fremont diets, as were tubers and roots. The people stored hard seeds and nuts and preserved meat and fish by drying them. In short, like the foragers who came before them, the Fremont people made the fullest possible use of the wild resources around them. But unlike their predecessors, they added cultivated plants to their diet.

Crafts

Gray-ware ceramics are signature Fremont artifacts. Earlier peoples did not make pottery, and Puebloan neighbors to the south decorated pots in different styles and produced contrasting forms. Fremont potters most often made plain, round-bottomed jars, often with a single handle attached to the rim, handled pitchers, and painted bowls. They burnished pot surfaces with rubbing stones and decorated some jars and pitchers with incised designs or finely executed corrugations. They also used a unique technique called coffee-bean appliqué to decorate vessels (plate 19) and clay figurines. Their painted vessels, almost always bowls, feature black designs on a gray or, in a few cases, white background produced by applying a slip—a thin layer of finely ground, liquid clay—over the vessel's surface. Sometimes Fremont potters applied ochre or hematite generously to the vessels to decorate them in red.

Looking at basketry also helps to define Fremont culture. Fremont basket makers created shallow trays and some bowls using whole or split willows or other kinds of slender, pliable wood as the "rod," or the horizontally coiled foundation. They wrapped the rod vertically with even more pliable, thin woody strips. A fiber bundle lay on top of the rod, leading archaeologists to call this the "one-rod-and-bundle" technique (see chapter 16). People also made twined bulrush and juniper bark mats to cover the floors of houses and line storage pits. From the dense bones of deer and other large animals they made whistles, needles, long, daggerlike awls, harpoons, rubbing tools for working hides, and what were probably weaving tools and gaming pieces. The ubiquitous awls served to split woody foundation rods for basket making and perhaps to repair clothing and footwear. Antlers served as wedges and flakers in tool making.

One type of artifact is uniquely Fremont: unfired clay figurines. These engaging, stylized human forms vary considerably in size and decoration across the region. Relatively elaborate specimens come from the northern Colorado Plateau. The most famous of these are the Pillings figurines, from a side canyon of Range Creek (chapter 15). Found in 1950 by Clarence Pillings of Price, Utah, these eleven figurines are notable for their large size (they average about 6 inches long) and elaborate decorations—necklaces, hair

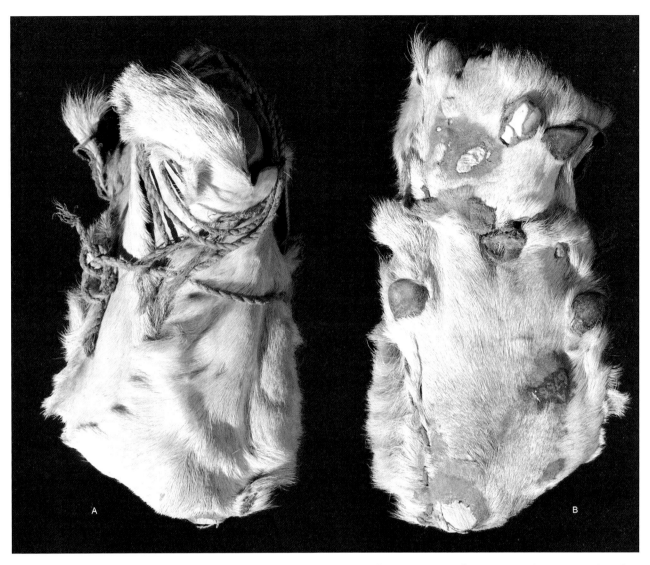

Figure 14.4. Top and bottom views of a pair of Fremont moccasins made from the hocks of a mountain sheep. Capitol Reef area, south-central Utah.

bobs, waist trappings, and red, buff, and brown face and body painting. Equally elaborate examples include a figure from the Nine Mile Canyon area that sports a face painted brilliantly in yellow-gold with vertical red stripes and a diagonal red "sash" across the torso (plate 9). Noel Morss found many figurines in the Fremont River sites he explored, but most were simple, formed of dark red clay with rounded heads and pinched noses.

In the early twentieth century Charles W. Lee, a collector exploring sites in the Capitol Reef area, discovered a spectacular figurine wrapped in tiny blankets of animal skin, juniper bark, and cotton cloth and resting in a finely crafted toy cradle-board. Other figurines featured skirts, elaborate hairstyles, earrings, and necklaces, giving us a glimpse of how the Fremont people clothed and adorned themselves. Actual items of clothing are surprisingly rare in Fremont sites, and we have to extrapolate what people wore from their figurines and rock art and from remnants found in burials. Kilts or skirts, occasionally decorated with bird or animal skins, may have been common. Rock art panels show figures with belts and possibly skirts, perhaps for both men and women. Another unique item associated with the Fremont is a type of moccasin that Morss found in the dry shelters of southern Utah. It was made from the lower leg skins of

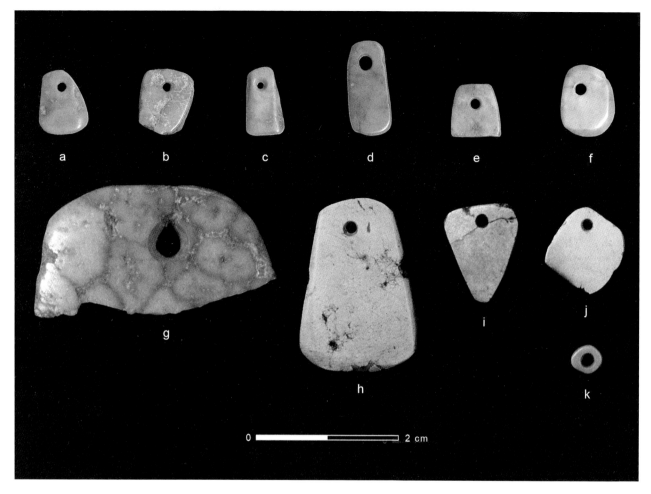

Figure 14.5. Turquoise pendants from Baker Village (top row) and Five Finger Ridge (bottom row).

mountain sheep and formed in such a way that the dew claws or hocks were on the sole (fig. 14.4).

Although we know little about Fremont people's clothing, we know a lot about their accessories. They adorned themselves with stone and bone beads and pendants. Archaeologists have found trapezoidal bone beads that look much like elements seen on rock art panels and in miniature on figurines. At Nawthis Village, careful excavations exposed a necklace consisting of hundreds of finely made bone and black lignite disk beads. Such beads turn up in Fremont sites from Utah Valley to Escalante Valley and seem to have been the preferred form. We also find larger stone beads with striking color patterns and a few exotic beads made of marine shells (mostly *Olivella* shells) and turquoise (fig. 14.5). Neither occurs locally, so

their presence shows that the Fremont traded with their neighbors to the south and west.

Besides jewelry, at least some Fremont people wore headdresses. Of the two that researchers have discovered, one is from Mantles Cave, in Dinosaur National Monument in northeastern Utah, and the other is from the Canyonlands area. The Mantles Cave example (plate 20) displays orange feathers from the red-shafted flicker, a bird common to the region. The feathers are arrayed vertically along a headband, making for a colorful display. The second example is made of a mountain sheep scalp with horn sheaths intact and decorated with *Olivella* shells. The considerable differences between these amazing specimens suggest that they served different cultural functions; possibly they even reflect the importance of individual choice in Fremont society.

Social and Ceremonial Life

We have few insights into Fremont social life. Indirect evidence for communal gatherings might be the many small, polished and decorated bone objects thought to be gaming pieces. These have been collected in large numbers at some sites—hundreds from the Parowan Valley, for example. Gambling was a popular pastime in many Native North American societies, especially during festivals that brought people together for social and ritual activities. It makes sense to think that the bone pieces from Parowan Valley sites and elsewhere were used similarly during community gatherings.

Annual and semiannual festivals are well documented in the historic-period Great Basin and Southwest. They were important social events that brought people together for courting, trading, gambling, competing, and feasting. Evidence for lavish communal meals appears at the Baker Village site, where excavators found thousands of rabbit bones in a large, adobe-walled central structure. Whether they were the result of a single feast or of many, we are unsure. The rabbits themselves might have been captured in a communal hunt.

Festivals also provided opportunities for trading. Archaeologists have found marine shell, exotic ceramics, obsidian, and locally unavailable minerals in Fremont sites. For instance, researchers found more than a hundred *Olivella* shell beads and a dozen turquoise pendants at Baker Village. The shells came from the Pacific coast. The turquoise sources may have been in Nevada to the west or south. Turquoise from the Five Finger Ridge site, on the other hand, looks more like the turquoise beads and pendants found in Arizona and New Mexico.

Fremont people traded pottery across the region as well. Black-on-white painted bowls most likely made in Castle Valley appear in many sites well away from the Fremont area. Similarly, corrugated and black-on-gray painted wares apparently made in the Parowan Valley found their way north and west. Obsidian, the volcanic glass highly prized for making sharp tools, came primarily from sources along the eastern margin of the Great Basin, and obsidian tools are common finds in that part of the Fremont area. Obsidian is less common at Fremont sites on the Colorado Plateau, but the specimens found are from the eastern Great Basin sources. Even though we can see that Fremont people traded, we do not clearly understand the nature of that trade. Tool makers might either have traveled to obsidian quarries or obtained blanks through down-the-line trade. Marine shell and turquoise probably passed from hand to hand along trade networks. Transporting pottery vessels would have been a challenge, and we still wonder how people moved them over such distances.

Not all social interaction, unfortunately, was friendly. Rock art panels portraying shield-bearing figures, some holding what may be trophy heads, evince conflict among the Fremont or between them and their neighbors (chapter 19). Charred, broken, and sometimes chopped human bones in houses raise the possibility of desecration or even cannibalism of enemies. The Turner-Look site yielded skull fragments, a possible "trophy" mandible, and the burial of a man who died from

Figure 14.6. Classic Fremont rock art panel, Nine Mile Canyon, Utah.

a blow to the head. Excavators of the Sky Aerie Charnel House site in northwest Colorado discovered a clay-capped hearth containing three human crania and other human bones. The excavators speculated that the heads had been roasted for consumption. Additional human bones lay scattered throughout the site, some near hearths and mixed with animal bones. These finds demonstrate that strife, even warfare, broke out on occasion during Fremont times.

On a more peaceful note, we find some evidence for community planning. At the Five Finger Ridge site in Clear Creek Canyon, the ancient residents positioned their adobe granaries along ridge lines and located most pit houses on slopes just below the ridge line. Perhaps this arrangement reflects coordination rather than simply personal preference. At Baker Village, Fremont people arranged both granaries and pit houses in a consistent way relative to the cardinal directions. This suggests directed group activity and implies the presence of a community head, an important indication of Fremont social and political structure. Researchers found an unusually large surface house

there that might have served as home for a person or family of some importance, perhaps indicating some ranking in Fremont society.

The way people treat their dead can tell much about their social hierarchy or lack of one. The Fremont placed their deceased in pits inside or near abandoned houses. Unlike some other peoples, they did not consistently orient bodies in a certain direction, and some of the bodies were flexed, or bent, whereas others were buried fully extended. Nor did Fremont people normally bury many mortuary goods with the dead—the usual marker of high status—although they did sometimes place grinding stones in the grave. Few excavated Fremont burials have contained goods such as ornaments and ceramic vessels. The sparse offerings in most Fremont burials stand in stark contrast to ancestral Pueblo mortuary goods, which typically included ceramic bowls and jars, beads, and other ornaments.

Exceptions to the rule include two burials of adult men in the Parowan Valley that contained bone tools and evidence of bird and weasel skins, perhaps clothing decorations. One Huntington

Canyon burial, also that of an adult man, lay beneath a house floor in a pit sealed with several grinding slabs. Two associated caches contained arrow points and miscellaneous chipped stone and bone tools. Many objects lay on a bench encircling the floor, among them several unfired but painted clay figurines, two unusual ceramic vessels shaped like cornucopias, a miniature clay cradleboard, red and yellow pigments, textiles, corncobs, beans, and other food items. A possible mass grave containing as many as seven persons was uncovered in the Great Salt Lake marshes. There the grave goods included ground stone, bone awls, gaming pieces, needlelike tools, and chipped stone items smeared with red ochre.

What status did these people with more elaborate grave goods hold in their communities? We do not know, but these remarkable collections of items, especially those with the Huntington burial, imply some kind of special status. Perhaps the deceased were shamans, respected leaders, or successful hunters.

Rock Art

Rock art is the remnant of Fremont presence that is easiest to see. Fremont artists left their marks on many stone canvases—sandstone cliffs, alcoves, and boulders. Panels attributed to the Fremont are among the best known in the world (fig. 14.6). Painted and pecked geometric, human, and animal shapes decorate these stone panels. Insightfully composed hunting scenes vie with hodgepodges of elements accumulated over time. Most resist easy understanding. Scholars Sally Cole and Polly Schaafsma have ably described the Fremont style of rock art (see chapter 19). Anthropomorphs—broad-shouldered, trapezoidal or hourglass-shaped human figures—are ubiquitous. Many of them wear elaborate headdresses and display body ornaments.

Despite shared features, the Fremont style varied geographically. West of the Wasatch Range, rock artists put greater emphasis on geometric textile or pottery designs, whereas on the Colorado Plateau they more often depicted anthropomorphs and developed the form more highly. Heroic figures wearing elaborate headgear and holding bags, trophies, or weapons intimidate viewers today and

may have in the past. Multiple humpbacked (or backpacking?) figures drawn in single file might depict the way goods were moved from place to place. Artists portrayed mountain sheep, elk, and other animals in ways that reflect intimate knowledge of animal behavior.

Understanding the function and meaning of rock art remains difficult. Scholars speculate that the images might have been parts of hunting rituals or shamanic activities, or perhaps they served to mark territory or record a concern with warfare. The frequency with which the panels portray large game, especially mountain sheep but also elk and deer, supports the notion that rock art was meant to convey information about animal behavior and perhaps success or failure in actual hunts. Polly Schaafsma has suggested that the elaborate headgear and attention to details of dress and associated paraphernalia in rock art indicate ritual or ceremonial activities. That some figures in Dinosaur National Monument and Capitol Reef National Park wear feathered headdresses similar to the piece discovered at Mantles Cave might mean that some rock art depicted actual persons. Although rock art panels exist throughout the Fremont area, certain places are treasure houses of Fremont rock art: among others, Clear Creek Canyon in central Utah, several places in the Uinta Basin, Nine Mile Canyon, Range Creek, and Capitol Reef National Park (see chapter 19 sidebar).

The End of an Era

Researchers find few Fremont sites dating after 1300 CE, but changes in this distinctive way of life began much earlier. People living in the Great Salt Lake marshes ceased to eat corn at about 1150, although those dwelling in the Salt Lake Valley to the south continued to eat this staple into the 1200s. Pit house dates from Five Finger Ridge bunch up between 1200 and 1300, but none falls after 1350. We find some evidence of continued farming as late as the 1400s in the northeastern portion of Fremont territory, but clearly people were giving up the practice in many areas. Reasons for the decline of farming are complex, but an important one may have been that shifts in summer rainfall made farming difficult and forced some people to emigrate to places where growing corn was still possible. Hunting and gathering continued as they had for millennia, but the Fremont style of combining these practices with farming disappeared. This shift might signal the arrival of the region's historic peoples, the Utes, Southern Paiutes, and Shoshones.

Joel C. Janetski is a professor of anthropology at Brigham Young University. His views on the Fremont culture are based on 25 years of archaeological research in the eastern Great Basin and on the Colorado Plateau.

Figure 15.1. Range Creek Canyon near Wilcox Ranch.

Range Creek Canyon

fifteen

Duncan Metcalfe

Range Creek Canyon scores the remote West Tavaputs Plateau of east-central Utah. It is one of two major drainages on the plateau; the other is Nine Mile Canyon, with its magnificent rock art (chapter 19). Few people besides local residents knew of Range Creek until June 2004, when an Associated Press article threw it into the national and international spotlight. Since then scores of articles and two video documentaries have publicized the place, which had long been protected by its remoteness and rugged terrain.

Why the intense interest in Range Creek? There is no single answer. Rather, several interwoven aspects of its location, its archaeology, and its history have captured the imaginations of both scientists and the public. The archaeology of Range Creek holds the potential to address long-standing and important questions about the early history of the Great Basin.

Range Creek is a perennial stream that heads at 10,200 feet above sea level at Bruin Point and flows about 37 miles to enter the Green River at an elevation of about 4,200 feet at the foot of Desolation Canyon. The higher, northern half of the canyon is largely privately owned; the lower half is divided between public ownership and land to which access is limited by the old Wilcox Ranch. The research that my colleagues and I have carried out has been confined to the lower half of Range Creek, primarily on land accessible through the ranch. It was a working ranch until the end of the twentieth century, and its houses, corrals, and work sheds are the headquarters of our research program.

The canyon itself is majestic. The creek has carved through the relatively soft, stratified mudstones, siltstones, and sandstones that were laid down during the Paleocene and Eocene geological epochs, some 68–54 million years ago and 54–35 million years ago, respectively. The result is a steep canyon flanked by stepped walls of alternating cliffs and scree slopes. Harder sandstones of the late Cretaceous period (about 144–68 million years ago) are exposed in the lower end of the canyon. In places the canyon rim is nearly 3,000 feet above the canyon floor, although the many side canyons prevent visitors from seeing its full vertical extent except from a few spots. The canyon floor is a sinuous, narrow strip of alluvium, or sediments left by flowing water, that winds back and forth between the toes of the remnant ridges separating the many side canyons. Weathered arches, pinnacles, and other wind-sculptured features adorn the long ridges.

The upper reaches of the canyon host open mountain meadows dominated by sagebrush and grasses with scattered, dense groves of aspen, Douglas fir, and subalpine firs. Lower down the meadows disappear into a carpet of Douglas fir and other firs. Halfway down the canyon, at about the northern limit of the Wilcox Ranch, firs give way to pinyon, juniper, mountain mahogany, Gambel oak, and broad sagebrush flats along the canyon bottom. Greasewood, saltbrush, shadscale, and sagebrush dominate the lowest reaches of the canyon. There, too, is a riparian zone flanking the creek, which is visually dominated by cottonwoods and box elder trees.

The main access to the canyon is by way of a dugway, a narrow dirt road cut into a steep canyon wall, with a summit at 8,700 feet above sea level (plate 21). The road breaches the Book Cliffs, the towering, undulating wall that marks the western and southern boundaries of the West Tavaputs Plateau. The road is impassable when wet or blocked by rock slides or fallen trees. Before the road was constructed in the early 1950s, visitors rode horses and mules into the canyon. And before Euro-American settlers arrived in the 1880s, people entered on foot.

My colleagues, students, and I have been conducting research in the canyon since the summer of 2002. We have recorded and described nearly 370 archaeological sites, the great majority of them in the main canyon near the valley floor. The sites with tell-tale artifacts are nearly all related to the Fremont archaeological complex, dated between about 400 and 1400 CE. Only a few sites have been recorded in the numerous side canyons, which we have yet to study systematically.

Away from the canyon bottom, the terrain becomes extremely rugged. We have found a few sites on the canyon walls well above the canyon floor—one of them a small residential village situated about 900 feet above the creek.

What is so valuable about these remote sites? Most important, they are in unusually good condition, so archaeologists can learn much more from them than from vandalized sites. Much public attention has been focused on the Wilcox family as stewards of the Range Creek archaeological sites, and rightly so. Budge and Pearl Wilcox purchased the ranch in the early 1950s and, with their sons Don and Waldo, ran cattle and grew crops there for about 50 years. They consistently discouraged casual visitation and thus kept vandalism of the archaeological sites to a minimum. The family also has a deep and abiding respect for the "ancient ones" who lived in Range Creek before them, and they have generally left the sites alone. As a result, most of the sites accessible from the ranch appear to be essentially untouched since they were abandoned. Stone tools, pieces of painted pottery, and beads lying on the surfaces of sites are the rule rather than the exception. Few of the pit houses and storage grana-

ries show signs of vandalism, and rock art panels show only the weathering of time. The excellent condition of the sites is even more remarkable in comparison with the state of sites immediately outside the ranch gates. There people have vandalized the pit houses, granaries, and rock art and often have collected all the recognizable tools.

Today no one lives in Range Creek Canyon year-round. Only a handful of Euro-Americans have ever resided there since the first settlement about 120 years ago. The resident population during Fremont times certainly exceeded 100 and may have approached or even exceeded 1,000. Only future research will tie that number down more tightly. Which brings me to an important point: We so far know very little about the Fremont occupation of Range Creek. All our efforts—stimulated largely by the increasing number of visitors to the canyon—have been directed toward surveying the canyon and inventorying its sites. We have done no systematic test excavations in any of the sites, so we have no dates or artifacts from the secure contexts that buried deposits provide. We hope to remedy this situation beginning in 2008.

What We Have Learned So Far?

We have made some progress in understanding the Fremont sites of Range Creek Canyon. They may be divided into groups based on the types of features and artifacts present or suggested by surface evidence. The more obvious features include the remains of residential structures, cliff-side granaries, and subterranean and semisubterranean cists, as well as rock art panels. We have recorded such sites from the upper end of Wilcox Ranch to the lowest reaches of Range Creek. We have learned that some sections of the canyon have many sites and others fewer, although we should not make too much of this until we have completed a more systematic survey.

We have learned from our survey where people lived. We have recorded 79 sites that likely were Fremont homesteads, sometimes called rancherias. These usually consist of one or more roughly circular to rectangular alignments of stone from 6 to about 25 feet in diameter. The alignments are made of water-rounded cobbles and boulders, large angu-

Figure 15.2. Stone alignments representing a possible pit house in Range Creek Canyon.

lar blocks, or thin tabular pieces of sandstone. Some alignments have sections of coursed stones; others have stones projecting vertically above the ground. Still others are a single course of stones, possibly the bases of less substantial structures. Stone alignments are surrounded by apparently collapsed remains of upper walls at some sites. Some of the alignments may simply be natural rings of stone; only test excavations in them will tell. Some or all of the alignments are probably the remains of shallow Fremont pit structures (fig. 15.2).

Residential sites are commonly one structure built on the toe of a ridge or low bench adjacent to the floodplain. Less commonly, clusters of structures are found in the same setting. The largest site recorded as of 2007 extends over 30,000 square yards and includes the remains of at least eight structures, a rubble mound of unknown function, six surface artifact concentrations, an exposed midden deposit, and three boulders with multiple grinding surfaces. We recorded more than 100 pro-

jectile points and other chipped stone tools and fragments, numerous gravers (small flaked stone tools used to score and cut wood and bone) and drills, as well as many stone chips. We also found manos and metates. There are corrugated and plain gray ceramics, some of the latter decorated by incising and appliqué, as well as black-on-gray, black-on-red, red ware, and polychrome potsherds.

Two rock alignments with artifacts are situated well above the valley floor. One is about 900 feet above the creek on a flat area of a long ridge that descends from the canyon rim to the valley floor. The other is even higher, on a small prominence of another ridge. We learned about both sites from Waldo Wilcox, the owner of the ranch, and caught our first glimpse of them when we viewed the documentary *The Secret Canyon*, produced by Scientific American Frontiers. Although not yet mapped, they appear to be substantial Fremont settlements. Their unusual locations, hundreds of feet above the farm fields and the creek, the nearest source of water,

Figure 15.3. A platform granary built onto a cliff face in Range Creek Canyon.

Figure 15.4. Cliff face where the platform granary stands.

suggest they were defensive. A radiocarbon date from one of the high sites is about 1050 CE, similar to dates obtained from sites near the canyon floor. Why some people lived in such easily defended sites while others lived safely on the valley floor is an unanswered question.

Perhaps the most intriguing sites are the remote granaries. We have recorded 62 of them so far. They have stone and mud walls and finely crafted roofs of wood and mud, and they often stand on the faces of cliffs. The only way to reach them, even for skilled climbers with modern equipment, seems to be by rap-

Figure 15.5. Fremont-style petroglyphs in Range Creek Canyon.

pelling down from above. Some are quite large, with interior capacities of 6 to 8 cubic feet; others are considerably smaller. Some have a single, undivided chamber, and others, multiple bins. Their contents, when we can get into them, are rat nests and corncobs, although earlier investigators reported beans, squash, and wild seeds in some. What strikes even casual observers is how much work was required to build the structures and the ongoing costs (and risks of injury and death) required to use them.

The extreme examples are granaries built on artificial platforms constructed on the faces of cliffs. The structure shown in figure 15.3 hangs about 60 feet up a cliff in the main canyon. Its builders first constructed wet-laid stone piers on narrow protrusions on the cliff face. The piers served as foundations for wooden support beams, which in turn supported a wooden platform. Having gone to all this effort, the builders then

erected an otherwise unremarkable granary on the platform. We have yet to get into the site.

The remote granaries generate much speculation. Why would anyone build storage bins in such precarious and difficult-to-reach places? Why not build them next to the houses? There people could have periodically monitored them for pest infestations, mold, and any number of other risks. They could have actively defended the stored food in times of conflict or famine and easily removed it for their next meal.

To answer these questions, we assume that the builders, given their circumstances, made economically rational decisions about the setting, construction, and function of the granaries. But what were those circumstances? Studies of animals that collect and store food show two general types of behavior: larder storing and scatter storing, or hoarding. Larder storing is usually centralized, and the stores can be defended. Scatter storing is what animals do when they cannot defend their stores in a central location or they leave the area for substantial lengths of time. If the Fremont people lived along Range Creek only seasonally, perhaps they protected foodstuffs or seeds of domesticated plants from both animal and human marauders by storing them in places very difficult of access—in effect, scatter storing. Similar granaries in hard-to-reach locations are found widely throughout the Colorado Plateau in areas inhabited by both Fremont and ancestral Pueblo people.

The remote granaries were not the only storage facilities the Fremont people used. They also dug storage pits in sheltered parts of the canyon. The pits are generally smaller in capacity than the remote granaries. They seem to have been purposefully placed in concealed settings, unlike the remote

Figure 15.6. Fremont-style pictographs in Range Creek Canyon.

granaries, and tend to be much more casually constructed. We often find them in groups, lined with juniper bark. They appear to represent a very different storage strategy from the remote granaries.

Rock Art

In addition to practical things like storage bins, the Fremont made art. To date we have recorded 66 sites with rock art panels. Some are associated with other archaeological features; many are not. There are pictographs (painted images) and petroglyphs (incised images) in both Fremont and Barrier Canyon styles (see chapters 14 and 19). Fremont motifs, including trapezoidal to triangular human figures and realistic images of mountain sheep, deer, elk, and snakes, are the most common (fig. 15.4). Most of the images are painted in white, yellow, red, blue, green, or black pigments. Few of the Fremont figures have body ornamentation other than what seem to be headdresses. One panel toward the south end of the canyon (see fig. 19.4) is remarkably similar in style to a collection of

unbaked clay figurines that the Pillings family found only a few miles downstream (chapter 14).

In contrast to the Fremont-style images, the Barrier Canyon style includes large, ghostlike human figures with long, tapered bodies (fig. 15.5). Some rock art scholars believe Barrier Canyon–style panels predate the Fremont people (chapter 19), although the question remains open.

Challenges and Opportunities

Range Creek has been protected by its anonymity, its remoteness, and its stewardship by the Wilcox family. In the five years we have been studying the archaeology of the canyon, we have barely scratched the surface. It is possible to design research projects for the canyon that will require many years to reach fruition. These projects include long-term studies of the canyon's natural resources; the planting of experimental gardens to grow Native varieties of maize, beans, and squash; and a range of paleoecological and paleoenvironmental studies similar to those carried out else-

Figure 15.7. Barrier Canyon–style pictographs in Range Creek Canyon.

Our work at Range Creek has the potential to illuminate more than the ancient past. It can perhaps help us understand how to cope with current and future climatic and environmental changes in the region. The Fremont people survived for hundreds of years by farming, hunting, and gathering in places whose climates and ecologies shifted over time. As conditions changed, they migrated to new areas, moved to higher elevations, or developed new food resources. Range Creek offers the possibility of studying a wide variety of such responses. The studies may also yield information useful to current occupants of the Great Basin in responding to changes in their natural world.

Duncan Metcalfe is curator of archaeology at the Utah Museum of Natural History and associate professor of anthropology at the University of Utah, Salt Lake City.

where in the Great Basin. To achieve these and other research goals, the University of Utah is negotiating with the Utah Division of Wildlife Resources, which owns the old Wilcox Ranch, to turn the ranch into a research station.

16.1. An incomplete Fremont coiled basketry parching tray from Hogup Cave, western Utah. Note the mending and signs of heavy use on the surface.

Fremont Basketry

James M. Adovasio, David R. Pedler, and Jeffrey S. Illingworth

Fremont basketry, although it varied across the Fremont homeland over time, is a principal defining attribute of the culture. Fremont weavers used two of the world's three basic basketry construction techniques: coiling, in which the interior foundation of the basket is made up of a spiraling core of material (the warp) that is sewn together with a single flexible fiber (the weft); and twining, in which a set of more or less rigid foundation materials (the warp) is joined by twisting two or more flexible fibers (the weft) between them (figs. 16.2, 16.3).

Archaeologists have found 342 specimens of basketry in 18 archaeological sites with Fremont or Fremont-related components. Most are pieces rather than whole baskets. About four-fifths of the pieces are coiled, and the rest are twined. Over the past 30 years, one of us, James Adovasio, has carefully examined all of these, as well as a large array of basketry materials from adjacent and earlier traditions. These studies, including the description and measurement of roughly a dozen technical features for each Fremont basket fragment, have taught us what we know about this craft tradition.

Archaeologists have found typical Fremont

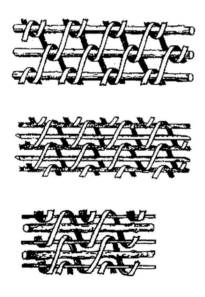

16.2. Basic structures of the three most common types of Fremont coiled basketry. Top: whole rod foundation, interlocking stitch; middle: half rod and bundle stacked, noninterlocking stitch; bottom: whole rod and welt stacked, noninterlocking stitch. All employ close coiling.

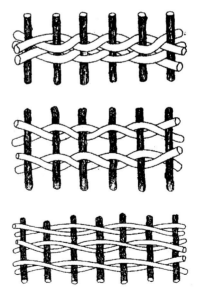

16.3. Basic structures of the three most common types of twined basketry in the Fremont range. Top: close simple twining, S-twist wefts; middle: open simple twining, Z-twist wefts; bottom: open diagonal twining, Z-twist wefts.

coiled basketry everywhere in Fremont territory. Our identification of baskets as "typically Fremont" relies on the presence of certain technical features, one of the most important being the basic foundation of the basket. Half of all Fremont coiled baskets were made with a foundation built on a core composed of half of a single rod of willow (genus *Salix*) along with a bundle of fibers from dogbane (*Apocynum*), milkweed (*Asclepias*), or occasionally juniper or yucca. This core is always so tightly stitched that the foundation is only rarely visible. (The core is identified by examining the cross section of a broken basket fragment with a strong magnifying glass.)

Examples of this distinctive type of coiling have been found at sites in southern Idaho and southwestern Wyoming, beyond the general range of the Fremont culture proper (fig 16.4). Perhaps

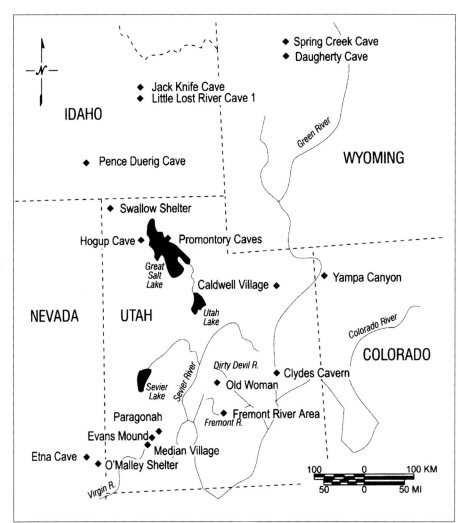

16.4. Fremont sites yielding basketry discussed in this chapter.

other ancient people traded for Fremont baskets, or perhaps Fremont people traveled to their country or intermarried with them. Fremont coiled baskets have not been found south of the Colorado or Virgin River, nor are they known in northeastern Nevada. The other chief technique, Fremont twining, is generally confined to northern Utah and northwestern Colorado, although it is more varied than the coiling.

People produced coiled basketry throughout the entire time span of the Fremont culture, from about 400 to 1300 CE. The tradition disappeared or was replaced by others at different times in different places. It became extinct in the Uinta area of present-day Utah about 950 but persisted in other core areas until the end of the thirteenth century. In

southern Idaho and Wyoming it may have persisted longer, but the dating there is uncertain. People also used twining techniques over the same time span, at least in the northern sections of the Fremont range.

Fremont coiled basketry remained recognizable over these centuries, but it was not unchanging. A gradual shift in technical features, such as that from mixed work directions to an almost uniformly right-to-left work direction; an increasing preference for the half-rod-and-bundle foundation; and an increasing tendency to employ noninterlocking or intentionally split stitches on the nonwork surface all appeared over time. We do not know why these subtle changes took place. The technical features of basket making are often learned habits passed on from teacher to pupil. Perhaps certain teachers became more influential.

Minor regional preferences existed among Fremont basket makers as well. Whole-rod foundation coiling, for example, was more common in the Uinta Basin and the Parowan Valley than elsewhere. A half-rod-and-welt stacked foundation was popular in the Parowan Valley but scarce or absent in other Fremont areas.

Different groups of basket makers also preferred specific stitch types. Interlocking stitches, in which the stitches of each successive row were linked into each other, were generally more common in northern Fremont areas. To the south, particularly in the Parowan Valley, basket makers favored noninterlocking stitches. The uneven distribution of S- and Z-twist wefts in twining, as well as the generally northern distribution of twining itself, may also reflect regional preferences.

Another way of understanding Fremont basketry is to look for its relationships to older basket-making methods and styles both inside and outside the Fremont heartland. The basic affinities of Fremont basketry, both twined and coiled, are to earlier Archaic industries from the same area. Very late Archaic (post-Fremont times) and historic-period baskets, which are part of the Shoshone, Southern Paiute, and Ute traditions, bear absolutely no relationship to baskets of those peoples' Fremont predecessors. But if we look at earlier Archaic basketry, we find all the basic Fremont coiling attributes. Similarly, all the Fremont twining attributes appear in Archaic baskets from the eastern Great Basin. The persistence of these construction techniques from Archaic into Fremont times is strong evidence that Fremont basketry and its makers derived directly from local Archaic industries and populations. The stark differences between these local Fremont basket-making practices and those of the historic-era Native residents of the region indicate that the two cultural groups were unrelated.

Earlier analysts proposed a close relationship between Fremont and ancestral Pueblo basketry of the American Southwest, but in fact there is virtually no relationship at all. Ancestral Pueblo coiling techniques included many varieties of both close and open stitch types, as well as a number of fancy stitch types never found among the Fremont. Also, a much greater range of foundation combinations existed among the ancient Puebloans than among the Fremont. The standard ancestral Pueblo foundation technique, two rods and a bundle bunched together and featuring noninterlocking stitches, never appears in Fremont sites. Nor, for that matter, do any of the later, standard ancestral Pueblo techniques ever appear in the Fremont range.

Unlike the Fremont people, ancestral Pueblo weavers made extensive use of unique ways to finish their baskets—for example, with false braid rims. They also used a variety of decorative weave patterns and painting and other technical features wholly unlike those to the north. The Puebloan weavers always worked from right to left and favored shapes and forms that are completely unknown in the Fremont area. In addition, the basic ancestral Pueblo coiling techniques are as old as the basic Fremont varieties, indicating that the two textile-making traditions and areas were separate for a very long time. Finally, the ancestral Pueblo style of twining was totally absent in the Fremont area during the time the two weaving traditions coexisted.

In short, the available evidence suggests that the basketry of the Fremont people constituted a distinct ethnic signature wholly derived from their Archaic predecessors and unrelated to any contemporary or later industries. Who the Fremont were, and where they went after the thirteenth or possibly early fourteenth century, remains unknown.

James M. Adovasio is a professor of anthropology and director of the Mercyhurst Archaeological Institute, Mercyhurst College, Erie, Pennsylvania. David R. Pedler is on the research staff of the Mercyhurst Archaeological Institute, and Jeffrey S. Illingworth is director of conservation for the institute's R. L. Andrews Center for Perishables Analysis.

Figure 17.1. Excavation of the Three Kids site in Clark County Wetlands Park, Henderson, Nevada.

Who Lived on the Southern Edge of the Great Basin?

Richard V.N. Ahlstrom and Heidi Roberts

It was June at the Three Kids site, sweltering hot, and not a breath of air anywhere. We stood 6 feet below ground level in a large pit we had excavated to expose the remains of a 1,500-year-old house, the first of its kind ever discovered in the Las Vegas Valley. The last group of visitors arrived, and we began our tour of the site.

We explained that the circular depression, 12 feet across, that we had exposed on the floor of the pit was the foundation of a semisubterranean earth lodge, or "pit house." The builders had erected the house over a 10-inch-deep pit dug out with sticks and baskets. Some time later the structure had burned, and the charred remains of roof poles strewn across the floor told us that the builders had wedged the poles around the perimeter of the house foundation and then joined them together over the center of the structure. We presumed that they had covered the framework of poles with mats or bundles of reeds and then a layer of earth, similar to the method used to cover historic Havasupai houses (fig. 17.2).

We told our visitors that the house's occu-

pants had hunted animals with bows and arrows, but we had not yet analyzed the fragments of bone collected from the house floor, so we did not know which animals. The people had also ground seeds using large grinding stones, and soon analysis of the microscopic pollen grains from floor soil samples would tell us the kinds of plants they had eaten. We particularly wanted to know whether the people who lived in the house were farmers who grew corn and other domesticated plants or whether they were solely foragers who gathered foodstuffs from cattails, mesquite trees, and other wild plants that grew in the vicinity. Because we had uncovered no

Figure 17.2. Havasupai house, about 1910, showing what the Three Kids pit house might have looked like.

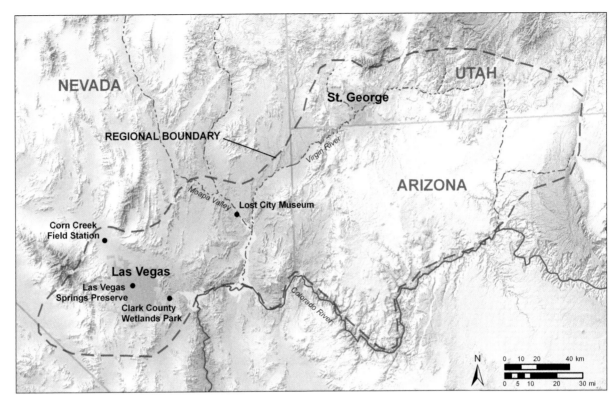

Figure 17.3. The western Pueblo region on the southern edge of the Great Basin.

pieces of broken pottery, we suspected that the house predated the arrival of ceramics in the Las Vegas Valley.

"Any questions?" we asked.

And of course our visitors replied, "Who lived here? Who were they?"

We had to answer, "Unfortunately, we don't yet know. People throughout the Southwest lived in simple pit houses like this one, and we haven't found any distinctive artifacts like pottery or arrowheads to link this house to the dwellings of other prehistoric cultures."

"But were they Pueblo Indians?" asked one of the visitors.

"Someday we hope to figure that out."

"Who lived here?" is one of the most popular questions visitors to archaeological sites ask. Archaeologists' ability to answer the question can vary widely, even for sites only short distances apart. This is true of the Moapa and Las Vegas Valleys, just 50 miles from each other along the southern edge of the Great Basin (fig. 17.3). Archaeologists have identified the early inhabitants

of the Moapa Valley as the far western representatives of the ancestral Pueblo culture, which centered on the Four Corners area of the Southwest. The modern descendants of the Puebloan peoples are the Pueblo Indians—the Hopis of Arizona, the Zunis of western New Mexico, and the Pueblo groups living along the Rio Grande.

Between 200 and 1200 CE, the people living in the lower Moapa Valley and adjacent sections of the Virgin River valley in present-day southern Nevada and southwestern Utah were village farmers whose lifeways were similar to those of the Puebloan communities to the east. Archaeologists call these people the Virgin Branch of ancestral Pueblo culture, after the river. We know that they relied on maize, or corn, as their staple crop. We presume that, like other Puebloans, they also planted beans and squash, but these crops leave few traces in the archaeological record.

The Moapa and Virgin River valleys receive less annual rainfall than most of the Puebloan world, so the farmers irrigated their crops with water drawn from the Muddy River, which flows through the

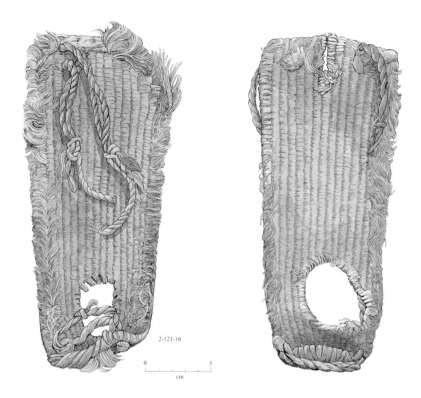

Figure 17.4. Two sandals from Black Dog Cave, Moapa Valley, Nevada. They closely resemble sandals made by people of the Puebloan Basketmaker culture in the Four Corners area.

Figure 17.5. Virgin Branch pottery vessels from the Moapa Valley, Nevada. The jar on the right has a "corrugated" surface.

Euro-Americans tilled the soil but are now gone. We know the people collected wild plants and hunted many species of animals along the rivers, in the uplands, and in the forested mountains that are within a day's walk or two from the valley bottoms.

The people relied on skillfully woven textiles, including nets, baskets, and sandals. Textiles from Black Dog Cave in the Moapa Valley were made in much the same way as contemporaneous forms to the east (fig. 17.4). About 600 CE, Virgin Branch people began to make pots from a gray-firing clay. They decorated some pots with black painted designs resembling those favored by Four Corners people at the same time. After about 1050 potters began to manipulate the surface of the clay, pinching it to produce a "corrugated" texture on cooking and storage vessels, a practice begun perhaps a hundred years earlier to the east (fig. 17.5).

Before 900 CE, Virgin Branch people lived in the same kinds of pit houses as other Pueblo peoples to the east (fig. 17.6). At first they stored foodstuffs outside the pit houses in individual, slab-lined storage bins dug partly underground. Later these pits developed into rows of attached bins, and still later the bins became rows of surface rooms built of stone masonry. Ultimately, people began to live in the stone structures as well as the pit houses (fig. 17.7).

Although the Virgin Branch shared many similarities with its eastern neighbors, there were some differences. In the Four Corners area, painted pottery designs changed with a regularity that allows archaeologists

Moapa Valley, and the Virgin River. Their fields were on the rivers' floodplains. Historic accounts tell of irrigation networks that still existed when the first

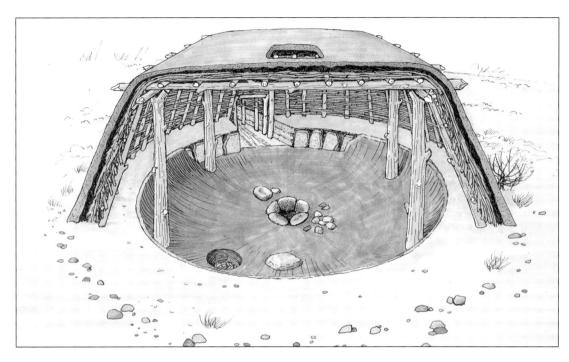

Figure 17.6. Interpretation of typical Virgin Branch pit house architecture, Black Dog Mesa, Nevada.

Figure 17.7. Reconstruction of a Virgin Branch pueblo, Lost City Museum.

to date sites to intervals of 50 to 100 years. Design change was not so regimented among Virgin Branch potters. It is as if they received some of the memos from the east indicating how design styles were changing, but not all of them. Thus Virgin Branch designs persisted for longer times.

Another difference lay in the construction and use of kivas—specialized, possibly ceremonial chambers. Ancestral Pueblo people developed kivas between about 950 and 1050, and they spread rap-idly throughout the Four Corners and adjacent Pueblo regions, but not to the Virgin Branch.

There are other architectural differences. Between 1000 and 1250, increasing numbers of people in the Four Corners area came together in large masonry pueblos containing dozens or even hundreds of rooms. Some pueblos were two and occasionally three or four stories high. Virgin Branch pueblos con-tinued to consist of alignments rather than blocks of rooms, and few, if any, rose more than a single story.

Figure 17.8. Las Vegas Southern Paiute encampment, about 1900.

agaves, desert tortoises, and desert bighorn sheep.

When Mexican and American explorers traveled through the Las Vegas Valley in the early 1800s, Southern Paiute people were living there (fig. 17.8). Their descendants continue to live in the valley and say they have done so "since time immemorial." From an archaeological perspective, the record suggests that the Southern Paiutes had ties to Puebloan cultures beginning around 200 CE, as well as to the Patayan, or ancestral Mojave, people. The nearest Pueblo communities lay in the Moapa and Virgin River valleys. The Patayan lived along the lower Colorado River to the south. The Southern Paiutes' historical range stretched outward from the Las Vegas Valley into portions of southeastern Nevada and sections of southwestern Utah, northwestern Arizona, and southeastern California.

The clearest archaeological evidence for connections between early Las Vegas Valley residents and Puebloan, Patayan-Mojave, and Southern Paiute groups is their pottery. Virgin Branch potters produced gray wares, Patayan potters made buff or tan wares, and Southern Paiutes made brown wares. Each style of pottery is easy to distinguish from the others. In the Las Vegas Valley, sherds from broken gray ware, buff ware, and brown ware vessels are found intermixed. Why?

We can suggest at least three answers. First, different people might have lived in the same favorable places in the valley repeatedly over a span of almost 2,000 years, each group leaving broken pieces of its own kind of pottery. Second, the valley's inhabitants might not have made their own vessels but obtained the few pots they needed by trading with their Puebloan and Patayan neighbors. This scenario fits the Las Vegas Valley record well, because sites typically contain only a few potsherds representing a small number of ceramic vessels. Third, archaeologists simply might not have found sites with unmixed collections of potsherds. Many such sites may have been destroyed by the explosive

Sometime in the 1200s the Virgin Branch culture disappeared from the archaeological record. Perhaps the Great Drought of the late thirteenth century caused crop failures and deaths. Perhaps Virgin Branch people migrated to the Four Corners area. Or they might have given up village life to become nomadic foragers and only part-time farmers, switching from farming to wild plant gathering as the need arose. Perhaps they made these changes but had in fact been speakers of Southern Paiute—the people living in this region in historic times—all along. These and other interpretations of the fate of the Virgin Branch are subjects of ongoing debate among Great Basin and Southwestern archaeologists.

Perhaps some of the answers will come from well-hidden sites in the Las Vegas Valley. Unlike the Moapa and Virgin River valleys, the Las Vegas Valley has no permanent streams. Instead, a scattering of life-giving springs existed there in the past. Thick stands of mesquite and marsh plants once flourished near flowing springs and major drainages. Mesquite trees produce abundant edible seed pods, and marshes host many edible plants, the most important of which, to early residents, were cattails. The mountains and foothills supplied several other staple foods, including pine nuts, growth of the Las Vegas metroplex over the past 50 years.

For most sites in the Las Vegas Valley we have only tentative answers to the question "Who lived here?" The answer depends on when people occupied each site. For instance, we recently investigated three sites in the Clark County Wetlands Park in the southeastern corner of the Las Vegas Valley. The first one we named the Larder site because it contained hundreds of storage pits. But we found little evidence suggesting that people lived there for any length of time. It might have served as a food storage site. Radiocarbon dates on plant remains suggest that the site served this function for almost 2,000 years, from about 300 BCE to 1600 CE.

The most surprising finding suggests that people were growing maize nearby—the earliest evidence of maize farming yet discovered in southern Nevada. Radiocarbon dates on maize from the storage pits range between 300 BCE and 200 CE. Who the farmers were, we cannot say. They had not yet begun to make pottery, so we can't identify them that way. And the storage pits are not culturally distinctive; many people made and used such pits over time.

The second site we investigated was the Three Kids site, which contained the pit house we described at the beginning of the chapter. Radiocarbon dates indicate that the house was built and used between 430 and 600 CE, a century or two before the beginning of pottery making in the Las Vegas Valley. That people built such a house rather than simply camping on the spot and building windbreaks or shade structures suggests that some attractive resources existed nearby. Pollen grains from the house floor indicated that the attraction was primarily marsh plants, particularly cattails.

These people did not cultivate maize or other crops, although they might have done so in places of moist soil adjacent to local patches of marsh vegetation. This is an important observation, considering that people were growing maize some 200 to 900 years earlier at the nearby Larder site. Also relevant is that Virgin Branch people had been farming for at least 200 years when the Three Kids pit house was inhabited. Why the residents of the house grew no maize remains puzzling.

The third site in our sequence, Scorpion Knoll, yielded another interesting bit of evidence. It demonstrated a link between people in the Las Vegas Valley and Virgin Branch communities to the northeast. People lived at Scorpion Knoll between 700 and 1000 CE, after the Three Kids pit house was abandoned. Few artifacts lay on the surface, but when we dug trenches with a backhoe, we found intact pit houses, cooking pits, and pottery. We found maize pollen on two pit house floors, indicating that the residents were farmers. People evidently lived there for only a short while. We think the site may been a "field house," used during the growing season by people tending farm plots nearby. Some 15 pieces of Virgin Branch gray ware pottery were found, suggesting that the occupants had some ties with their Puebloan neighbors.

Did Virgin Branch people live at Scorpion Knoll? Perhaps, given the gray ware pottery and the evidence of farming and short-term use. Other sites also suggest a link. Two other recently excavated Las Vegas Valley sites have pit houses associated with Virgin Branch pottery. A pit house dating between 700 and 900 CE at the Las Vegas Springs Preserve yielded fragments of charred maize and Virgin Branch potsherds. What might be a cluster of pit houses sits at the north end of the valley, adjacent to several springs. One structure, dated between 550 and 700, contained Virgin Branch gray ware sherds, although no evidence of maize pollen.

These cases suggest two scenarios. In one, small numbers of Virgin Branch people visited and farmed in the Las Vegas Valley over several centuries. In the other, some valley occupants used Virgin Branch pottery, built and lived in pit houses, and grew corn. Which scenario is correct requires further research. Was the gray ware pottery found at these sites made in the Las Vegas Valley or brought from the Moapa and Virgin River areas? How closely the pit houses resemble Virgin Branch structures will also shed light on the identity of the residents of the Las Vegas Valley sites.

Patayan buff ware pottery appeared in southern Nevada after about 1200 CE and continued into the 1800s. This pottery suggests ties to Patayan-Mojave people living along the lower Colorado River.

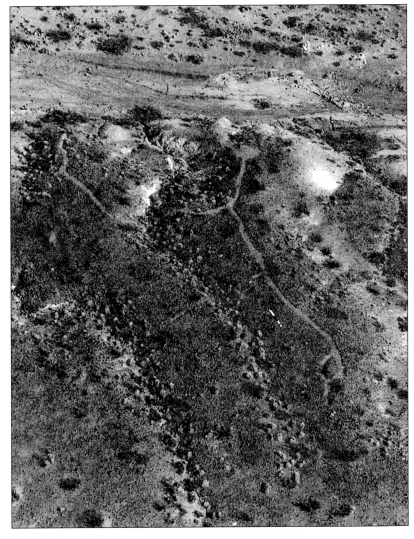

Figure 17.9. Aerial view of the Las Vegas Wash intaglio, near Clark County Wetlands Park.

Euro-Americans arrived. We find bits of their brown ware pottery dating back to about 1200. By the early 1800s Paiute people had access to manufactured goods, including glass trade beads, ammunition, and guns. They used imported glass and metal objects to make traditional arrowheads. Anthropologist Isabel Kelly interviewed Southern Paiute people who lived in the Las Vegas Valley in the 1930s. Their accounts provided details of their ancestors' lives extending back into the mid-1800s. They described farm plots adjacent to, and watered from, some of the valley's important springs. The accounts even gave the names of some of the people who owned the springs. A radiocarbon date of 1430 to 1620 CE on corn pollen collected from a pit at the Larder site shows that people stored corn there in the early Paiute period, before Euro-Americans arrived.

Who, then, were the people who lived along the south-central edge of the Great Basin? The archaeological records from two areas in southern Nevada back different answers. Virgin Branch people, participants in the Southwestern Puebloan culture, seem to have used the Moapa and Virgin River valleys for a thousand years. The story of the Las Vegas Valley, on the other hand, seems to involve the histories of several neighboring peoples. A definite ending to that story is not yet in our grasp.

Richard V.N. Ahlstrom joined HRA, Inc., Conservation Archaeology in Las Vegas, Nevada, in 1999, after 25 years of working in archaeology and dendrochronology in the American Southwest. Heidi Roberts founded HRA, Inc., Conservation Archaeology in 1998. She has worked in contract archaeology throughout the western United States since 1979.

Other evidence of some relationship between Las Vegas Valley people and Patayan-Mojaves is a trail system linked to a 40-foot-long intaglio, or ground figure. The Las Vegas Wash intaglio is a humanlike figure scraped into the surface of the desert soil (fig. 17.9). Intaglios are relatively common along the lower Colorado River, where they are associated with the ancestors of the modern-day Mojave Indians and, farther south, with other Yuman-speaking peoples. Did visiting ancestral Mojaves create the Las Vegas Wash intaglio, or did local people borrow this art form from their neighbors?

Finally, we know that Southern Paiute people were living in the Las Vegas Valley when the first

Figure 18.1. Human figure with bow and arrow and bighorn sheep, Long Lake area, southeastern Oregon.

Rock Art in the Western Great Basin

eighteen

Alanah Woody and Angus Quinlan

Rock art is a familiar but enigmatic trace of ancient people in much of the Great Basin, one that fascinates those who see it and sparks much debate among scholars. Rock art glyphs are easy to identify but difficult for modern-day people to understand. Native people in the Great Basin made rock art and incorporated it into their social practices for perhaps as long as 10,000 years. Their art included visually arresting figures and motifs such as naturalistic depictions of bighorn sheep apparently being hunted (fig. 18.1). Such images appeal to modern viewers because they seem to show actual scenes of daily life. Other figures and motifs are more mysterious to viewers today (figs. 18.2, 18.3).

However we interpret it, rock art remains in the place where its makers intended for people to see and interact with it. For this reason, few viewers

can escape a sense of place and the sweep of human history when looking at rock art in its natural setting. What can we make of this ancient art form?

First, what exactly is it? Rock art is the general name for markings people made on landscape features such as boulders, cliff faces, and cave walls and ceilings. Although rock art can be made in a variety of ways, in the Great Basin it was done by engraving, pecking, abrading, or scratching the rock surfaces, which produced images now known as petroglyphs, or by painting on a rocky surface using mineral pigments, which produced what researchers call pictographs. Petroglyphs are seen far more commonly than pictographs in the western and central Great Basin, because they are more likely to have

Figure 18.2. Motifs on boulder, Dry Lake area, northern Nevada. The heavier patination on the motifs on the left side indicate greater age.

Figure 18.3. Representational and abstract rock art figures, Long Lake area, southeastern Oregon.

survived in open environments exposed to the elements. Pictographs tend to be found in caves, rockshelters, and other protected places. The questions that both public viewers and archaeologists ask about rock art are three: When was it made, who made it, and why was it made?

Dating Rock Art

Knowing when people created a panel of rock art is an important starting point for understanding it. But rock art is notoriously difficult to date. Although some scientific methods exist for dating pictographs, they have not been widely applied in the Great Basin because they are expensive and require removing pigment samples from the image. Petroglyphs currently cannot be directly dated at all. Instead, most estimates of the ages of rock art are based on relative dating methods.

Figure 18.4. Abstract figures on boulder, Lagomarsino Canyon, northwestern Nevada. Petroglyph figures and elements occur on many of the talus slope boulders and all along the rim of the canyon, at the top of the picture.

Sometimes the relative dates of rock art are revealed by the artists' having placed new motifs directly on top of older ones. Perhaps this was one way people connected themselves to the past. Occasionally this superpositioning obliterated older motifs or figures, possibly to cancel their power or meaning. Of course people might also have reused rock art sites without making new figures or modifying older ones. Studying the archaeological remains found around the sites may be the only way to discern their continued use over time.

Another clue to relative dates is the degree to which rock art images have been darkened by "desert varnish," the patina that forms on rocks long exposed to air and water. Because rock art is so visible in the cultural landscape, people reused and reinterpreted it long after it was first made. They enhanced, modified, or otherwise reworked some

rock art panels, and the newer figures and motifs appear much lighter and fresher than older ones (fig. 18.2).

Estimating the age of rock art from its contents or style can be deceptive and generally results only in broad guesses. Some researchers, for example, think an apparent elephant motif in the Black Rock Desert in northwestern Nevada portrays a mammoth. But the image could be a historic representation of circus elephants observed on the nearby railroad. Even when the interpretation of an image is uncontroversial, it may offer only an "earliest" date for the rock art. For instance, we know that bows and arrows replaced atlatls some 1,500 to 2,000 years ago, so depictions of bows and arrows had to have been made after that time. We seldom know for certain how long after.

Styles of Great Basin rock art are defined by the way the images were made and the types of motifs or themes represented. The oldest style, widespread across North America and around the world, is believed to be the "pit-and-groove" style, more commonly known as cupules. Cupules are circular

Figure 18.5 Petroglyph in the carved abstract style, Long Lake area, southeastern Oregon. Note the heavy patination at upper left. The petroglyph was partly reworked at a later time with additional motifs.

Figure 18.6. Petroglyphs in the carved abstract style, Winnemucca Lake area, northwestern Nevada.

depressions, usually 1 to 2 inches wide and deep, made on boulders, apparently in random patterns. Their great antiquity is apparent at the Grimes Point site in western Nevada. The cupules made on basalt boulders there have been completely revarnished and are now indistinguishable from the rock's natural patina. They may 8,000 years old or more.

Another of the oldest known styles is the Great Basin carved abstract style. First defined by Mary Ricks and William J. Cannon at the Long Lake site in southeastern Oregon, this style is found only at sites in southern Oregon and northwestern Nevada (figs. 18.5, 18.6). It is distinguished by deeply engraved motifs in which wide lines create intricate, tightly packed designs. We know the style is at least 7,600 years old because at the Long Lake site a panel with carved abstract designs was covered with ash from the eruption of Mount Mazama.

The most common styles in the western Great Basin are rectilinear and curvilinear abstract styles collectively called the Basin and Range Tradition. The carved abstract style is a variant of this tradition. The curvilinear style features individual circles, concentric circles, connected circles, and meandering lines. The rectilinear style is composed of rows of dots, grids, rectangles, squares, triangles, lines, and cross-hatching.

The rectilinear and curvilinear styles frequently appear in the same places throughout the region, often in association with other styles. Sites displaying fine examples include the Lagomarsino Canyon petroglyph site in western Nevada (fig. 18.7, plates 17, 18) and the Grapevine Canyon and Sloan Canyon petroglyph sites in southern Nevada. It is difficult to date Basin and Range Tradition styles, but they span perhaps 10,000 years, from early Paleoarchaic until recent times. We know that the tradition covers a very long time because panels exhibit different degrees of varnishing, from complete repatination to none at all.

Many researchers believe that another type of petroglyph, the incised or "scratched" style, was made in relatively recent times, because few examples show much revarnishing, if any. The makers used sharp stone tools to incise lines in the form of dense cross-hatching, squares, rectangles, and circles with lines radiating from them. The style is scattered throughout the Great Basin but rarely dominates at any single site. Researchers think it

Figure 18.7. Petroglyphs in the curvilinear abstract style, Lagomarsino Canyon, northwestern Nevada.

dates from perhaps 1,000 years ago to historic times, but some examples could be as old as 3,000 years. Robert Bettinger and Martin Baumhoff have suggested that Numic peoples migrating into the Great Basin made scratched-style rock art to obliterate older rock art made by preceding groups.

Representational rock art in the Great Basin includes depictions of people (anthropomorphs) and animals (zoomorphs). The simplest examples are schematic human "stick figures" and naturalistic animals. These often appear together with abstract petroglyphs and represent local treatments of widespread symbolic themes. We find naturalistic representations of bighorn sheep, for example, throughout the Great Basin. They are most abundant at sites in the Colorado River drainage and the eastern Great Basin and in the spectacular rock art complex of the Coso Range of eastern California.

Indeed, a distinct style has been defined for

Figure 18.8. Bighorn sheep panel, Coso Range, southeastern California.

the Coso Range. Representational forms predominate there, although abstract elements are present. Researchers have recorded several thousand finely executed bighorn sheep, some of them life-size with boat-shaped bodies (fig. 18.8). Elaborate anthropomorphs display patterned bodies and wear elaborate headgear or hairstyles (fig. 18.9). They seem to depict clothed people, perhaps ritual or social leaders

Figure 18.9. Human figures with patterned bodies, Coso Range, southeastern California.

Figure 18.10. Pahranagat-style figures, Pahranagat Valley, southeastern Nevada. "Patterned-body" figures can be seen on the left, with a bighorn sheep between them; the element to the right of the upper figure may represent an atlatl. A Pahranagat figure with four-fingered hands is in the lower center.

wearing regalia. Some Coso-style figures may be as much as 9,000 years old, but most of them probably date between about 3,000 and 500 years ago.

A distinctive style of anthropomorphs charac-

terizes the Pahranagat Lake area and the adjacent Mount Irish Archaeological District in eastern Nevada. The Pahranagat style encompasses two types of anthropomorphs: patterned-body figures and "Pahranagat" figures (fig. 18.10). The patterned-body figures are generally rectangles with a fringe at the bottom between two stick legs. They have no heads but do have short arms that sometimes hold something resembling an atlatl. The rectangular bodies have internal geometric designs. Pahranagat figures are either rectangular or oval and have large eyes; sometimes vertical lines protrude from the heads. The two types of figures often appear together, along with other representational forms, principally bighorn sheep. They probably date from 1,500 to about 200 years ago.

What Does It Mean?

What do the enigmatic rock art panels, motifs, and figures mean, and why did people make them? One answer is that ancient people were trying to enlist magical aid to ensure success in the hunt, increase the numbers of game animals and other resources, or symbolically manage prized or feared animals. Scholars used this explanation, known as the hunting-magic theory, throughout the twentieth century to interpret the art in European Upper Paleolithic caves, which date from 35,000 to about 12,000 years ago. In the 1960s Robert Heizer and Martin Baumhoff adopted it as an explanation for Great Basin rock art.

In this view, representations of bighorn sheep and deer portray the game animals that hunters most desired. By making pictures of the animals, hunters could exert some kind of magical control over them. Heizer and Baumhoff thought scenes of people hunting animals either depicted actual hunts or were made as magical exercises to ensure the success of the hunt by portraying the desired outcome. They also noted that many Great Basin rock art sites lie along game trails, in good places for ambushes, and near other hunting-related features such as hunting blinds and projectile points.

One problem with the hunting-magic explanation is that it cannot account for the many rock art sites that have no animals or hunting scenes. In the western Great Basin, abstract Basin and Range Tradition motifs dominate most sites, and in the eastern part anthropomorphs are most prominent. Also, many rock art sites are near the remains of domestic camps—house rings and tools used for processing plants and seeds—which implies that women as well as men made and used rock art.

Other scholars have offered alternative explanations. Since the 1970s some researchers have interpreted Great Basin rock art in terms of sham-anistic practices (see chapter 19). David Whitley, for example, has advanced shamanistic theory to interpret geometric and other abstract motifs in western Great Basin rock art as representations of mental imagery that we all potentially experience during sleep or by rubbing our eyes, as well as in trance states. He believes representational images to be figurative compositions that express univer-sal shamanistic themes. In some parts of the world shamans liken entering a trance to dying because they are "dead" to the mundane world during trance. Accordingly, rock art motifs of hunters killing bighorn sheep would be not hunting scenes but visual metaphors of trance, because they portray death.

Whitley considers the Coso Range patterned-body anthropomorphs to be representations of shamans wearing clothing decorated with the geometric images they experienced during trance and that were the sources of their supernatural power. Bighorn sheep images in the Coso Range and else-

Figure 18.11. Eugene Hattori (left) and David Turner recording a large petroglyph site in Meadow Valley Wash, southwestern Nevada, in 1967.

where in the Great Basin might be the spirit helpers of rain shamans.

Both the hunting-magic and shamanistic interpretations may, in many instances, tell us more about the theoretical preferences of modern interpreters than about the beliefs of people in the past. When we consider the landscape settings of all known rock art sites in the Great Basin, any single interpretation seems unlikely. Some might have been vision-quest places; others, along game trails and near hunting blinds, could have been hunting related. Others, in direct association with house rings, middens, and food processing tools, might have been visible to many people as they went about their daily routines, rather than having been solely the preserve of shamans or hunters.

The multiplicity of possibilities is not unusual. In archaeology it is rare for individual artifacts to answer many questions. Rather, the contexts in which they are found and their associations with other artifacts and landscapes provide a better understanding of their purposes, intended audiences, and uses. For rock art such uses could have

been shamanistic or related to hunting or food collecting. Rock art panels might have depicted domestic activities, marked trail routes, signaled social or ethnic differences and territorial boundaries, or been simply "art for art's sake," even doodling. People might have used individual sites for several such purposes and for others that we cannot yet fathom.

Rock art is an enduring and widespread form of human cultural expression, one that fascinates modern viewers. It is of great significance to contemporary Great Basin Indian peoples, who continue to connect with their past and maintain their relationships with the places and landscapes of their ancestors. The striking visual images seem

to have played important roles in the lives of past peoples. Although today we can only dimly apprehend their original cultural significance and possible meanings, rock art images still exert the power to provoke novel rereadings.

The late Alanah Woody received her bachelor's and master's degrees from the University of Nevada, Reno, and her doctorate from the University of Southampton. At the time of her death in July 2007 she was the founding executive director of the Nevada Rock Art Foundation. Angus Quinlan holds a doctorate in anthropology from the University of Southampton and is executive director of the Nevada Rock Art Foundation.

Figure 19.1. Ghostly human forms in the Barrier Canyon style appear to encircle a central figure about 6 feet tall. The ethereal appearance of the large figure was achieved by applying the paint with a spraying technique. Great Gallery, Horseshoe (Barrier) Canyon.

Shamans, Shields, and Stories on Stone

nineteen

Polly Schaafsma

East of the Wasatch Range, deep gorges slice the Colorado Plateau, cutting their way to the Green and Colorado Rivers. For almost as long as people have called this rugged landscape home, the canyon walls of colorful sandstones have served as a medium on which they inscribed and painted images that derived from and sustained their mythologies, stories, and religious rites. Today this rock art provides insights into a past for which material remains are often scant. But as the rock art indicates, the abstract and mental dimensions of these human lives were spiritually rich and complex. Much of the imagery is best explained as the work of shamans, a tradition that was long-lived, probably spanning thousands of years.

The Barrier Canyon Style

Rock art classified under the rubric Barrier Canyon style is one of the predominant styles in the canyons and uplands of present-day eastern Utah. Most examples are painted pictographs, but we also find incised petroglyphs. The Barrier Canyon style features large anthropomorphic figures (fig. 19.1) that dominate integrated scenes with bighorn sheep, birds, snakes, and other animals. Entities with no natural counterparts also appear in these scenes (plate 10).

Rendered in a variety of painting techniques, the abstracted, ghostlike human forms, commonly portrayed in large groups, evoke a sense of awe. These human silhouettes, often lacking arms and legs, imply associations with the supernatural realm—they appear to be either shamans fixed in trance or in some cases possibly deities. The figures are typically painted in red and are sometimes larger than life-size. Details often include large eyes, thin antennae-like headgear, a "crown" of white dots, and torsos divided into panels or textured with dot patterns or with painted or incised lines (plate 14).

Snakes are commonly featured within the body, alongside a figure, or held in a hand if a hand is shown. Curly-tailed dogs sometimes attend the human shapes. In many cases tiny, finely painted renderings of bighorn sheep approach the figures, or birds perch on their shoulders or flutter around their heads. One site pictures dragonflies (fig. 19.2).

Figure 19.2. Anthropomorphic beings with animal spirit helpers and a possible transformation scene attended by dragonflies. Green River drainage.

We can infer that the human figures and the associated life forms, including plants, might be spirit helpers and were in some kind of close communication. At some sites human figures with arms and legs in active poses join the static anthropomorphic forms, but even these humans with limbs may be transforming into birds, serpents, and plants. In a few instances roots grow from the feet. Such transformational figures appear to be part of a ceremony or shamanic ritual (fig. 19.3).

Researchers think the painters of these compelling scenes were shamans and associated ritual participants. Shamans would have been important members of the small bands of hunter-gathers who made seasonal rounds to glean their living from the canyons and nearby uplands. Among such peoples it is commonly the shaman's responsibility to cure the sick, restore harmony, foster success in the hunt, and control the weather, thus ensuring some control over a group's destiny. Shamans in all cultures acquire their power through journeys to a supernatural realm, and it is the shaman on his journey, aided by spirit helpers, who seems to be pictured in much eastern Great Basin rock art. Painting on stone may have been a shaman's means of validating such journeys and communicating the experience to a wider group, including initiates. As Peter Furst notes, "performance, verbal and theatrical, is everywhere a vital aspect of shamanism." He adds that dramatization of the sacred includes the visual arts. This model of the shaman-artist provides one plausible interpretation for nearly all the elements in the Barrier Canyon style, a rock art style for which no specific ethnographic information exists today. No living descendants of the people who made it exist to guide us in interpreting it. These paintings clearly show the perception of unity with all life that universally underlies shamanic practices.

In recent years researchers have made several attempts to secure radiocarbon dates on organic pigments from Barrier Canyon–style paintings. So far the reliability of this dating method is open to question, but the varied results are interesting. Sites in Horseshoe (also known as Barrier) and Black Dragon Canyons have yielded early Archaic dates of 8,650 and 8,500 years ago. In contrast, a Salt Creek

Figure 19.3. A Barrier Canyon–style composition in which two figures border a central, highly abstracted human form. The figure on the left holds a plant, and roots grow from its feet. San Rafael Reef.

site in Canyonlands National Park produced middle Archaic dates of about 2,700 years ago. Archaeologists think people made the Salt Creek figures between about 1900 BCE and 300 CE. Yet until the results of radiocarbon dating of these paintings can be better evaluated, no certainty exists. Stylistic considerations support both time frames.

Some likenesses in form and body decoration between Barrier Canyon–style paintings and clay figurines excavated from the Cowboy Cave and Sudden Shelter sites in central Utah favor the early dates. The figurines came from layers dating to around 6,300 years ago. On the other hand, similarities between Barrier Canyon–style and later Fremont art in the region are more easily explained if some kind of chronological and cultural continuity existed between them.

We do not know how long the Barrier Canyon style lasted, but cultural change was slow during Archaic times, and long-term continuity was the norm. This rock art tradition and the ideology and beliefs that gave rise to it may have been stable over several millennia. Such stability might account for the variation in the radiocarbon dates as well as the stylistic relationships on either end of the time spectrum.

Fremont Rock Art

The later Fremont people of Utah probably made another category of rock art featuring large human figures (fig. 19.4). As Joel Janetski points out in chapter 14, archaeologists differ over what defines "Fremont" in an archaeological or cultural sense. Unlike the contemporaneous ancestral Pueblo remains to the south, which are relatively uniform,

Figure 19.4. Broad-shouldered Fremont figures with splayed fingers, wearing (right) an elaborate necklace and (left) a bandoleer. Range Creek Canyon, Utah.

Visiting Great Basin Rock Art Sites on Public Land

The 1979 Archaeological Resources Protection Act attempts to keep the locations of many rock art sites on federal land concealed, to protect them from vandalism. But federal and state agencies have developed and interpreted some important rock art sites for the public to visit. These include the spectacular panels in Horseshoe (Barrier) Canyon in Canyonlands National Park; the numerous galleries in Nine Mile Canyon, Utah; specific groups of panels in Buckhorn Wash in the San Rafael Swell area of Utah; the Fremont Petroglyphs in Capitol Reef National Park; the Fremont Indian State Park in Utah; the Parowan Gap Petroglyphs in Utah; the Grimes Point, Hickison Summit, Mount Irish, Valley of Fire State Park, and Sloan Canyon sites in Nevada; and the Coso Range petroglyphs in California. Besides those listed, some federal and state recreation areas have rock art panels that the public can view.

The easiest way to find information about Great Basin rock art sites that you can visit is to check federal and state government Internet sites. Some of the most useful as listed here.

- National Park Service parks, monuments, and recreation areas: www.nps.gov
- US Bureau of Land Management for Nevada and Utah: www.nv.blm.gov; www.ut.bl.gov/Recreation
- US Forest Service Intermountain Region: www.fs.fed.us/r4/
- Utah State Parks: www.stateparks.utah.gov; www.utah.com/State Parks/
- Nevada State Parks: www.parks.nv.gov; www.travelnevada.com
- Coso Range petroglyphs: These are on the US Naval Weapons Center, China Lake facility; tours can be arranged through the Matrango Museum in Ridgecrest, California (www.matrango.org).

When you go, remember the cardinal rule of visiting all archaeological sites, and particularly rock art sites: Look, appreciate, and take pictures, but do not touch!

Figure 19.5. Imposing classic Fremont figures wearing heavy necklaces. One holds a head trophy. Northeastern Utah.

Fremont culture is composed of a patchwork of components that might or might not resemble each other all across Fremont territory. Date estimates vary regionally, but a range roughly between 100 and 1350 CE is generally accepted.

One of the more stable components of things Fremont is its rock art, in which the hallmark is again a dominating human figure—but now rather angular and commonly shown with arms and legs, as well as often horned and wearing an elaborate necklace. This anthropomorph is widespread throughout the northern Colorado Plateau, through the Clear Creek drainage in the Wasatch Plateau, and as far west as eastern Nevada. Across this territory, local Fremont people used different styles of architecture and pottery and different subsistence strategies. The common element is the Fremont anthropomorphic figure. Its easily recognized attributes suggest an ideological link among these far-flung groups, as well as cultural conservatism among Fremont people over roughly 1,200 years.

In some cases, stylistic similarities between

Barrier Canyon–style figures and Fremont figures dating from about 500 to 1300 CE suggest that either the Fremont people were continuing an earlier tradition (implying that late dates for at least some of the Barrier Canyon–style art are correct) or that Fremont artists were heavily influenced by the older images they saw in their surroundings. In general, however, Fremont anthropomorphs are readily distinguishable from earlier forms. Also, the subject emphasis is not a shamanic journey but often explicitly the hunt or, in the Uinta Basin region, human conflict. We can infer from this change in focus that Fremont rock art fulfilled a function different from that of Barrier Canyon rock art.

In Dry Fork Valley in the Uinta Basin, seemingly celebratory scenes feature large, commanding, broad-shouldered human figures standing in lines across cliff faces (fig. 19.5). Many are elegantly bedecked with towering headdresses. They also wear large, circular earrings—also called "earbobs" —heavy yokes or stone necklaces, beaded girdles or belts, and fringed breechclouts. Some of these fig-

Figure 19.6. Fremont figures with feathered headgear and fancy, multistrand necklaces. Lines fall from their eyes, which are indicated as mere slits. Capitol Reef National Park.

ures hold human trophy heads or scalps in their hands. The protagonists and the heads they carry may display similar facial features, suggesting a ritual identity between them. Staffs and shields are among their other accoutrements. Larry Loendorf reports that one less elaborate shield-bearing warrior was radiocarbon dated to between 750 and 850 CE.

Farther south these paragons of power are less imposing, although they may retain much of the same attire (fig. 19.6). To the north of the Dry Fork Valley area, hunting scenes replace the trophy bearers, with bighorn sheep featured prominently and hunted with bows and arrows. Some of the horned anthropomorphs in these scenes may depict hunt shamans empowered in their horned headgear. On the Tavaputs Plateau and in Nine Mile Canyon the typical Fremont human figure

wears a tall headdress of deer or elk antlers. Some figures wear plain curved horns that are less easily associated with any particular game animal, although researchers have suggested that they might be bison horns. In some cases the figures boast tall feathers. These figures have heads but may or may not have facial features. They wear earbobs, a variety of necklaces, bandoleers, garments that resemble kilts or skirts, and sometimes beaded girdles. Human figures with arms and legs as well as some without (resembling clay figurines from the Fremont region) also appear.

Bighorn sheep and snakes with sheeplike horns and ears appear in these panels along with the human figures. But except in hunting scenes and the famous Cottonwood Canyon scene, which depicts a horned shaman among bighorn sheep (fig. 19.7), animals and human figures seldom engage explicitly with one another. Other elements include zigzags, rainbows, lines of triangles, spirals, and rows of dots. Gridlike designs may represent hunting nets. In Nine Mile Canyon, rock art occurs in the vicinity of habitation and storage sites dating between 1000 and 1300 CE.

A variant on the Fremont anthropomorph theme is the "faces" motif found in the Canyonlands region (plate 13). These are paintings of human forms ranging from single figures to sets of as many as 13. Researchers have found these sequences alongside ancestral Pueblo storage units, together with Pueblo pottery types. Puebloan archaeological remains in this area represent seasonal use of the canyons between about 900 and 1200 CE. For this reason, some writers have described the rock art panels as ancestral Pueblo. I find this attribution problematic on several counts.

The human figures in these panels are large scale and share most of their significant features with other Fremont rock art anthropomorphs throughout the San Rafael region, as well as with the famous Pillings clay figurines from Range Creek (chapters 14, 15). Similar figurines come from the Old Woman site in south-central Utah. Both Range Creek and the Old Woman site are some distance from Canyonlands. The figurines

Figure 19.7. Hunt scene showing a horned shaman near the center of the top row of animals. The figures in this composition are joined by lines in a nearly unbroken sequence that suggests a metaphysical continuity between them. Cottonwood Canyon in Nine Mile Canyon, eastern Utah.

have large, well-defined heads with facial features, hair tied in thick "bobs" on each side of the face below a rounded chin, a variety of heavy necklaces, kilts or skirts, and beaded girdles at the waist. Some of the rock art faces motifs have feather headdresses in addition and, more rarely, bandoleers. Human figures pictured in indisputably ancestral Pueblo territory do not have these attributes.

That the faces motifs are Fremont in every detail poses fascinating questions. If the same seasonal farmers who constructed the nearby rooms and granaries painted them, then we are looking at the remains of a people not confined to a single cultural box, so to speak. They might have combined Puebloan and Fremont practices. David Madsen has urged Fremont researchers to look for more "elastic," unbounded social environments, recognizing that there is a great deal of regional variation within the Fremont region.

We also know that Fremont and ancestral Pueblo people lived in rockshelter sites in the Escalante River drainage just west of the Canyonlands area at different times. Evidence for the time difference comes from radiocarbon dating of the distinct forms of corn grown by the two peoples. The Fremont corn is earlier. Thus the Canyonlands figures could easily be Fremont in origin, the other features having been left by later Puebloan people. Whoever made the paintings subscribed to an ideological framework that had its origin in Fremont and not in Puebloan culture.

More Rock Art

Besides the dramatic imagery of the Barrier Canyon and Fremont rock art styles, we find a wealth of other inscribed and painted motifs in the eastern Great Basin that is more difficult to categorize in terms of cultural origins and dates. Some petroglyph panels in Desolation Canyon of the Green River contain few diagnostic figure types and display layers of graphics that seem to defy chronological ordering. Among them are square-bodied anthropomorphs with a fringed baseline, interior decoration, and short, horizontal arms terminating in splayed fingers (fig. 19.8). They relate more closely to a style of rock art, found in Wyoming,

Figure 19.8. A palimpsest of petroglyphs in Desolation Canyon on the Green River, Utah. The rectangular human figures higher up in the panel share features with those of interior-line-style rock art in Wyoming.

called "interior line," than to Barrier Canyon–style figures. Their estimated dates range from 1 to 1000 CE. Hunting and gathering bands ethnically distinct from and later in time than the makers of Barrier Canyon–style paintings seem to have executed these petroglyphs.

Much more recently, historic Ute people, who today live on reservations in the region, also left their records on stone in both eastern Utah and western Colorado. Their rock art often reflects elements of Euro-American cultures (fig. 19.9). Traditional mythic or religious symbolism features bears, bear tracks, and even bear shamans, but more common are panels that incorporate items valued historically as self-promotional, such as horses, shields, and even portraits. Loosely defined narrative scenes depict people on the move or engaged in conflicts. At the same time, some of the panels include copies of older figure types, a prac-

tice that probably happened in earlier times as well.

The walls of the canyons of the eastern reaches of the archaeological Great Basin have encoded on them motifs depicting millennia of beliefs and the religious and cultural practices of the varied groups who lived there. Through the fragmentary remains of their campsites, tools, houses, and granaries we can trace how and where the people lived and even what they ate. But among all their remains, their tantalizing carvings and paintings on stone provide the clearest insights into their minds and into the cosmological milieus that framed their perceptions and their daily existence.

Polly Schaafsma is a research associate at the Museum of Indian Arts and Culture/Laboratory of Anthropology in Santa Fe, New Mexico. *Indian Rock Art of the Southwest*, *The Rock Art of Utah*, and *New Perspectives on Pottery Mound Pueblo* are among her many publications.

Figure 19.9. Ute petroglyphs of horses and riders, a bison, and a person carrying a shield and spear. Capitol Reef National Park.

Rediscovering and Appreciating Ancient Knowledge

Twenty

David Hurst Thomas

First-time visitors often perceive the Great Basin as a vast sagebrush sea, a monotonous and barren landscape separating the Sierra Nevada from the Rocky Mountains. As Don Fowler noted in the 1970s, the Great Basin has long suffered from this "view from" syndrome—persistent and unfavorable comparisons to allegedly better places elsewhere.

A transplanted Scotsman named John Muir, for instance, warned future travelers in 1878 about the disappointing landscape to the east of his beloved Sierra Nevada: "From the very noblest forests in the world [one] emerges into free sunshine and dead alkaline levels. Mountains are seen beyond…[but] these always present a singular barren aspect, gray and forbidding and shadeless, like heaps of ashes dumped from the sky." Pretty grim stuff, but Muir was hardly alone. Southwestern archaeologists long followed the lead of A. V. Kidder, who once called Utah a land of "low adobe mounds…and minor antiquities" and dismissed the Great Basin as the "northern periphery" of the ancient Puebloan world.

The contributors to this book suggest another view. Let's drop the California-colored glasses and the Southwestern Puebloan perspectives, they advise, and view the Great Basin for what it really is—not what it isn't.

The most important theme permeating these chapters is a deep appreciation for what the late Margaret Wheat called the "survival arts" of Great Basin people, the old ways as passed down for countless generations. Steve Simms, for example, eloquently conveys the affection and insight still attached to the high desert by those reared there,

whose ancestors knew the Great Basin as their only home. These subtle survival skills—from setting a deadfall and running a trout line in desert waters to chain-linking a hundred rabbit skins into a winter blanket—are reflected in every aspect of the archaeological record the ancestors left behind.

Great Basin people were not "cave dwellers" in any sense of the term, but they long used caves and rockshelters to their advantage. As prominent and easy-to-relocate features on the enduring desert landscape, caves have always offered shelter in a storm and a place to store things for the future. Great Basin caves were often decorated with pictographs and petroglyphs, rock art reflecting their special spiritual significance as well.

Sheltered caves, dry and relatively cool, can preserve perishable and fragile artifacts for thousands of years, an important fact for ancient people and archaeologists alike. This is exactly what happened at Hidden Cave, overlooking the Carson Sink, where we found dozens of ancient cache pits, many of them unopened for millennia. Thousands of artifacts had been stored there—unbroken obsidian spear points, traps for snaring rodents, basketry-making tools, grinding stones, fishhooks, digging sticks, and fire-making apparatus. Archaeologists call such artifacts "passive," in the sense that they were not left in place in the course of daily use. Most modern-day attics and garages contain dozens of passive artifacts—the skis used last February, the fly rod ready for opening day, the stadium blanket from last fall's football game. Because passive gear is used only seasonally, it must be cared for and stored away at times, always ready to return to active duty. Usually, the more seasonally variable the environment, and the more ancient people moved around during the year, the greater the proportion of their implements they carefully stored until needed. The ancient people of the Carson Sink also stashed away food in anticipation of future need, mostly seasonally available resources including pine nuts, dried fish, seeds of Indian rice grass, and cattail pollen. The caches of Hidden Cave reflect an obsession with planning, part of the subtle survival skills that permeated the old way.

Archaeologists have long studied passive artifacts collected from cache caves, but dating them has been problematic. With the advent of the AMS technique for radiocarbon dating, Great Basin archaeologists can now obtain "direct" dates on tiny fragments of baskets, sandals, and wooden tools found in the dry caves. The extraordinary woven fiber bag from Spirit Cave that Catherine Fowler and Eugene Hattori discuss in chapter 8 is now known to have been made more than 10,600 years ago. The Spirit Cave environment preserved masterpieces like this for millennia, even though the skills that created them vanished long ago.

Some of the maker's knowledge can now be recovered. Adopting a weaver's perspective, Fowler and Hattori have painstakingly reconstructed the way the raw materials must have been collected and the way the weaver tied the elements together, integrating brown and white duck feathers into diagonal decorative lines. Hands-on experimentation with reproducing the large bulrush mats from Spirit Cave demonstrates the near impossibility of simultaneously manipulating the more than 700 bulrush stems. The details of this ancient technology remain to be rediscovered, but they suggest that an upright frame loom was required to keep the materials in order and the stitching tight. This is a solution weavers have reached many times in many places in the world.

Hiding valuables in a cave seems an obvious survival strategy. But my archaeological surveys and excavations in the Toquima, Toiyabe, and Monitor Ranges of central Nevada suggest that ancient people's choices of caves and rockshelters in the Great Basin were subtler than they first appear. People deliberately chose south-facing caves and rockshelters for their short-term camps, reflecting, I believe, a purposeful understanding of passive solar heating principles. East- and especially west-facing shelters are unbearably hot in summer, and caves in north-facing cliffs remain dank all day. But in relatively shallow, south-facing rockshelters, the high arc of the summertime sun creates ample patches of shade along the rear of the overhanging cliff walls. In winter the low solar angle directs sunshine onto the rear of a south-facing shelter, storing solar radiation in the naturally insulated cave walls during the daytime and releasing it at night.

In other words, a rockshelter with a southern exposure receives more solar energy when air temperatures are cool and considerably less when the ambient temperature is high. The bedrock surrounding the south-facing shelter functions as a latent heat sink, absorbing solar energy during the hot summer months and releasing stored heat with the onset of winter weather. Understanding these basics of passive solar gain, Great Basin people used upland caves and rockshelters to buffer the extremes of hot summers, cold winters, and daily temperature shifts.

For decades Great Basin archaeology was pretty much cave archaeology: Lovelock Cave, Fort Rock Cave, Danger Cave. And why not? The caves were easy to find and the payoff was big. As the chapters by Mel Aikens, Bryan Hockett, Ted Goebel, and Kelly Graf clearly demonstrate, caves still contribute critical knowledge about the ancient desert West—witness the important ongoing excavations at Bonneville Estates Rockshelter. But caves tell only part of the story, and archaeologists in recent decades have developed more systematic approaches

to exploring the outdoor archaeological record of the desert West.

We now recognize that the nearly 200 diverse desert valleys of the Basin and Range province contain important dwelling and special use sites with evidence quite different from that uncovered in caves. David Madsen and Robert Kelly, for instance, describe the marshside settlements that figured so prominently in the lives of desert people, sometimes as year-round villages and sometimes as places for seasonal stopovers integrated with trips to the mountains for piñon nuts, bighorn sheep, and other upland resources. Robert Elston writes about the Tosawihi quarries, where for 10,000 years flint knappers mined high-quality white chert for tools and trade. Western Shoshone people still return to Tosawihi, a sacred site providing not just tool stone but also red and white mineral pigments used as medicine and ornamentation.

Exploration of the Great Basin uplands lagged far behind the exploration of caves and valley floors, perhaps because most of us felt, at least tacitly, that "if I don't want to climb that mountain, then neither did ancient people." We were wrong. When archaeological teams finally began systematically searching the alpine reaches of the Great Basin, they immediately came upon a rich record of high-altitude hunting spanning 5,000 years—hunting blinds, rock cairns, and thousands of spent projectile points lost in the pursuit of bighorn sheep and the occasional pronghorn.

Robert Bettinger, in chapter 12, describes his startling discovery of several alpine villages at extreme elevation in the White Mountains and discusses my own archaeological research at Alta Toquima, a habitation site with 31 rock house foundations at 11,000 feet, overlooking Monitor Valley. People's having situated these remote, isolated villages at such height differs radically from known historic practices, and so far the villages appear to be unique in the Great Basin. Although we are still struggling to understand their meaning, there are some clues.

At a minimum the alpine villages underscore the importance of seasonality and verticality as components of Great Basin survival strategies. All Great Basin people understood the importance of being in the right place at the right time of year. To harvest piñon nuts they had to be in the piñon-juniper woodland in the fall; to gather fresh cattail shoots they had to be in the marshes in springtime; to catch spawning cutthroat trout and cui-ui they had to be alongside the Truckee River in late April or early May. For millennia, monitoring the when and where of subsistence was the most important survival strategy of all.

The alpine tundra is just another kind of desert, but it requires a special set of skills to make a living there. People knew that the verticality of the Great Basin landscape constituted another element in timing the seasons. Within a relatively short walking distance, it was literally possible to follow the progress of the seasons up and down the mountain slopes. Wildflowers and edible roots appear in the low desert in April. By early June they are growing on the lower mountain slopes and in the canyons. Springtime comes late to the high country, in late June or so, and so do the wildflowers and the root plants. On the mountaintops, summer is generally restricted to July, and fall arrives in early September. One must retreat or risk being caught when early snow blocks the best routes of access. But on their way back to the lowlands, alpine visitors knew they could harvest fall-ripening plants as they moved downhill. Although alpine seasonality is compressed, rapid, and unforgiving, the verticality of the landscape offered people a unique way of spreading out their seasonal harvests

The alpine villages also pose serious questions about climate change. Were these high-elevation settlements a survival response to extreme drought? Several of the contributors, including David Madsen, Robert Kelly, Donald Grayson, and David Rhode, have detailed the evidence pointing to tremendous environmental changes during the human tenure in the Great Basin. The "bathtub rings" around lake margins document environmental change on a biblical scale. Relic tree lines in the White Mountains show that bristlecone pines once lived at much higher elevations than they do now. Tree stumps submerged beneath Lake Tahoe and Fallen Leaf Lake reflect much drier times and lower lake levels. Bone and plant remains from owl pellets and wood rat nests signal significant changes in vegetation patterns, even in the recent past. Desert lakes appeared and disappeared, marshes developed and then dried up, the piñon woodland expanded its range across three states, and century-long droughts sometimes withered the landscape.

The American West has suffered six multiyear droughts in the last 150 years, each with environmental and social effects. But these historic-period droughts were dwarfed by the sequence of megadroughts that struck the West between about 900 and 1400 CE. The Great Basin is rich with high-resolution records that document these events. They are undoubtedly part of a long-term global pattern, and considerable evidence suggests that long and unrelenting droughts are a recurring aspect of North American climates.

If such a megadrought were to strike today, it could disrupt and perhaps paralyze the American West. This is why paleoclimatic data, from the Great Basin and elsewhere, have become critical as water supply planners regulate reservoir levels, allocate groundwater resources, and plan for upcoming droughts across the American West. Increasing demands on limited water clearly require both short- and long-term collaboration among resource managers, decision makers, and scientists familiar with the long-term environmental record.

Over the decades, archaeologists have learned to appreciate the diversity and variability of the ever-changing Great Basin landscape and have worked to document the remarkable stories of human ingenuity, persistence, and above all survival that played out in that extraordinary place.

David Hurst Thomas is curator of anthropology at the American Museum of Natural History.

Suggested Reading

Beck, Charlotte, ed.
1999   *Models for the Millennium: Great Basin
        Anthropology Today.* University of Utah
        Press, Salt Lake City.

Beck, Charlotte, and George T. Jones
1997   "The Terminal Pleistocene/Early Holocene
        Archaeology of the Great Basin." *Journal of
        World Prehistory* 11, no. 2: 161–236.

Cressman, Luther S.
1942   *Archaeological Researches in the Northern
        Great Basin.* Publication 538, Carnegie
        Institution of Washington, Washington,
        DC.

d'Azevedo, Warren L., ed.
1986   *Handbook of North American Indians*, vol.
        11: *Great Basin.* Smithsonian Institution,
        Washington, DC.

Fowler, Catherine S.
1992   *In the Shadow of Fox Peak: An Ethnography
        of the Cattail-eater Northern Paiute People of
        Stillwater Marsh.* US Fish and Wildlife
        Service, Region 1, Cultural Resource Series
        5. US Government Printing Office,
        Washington, DC.

Fremont, John C.
1845   *Report of the Exploring Expedition to the
        Rocky Mountains in the Year 1842, and to
        Oregon and California in the Years
        1843–1844.* Reprinted in several editions in
        the twentieth century.

Graf, Kelly E., and Dave N. Schmitt, eds.
2007   *Paleoindian or Paleoarchaic? Great Basin
        Human Ecology at the Pleistocene-Holocene
        Transition.* University of Utah Press, Salt
        Lake City.

Grayson, Donald K.
1993   *The Desert's Past: A Natural Prehistory of the
        Great Basin.* Smithsonian Institution Press,
        Washington, DC.

Heizer, Robert F., and Martin A. Baumhoff
1962   *Prehistoric Rock Art of Nevada and Eastern
        California.* University of California Press,
        Berkeley.

Janetski, Joel C., and David B. Madsen, eds.
1989   *Wetland Adaptations in the Great Basin.*
        Occasional Papers 1, Museum of Peoples
        and Cultures, Brigham Young University,
        Provo, Utah.

Jenkins, Dennis L., Thomas J. Connolly, and
C. Melvin Aikens, eds.
2003   *Early and Middle Holocene Archaeology of the
        Northern Great Basin.* Anthropological
        Papers 62, University of Oregon, Eugene.

Jennings, Jesse D.
1957   *Danger Cave.* Anthropological Papers 27,
        University of Utah, Salt Lake City.

Kelly, Robert L.
2001   *Prehistory of the Carson Desert and Stillwater
        Mountains: Environment, Mobility, and
        Subsistence in the Great Basin Wetland.*
        Anthropological Papers 123, University of
        Utah, Salt Lake City.

Loud, Llewellyn L., and Mark R. Harrington
1929   "Lovelock Cave." *University of California
        Publications in American Archaeology and
        Ethnology* 25, no. 1: 1–83. Berkeley.

Madsen, David B., and David Rhode, eds.
1994   *Across the West: Human Population
        Movement and the Expansion of the Numa.*
        University of Utah Press, Salt Lake City.

Quinlan, Angus R., ed.
2007   *Great Basin Rock Art: Archaeological
        Perspectives.* University of Nevada Press,
        Reno.

Schaafsma, Polly
1994   *The Rock Art of Utah.* University of Utah
        Press, Salt Lake City.

Simms, Steven
2008   *The Ancient Peoples of the Great Basin and
        Colorado Plateau.* Left Coast Press, Walnut
        Creek, California.

Picture Credits

Abbreviations:

AMNH	American Museum of Natural History
ACDAUU	Archaeological Center, Department of Anthropology, University of Utah
ASM	Arizona State Museum
BLM	Bureau of Land Management
BYU	Brigham Young University
HRCES	Harry Reid Center for Environmental Studies, University of Nevada, Las Vegas
IM	Intermountain Research
NMAI	National Museum of the American Indian
NRAF	Nevada Rock Art Foundation
NSM	Nevada State Museum
SAR	School for Advanced Research
SI	Smithsonian Institution
UOMNCH	University of Oregon Museum of Natural and Cultural History
USUDA	Utah State University Department of Anthropology
UMNH	Utah Museum of Natural History

Color section after page 50: Plate 1, courtesy Linda Dufurrena, photographer; plate 2, courtesy NSM; plate 3, photograph by Eugene M. Hattori, courtesy NSM; plate 4, courtesy NMAI; plate 5, courtesy David Rhode; plates 6–8, photographs by Ruth Jolie and Eugene M. Hattori, courtesy NSM; plate 9, courtesy Museum of Peoples and Cultures, BYU; plate 10, courtesy Polly Schaafsma, photographer; plates 11–12, courtesy Linda Dufurrena, photographer; plate 13, courtesy James Duffield, photographer; plate 14, courtesy Polly Schaafsma, photographer; plates 15–16, courtesy Linda Dufurrena, photographer; plates 17–18, photographs by Angus Quinlan, courtesy NRAF; plate 19, courtesy Price Prehistoric Museum; plate 20, courtesy University of Colorado Museum, Boulder; plate 21, courtesy Don D. Fowler, photographer; plate 22, courtesy Robert L. Kelly; plates 23–24, courtesy Linda Dufurrena, photographer.

Front matter: Frontispiece, adapted by Cynthia Dyer from Heizer and Baumhoff, *Prehistoric Rock Art of Nevada and Eastern California* (Berkeley: University of California Press, 1962): ii; maps 1–3, drawn by Molly O'Halloran, courtesy SAR.

Chapter One: Fig. 1.1, courtesy Linda Dufurrena, photographer.

Chapter Two: Figs. 2.1–2.8, courtesy Donald K. Grayson.

Chapter Three: Fig. 3.1, drawing by William Henry Holmes, reproduced from Grove Karl Gilbert, *Lake Bonneville* (Washington, DC: US Geological Survey, 1890); fig. 3.2, courtesy ASM, University of Arizona, neg. NT 03.NV.001-008; fig. 3.3, after Malcolm K. Hughes and Lisa J. Graumlich, "Multi-millenial Dendro-climatic Studies from the Western United States," in *Climatic Variations and Forcing Mechanisms of the Last 2000 Years*, eds. P. D. Jones, R. S. Bradley, and J. Jouzel (Berlin, Springer-Verlag, 1996), pp. 109–124, courtesy David Rhode; figs. 3.4–3.8, courtesy David Rhode.

Chapter Four: Fig. 4.1, courtesy NMAI, SI, neg. NO9453; fig. 4.2, photograph by Donald Tuohy, courtesy NSM; fig. 4.3, courtesy NMAI, SI, neg. N41757; fig. 4.4, photograph by F. H. Stross, courtesy Phoebe Hearst Museum, University of California, Berkeley; fig. 4.5, courtesy UOMNCH; fig. 4.6, photograph by Luther Cressman, courtesy UOMNCH; fig. 4.7, courtesy UMNH; fig. 4.8, courtesy Don D. Fowler, photographer; fig. 4.9, courtesy ACDAUU.

Chapter Five: Fig. 5.1: courtesy UOMNCH; fig. 5.2, courtesy Bryan Hockett, photographer; fig. 5.3, courtesy Ted Goebel, photographer; figs. 5.4–5.5, photographs by Eugene M. Hattori, courtesy NSM; fig. 5.6, courtesy Ted Goebel, photographer; fig. 5.7, courtesy UOMNCH; fig. 5.8, courtesy Bryan Hockett, photographer; fig. 5.9, courtesy Ted Goebel, photographer.

Chapter Six: Fig. 6.1, courtesy ACDAUU; fig. 6.2, courtesy NSM; fig. 6.3, drawing by Simon S. S. Driver, reproduced by permission from Stephen Plog, *Ancient Peoples of the American Southwest* (New York: Thames and Hudson, 1997), 45; fig. 6.4, drawing by and courtesy of Charlotte Beck; figs. 6.5-6.6, photographs by Eugene M. Hattori, courtesy NSM; fig. 6.7, drawing by and courtesy of Charlotte Beck; fig. 6.8, after R. Hughes and J. Bennyhoff, "Early Trade," in *Handbook of North American Indians*, vol. 11, *Great Basin* (Washington, DC: SI, 1986), 238; fig. 6.9, drawing by and courtesy of Charlotte Beck.

Chapter Seven: Fig. 7.1, photograph by Robert Elston, courtesy IM; fig. 7.2, photograph by Bryan Hockett, courtesy BLM, Elko District, Nevada; figs. 7.3–7.5, photographs by Robert Elston, courtesy IM; fig. 7.6, drawing by Cari Inoway, courtesy IM; fig. 7.7, photograph by Robert Elston, courtesy IM.

Chapter Eight: Fig. 8.1, drawing by Karen Byers, courtesy NSM; fig. 8.2, drawing by Catherine S. Fowler, courtesy NSM; figs. 8.3–8.4, drawings by Karen Byers, courtesy NSM; figs. 8.5–8.6, drawings by Steve Stern, courtesy NSM; figs. 8.7–8.8, photographs by Eugene M. Hattori, courtesy NSM.

Chapter Nine: Fig. 9.1, drawing by Kris Kirkeby, courtesy UOMNCH; fig. 9.2, map by Kris Kirkeby, courtesy UOMNCH; fig. 9.3, courtesy Tom Connolly; fig. 9.4, drawing by Karen Byers, courtesy NSM.

Chapter Ten: Figs. 10.1–10.3, photographs by Ruth Jolie and Eugene M. Hattori, courtesy NSM.

Chapter Eleven: Fig. 11.1, photograph by Jeff Mackey, courtesy US Fish and Wildlife Service, Ruby Marshes National Wildlife Area; fig. 11.2: photograph by Mary Freeman, courtesy of Special Collections Department, University of Nevada, Reno; fig. 11.3, courtesy Joel C. Janetski; fig. 11.4, courtesy Robert L. Kelly.

Chapter Twelve: Figs. 12.1–12.3, photographs by Robert L. Bettinger, courtesy Department of Anthropology, University of California, Davis; fig. 12.4, photograph by David Hurst Thomas, courtesy AMNH, New York.

Chapter Thirteen: Fig. 13.1, photograph by Steven R. Simms, courtesy USUDA; fig. 13.2, courtesy Steven R. Simms; fig. 13.3, photograph by Steven R. Simms, courtesy USUDA; figs. 13.4 and 13.5, drawings by Eric Carlson, courtesy USUDA; fig. 13.6, photograph by Steven R. Simms, courtesy USUDA; fig. 13.7, drawing by Eric Carlson, courtesy USUDA.

Chapter Fourteen: Fig. 14.1, drawn by Molly O'Halloran, courtesy SAR; fig. 14.2, courtesy University of Utah Marriott Library Special Collections; fig. 14.3, courtesy Museum of Peoples and Cultures, BYU; fig. 14.4. copyright 2007 Peabody Museum, Harvard University, 29-5-10/A6766.1; fig. 14.5, courtesy Museum of Peoples and Cultures, BYU; fig. 14.6, courtesy Ray T. Matheny.

Chapter Fifteen: Figs. 15.1–15.7, photographs by Duncan Metcalfe, courtesy UMNH.

Chapter Sixteen: 16.1, courtesy UMNH; figs. 16.2–16.4, courtesy Mercyhurst Archaeological Institute.

Chapter Seventeen: Fig. 17.1, courtesy US Bureau of Reclamation, Lower Colorado River Office, Las Vegas; fig. 17.2, photograph by Edward S. Curtis, courtesy Library of Congress, no. LC-USZ62-51436; fig. 17.3, map by Jerry Lyon, courtesy HRA, Inc.; fig. 17.4, illustration by David C. Smee, courtesy HRCES; fig. 17.5, courtesy Lost City Museum, Overton, Nevada; fig. 17.6, illustration by David C. Smee, courtesy HRCES; fig. 17.7, courtesy Lost City Museum, Overton, Nevada; fig. 17.8, courtesy Elizabeth V. T. Warren, HRA, Inc.; fig. 17.9, courtesy HRA, Inc.

Chapter Eighteen: Fig. 18.1, courtesy William J. Cannon, photographer; fig. 18.2: photograph by Alanah Woody, courtesy NRAF; fig. 18.3: courtesy William J. Cannon, photographer; fig. 18.4: photograph by Angus Quinlan, courtesy NRAF; fig. 18.5, courtesy William J. Cannon, photographer; fig. 18.6, courtesy Catherine S. Fowler, photographer; fig. 18.7, photograph by Angus Quinlan, courtesy NRAF; figs. 18.8–18.10, photographs by Alanah Woody, courtesy NRAF.

Chapter Nineteen: Fig. 19.1, courtesy Polly Schaafsma, photographer; fig. 19.2, courtesy Jim Duffield, photographer; figs. 19.3–19.9, courtesy Polly Schaafsma, photographer.

Index

Numbers printed in *italics* refer to illustrations; numbers beginning with uppercase P refer to plates; numbers in **bold** refer to maps or plans.